English

Ian Barr
John Reynolds

John Murray

Acknowledgements

The publishers would like to thank Alison Baxter for her assistance in preparing this book and for her constructive and practical suggestions. Thanks also to Lucy Purkis of Cambridge International Examinations for her assistance and encouragement.

Examinations acknowledgement

All the IGCSE examination questions used in this book are reproduced by permission of the University of Cambridge Local Examinations Syndicate.

Picture and text acknowledgements

The authors and publisher are grateful to the following for permission to include material in the text:

p.11 *A Voice Across the Sea* by Arthur C. Clarke, Harper and Row, 1958; **p.12** *The Independent*, 1998; **p.16** *The Discovery of the Titanic* by Robert Ballard, The Orion Publishing Group, 1995; **p.19** Text from The Worldwatch Institute, www.worldwatch.org; **p.22–23** *The Road from Coorain: An Australian Memoir* by Jill Ker Conway, Vintage, 1992; **p.28–29** Children's Aid Direct (formerly Feed the Children), 12 Portman Road, Reading, Berks, RG30 1EA; **p.36** *In the Castle of my Skin* by George C. Lamming, Longman, 1979; **p.37–38** *Malgudi's Days* by R.K.Narayan, Penguin, 1994; **p.39** *The Endless Steppe* by Esther Hautzig, Puffin, 1993; **p.42–43 & 151** UniChem Pharmacies; **p.44–45** *The Mail on Sunday*, 1997; **p.47–50** From *The Habit of Loving*, Flamingo, 1993; **p.59** *The Guardian*, 14 September 1994; **p.63–64 & 104–106** *From Pole to Pole* by Michael Palin, BBC Consumer Publishing (Books), 1995; **p.66–67 & 112–113** *The Calcutta Telegraph*, 30 March, 1993; **p.68–69 & 114–115** *Les Misérables* by Victor Hugo; **p.72–73** *The New Straits Times*, 5 July 1994; **p.77** *The Environment and Health* by Brian Ward, Franklin Watts, 1989, *Wake Up to What You Can Do for the Environment*, The Department of the Environment (DETR); **p.79–80** *The New Straits Times*, 8 July 1994; **p.86** The Whale and Dolphin Conservation Society;

p.92–93 *A Drink of Water* by Samuel Selvon; **p.96–97** From *The Politician and Other Stories*, by Khamsing Srinawk, Oxford University Press, 1992; **p.98–99** *The Observer*; **p.110–111** *Which?* Magazine; **p.120–121** *The Mail on Sunday*, 1997; **p.122–123** *The Observer*; **p.124** *The Guardian*, 14 September 1994; **p.125–126** *Adscene*, September 1994, Kent Regional Newspapers; **p.144 & 146–147** From *The Stench of Kerosene – Short Stories* by Steve Bowles, Cambridge University Press, 1991; **p.150** *Simple Lust: Collected Poems of South African Jail and Exile, Includes Letters to Martha*, Heinemann, 1973.

Cover David Greenwood/Telegraph Colour Library Stock Directory; **p.3** *t* John Walmsley, *b* Last Resort; **p.4** John Walmsley; **p.8** Patrick Fagot/NHPA; **p.16** Ralph White/Corbis; **p.19** Red List, www.redlist.org; **p.20** Glyn Kirk/Action Plus; **p.23** J Hartley/Panos; **p.29** Liba Taylor/Panos; **p.59** Matthew Clarke/Action Plus; **p.66 & p.112** Heldur Netocny/India/Panos; **p.68 & p.114** Performing Arts Library; **p.72** Robert Harding; **p.99** Neil Libbert; **p.106** Heidi Bradner/Rex Features; **p.125** Kent Regional Newspapers; **p.139** Chris Stowers/Panos; **p.140** Photofusion.

Every effort has been made to trace all copyright holders, but if any have been inadvertently overlooked the Publishers will be pleased to make the necessary arrangements at the first opportunity.

> **Teacher's Notes**
> Answers, marking schemes and 'mock' IGCSE English papers can be found in the accompanying IGCSE English Teacher's Notes (ISBN 0 7195 7034 4), free on request from the Publisher.

© Ian Barr and John Reynolds 2001
First published in 2001
by John Murray (Publishers) Ltd
50 Albemarle Street
London W1S 4BD

Layouts by Amanda Easter
Illustrations by Richard Duszczak, Malcolm Stokes/Linden Artists
Cover design by John Townson/Creation
Typeset in Galliard by Dorchester Typesetting Group Ltd, Dorchester
Printed and bound in Great Britain by Butler & Tanner Ltd, Frome and London

A CIP record for this book is available from the British Library

ISBN 0 7195 7033 6
Teacher's Notes ISBN 0 7195 7034 4

Contents

4 Applying your writing skills

5 Writing summaries

6 Writing essays and coursework

7 Speaking and listening skills

Introduction

Your route to the examination

When choosing your route through the course, there are some important decisions that you and/or your teacher have to make.

The first decision is to select the appropriate examination level: **core** or **extended.** Your teacher will be able to explain in detail what is involved at each level, but the key points are as follows.

At both levels there are two compulsory areas of work:
- Reading and Directed Writing (Paper 1 (core) **or** Paper 2 (extended));
  and
- Continuous Writing (Paper 3) **or** Coursework (Paper 4).

There is also one optional area of study:
- Assessment of Speaking and Listening Skills: you can take the exam (Paper 5) **or** do your speaking/listening as coursework (Paper 6)

The next decision is to choose between the Continuous Writing examination (Paper 3), and Coursework (Paper 4).

Finally, you and/or your teacher have to decide whether or not you will take the Listening/Speaking option, and if so, whether you will do it as coursework or as an oral exam.

Here is a bit more information about what the different parts of IGCSE English involve.

Reading and Directed Writing (Paper 1 (core) or Paper 2 (extended))

At both core and extended levels, the Reading and Directed Writing Paper has to be sat as a written examination test. This paper requires you to read two or three different pieces then use what you have read in different ways. You might have to answer some basic comprehension questions or you might be asked to summarise the material: both ways show the examiner that you have understood what you have read.

Continuous Writing (Paper 3) or Coursework (Paper 4)

Both these options require you to write at some length.

- If you sit the Continuous Writing examination, you have to choose one of nine essay titles, and write 350–500 words on that topic.
- If you are doing coursework instead of the examination, you will have to submit three pieces of written work, each of around 500 words.

Speaking and Listening Skills (Paper 5 or Paper 6)

Although this part of the course is optional, it is worth remembering the following story which we were once told by a teacher in Cyprus.

> A student followed a course which was not IGCSE and which did not offer the possibility of an oral examination. The student achieved success, getting a Grade B, and on the strength of that was given a job in a bank. To their horror, her employers found that, although she could write letters, she had real problems when speaking to customers, either in the bank or on the phone. Without effective speaking skills, she had difficulties in doing her job well.

You might decide that it is worth doing the oral. There are, after all, four areas of skill when using any language: reading, writing, speaking and listening. Make sure you acquire them all.

Structure of the book

In this book you will find the chapters follow the requirements of the course very closely.

Chapter 1 aims to improve and develop your **reading** skills, to help you achieve the best possible grade in the Reading and Directed Writing paper.

Chapter 2 covers reading comprehension, practising the skills needed for the reading aspects of the Reading and Directed Writing paper.

Chapter 3 aims to improve and develop your **writing** skills, to help you achieve the best possible grade in the Reading and Directed Writing paper, and in the Continuous Writing paper.

Chapter 4 helps you to practise the specific skills you will need for the writing aspects of the extended Reading and Directed Writing paper.

Chapter 5 looks at the particular skills needed when writing a summary – one of the tasks on every extended Reading and Directed Writing paper.

Chapter 6 advises you on continuous writing and gives you the opportunity to develop the necessary skills. It is divided into two sections – one on essay writing, for those taking paper 3, and one on coursework.

Chapter 7 outlines the requirements of the Listening and Speaking examination, and gives you some opportunities to practise for the oral exam or prepare for your coursework assessment.

Authors' note: In the examples of candidates' work throughout the book, the original spellings and punctuation have been retained. Many errors are identified but many are left unmarked, reflecting the principle that teachers and examiners reward merit in writing and do not seek only to highlight mistakes.

Examiner's analysis: is printed in blue like this
Teacher's comments: are written in red like this

Becoming a better reader

■ Why do you read?

The written word is all around us. It is almost impossible to spend a day without reading something. Here are a few examples.

- If you catch a bus, you will probably read the destination board to make sure that it is the bus that you need.

- If you go to a fast-food restaurant, you need to read the menu before deciding which delicious meal you are going to order.

- Whenever you work on a computer, you need to read the different messages that appear on the screen.

- When you settle down to relax after a hard day's study, you might decide to watch television. How do you find out which programmes are on? Most probably you will turn to a television guide. How do you know when the programme you intend to watch is about to start? Almost certainly because you will read the title as it flashes upon the screen in front of you.

- Of course, you may decide that the most enjoyable way to relax is not by watching television at all, but by reading. But what will you read? Will you choose your favourite sports magazine or will you return to the novel that you left by your bed last night?

▨ Passive and active reading

So, reading is something we spend our lives doing, often without being conscious of the fact that we are doing it. In fact, you might think that the printed word is so much a part of our lives that we take very little notice of it; it is just *there*. We take it for granted and, as a result, we frequently recognise familiar (and less familiar) words without really thinking about what they mean – we're reading **passively**, just accepting what we see. Most of the examples given earlier are of passive reading, but reading can be an **active** process, in which you really think about what you are seeing and try to get as much out of the text as you can. For examination success, it is the skill of **active reading**, in other words **reading for understanding**, that you need to develop.

English Language is unlike most other examination subjects in that there are very few facts and details which you need to revise in advance. However, there is still important preparation to do! Your performance in this examination will be much better if you spend some time developing the **skills** you need. For IGCSE English you need to be able to:

■ understand and convey information
■ understand, order and present facts, ideas and opinions
■ evaluate information and select what is required for specific purposes
■ recognise implicit meaning and attitudes.

If you improve your skill in active reading, this will help your examination performance in many other subjects as well.

The English examination will test your reading of different types of material. You might be presented with:

■ a piece of non-fiction (possibly taken from a newspaper)
■ an extract from a novel or short story
■ a piece of personal writing such as an autobiography

to give just three examples.

It is quite possible that you will also have to read a leaflet, or something similar, in which pictures or diagrams as well as words are used to convey the writer's meaning.

▨ How do you develop the skill of active reading?

In the build-up to the examination, it is a good idea to practise reading the types of writing on which you will be tested. So, as well as reading novels and magazines, spend some time reading:

■ newspaper articles – in particular, feature articles in which the writer develops an argument
■ any leaflets or pamphlets you can find.

Remember, revising for other subjects, such as History or Sociology, also requires you to read non-fiction books which contain complicated and well-structured arguments. As a general rule, try to read as wide a range of non-fiction as you can.

When you are reading, make sure that you think carefully about what the words, sentences and paragraphs actually mean. It may help to:

- ask yourself questions as you go along, or
- imagine what you would ask someone else if they had read the article and you hadn't.

When you are working on comprehension passages in class, it is almost certain that your teacher will keep prodding you with questions, to help you gain a complete understanding of what you have read, and to ensure that your answers are as precise and specific as possible. So, when you are reading on your own, try to think about what questions your teacher would ask if he/she were there with you. This should help to ensure that you have thought about the main concerns of the passages and understood them to the best of your ability.

Once you have mastered this approach, you will find that you are reading with a much clearer and more focused understanding, and if you apply this new skill in the examination itself it will really raise your performance.

Skimming and scanning – getting the gist

When you are actually taking the examination, you must be able to read as much as you can and understand it as fully as you can, in a limited period of time. This is why the preparation above is so important. You must read through the whole question paper carefully, but if you are skilled at reading actively, then you can save some time by employing the techniques known as **skimming** and **scanning**. **Skimming** means reading quickly through a passage in order to gain a clear, overall view of what it is about. **Scanning** is a refinement of this approach, as it means you are reading in order to extract specific details which are relevant to the questions that you are required to answer. Before we look a little more closely at how to apply these techniques, there is one other very important point to consider, and it is also one which is easy to overlook.

Identifying key words in the question

At the beginning of this section we mentioned the importance of reading through the whole question paper. This means, of course, not only reading through the passages on which you will be tested, but also reading through the *questions* on those passages as well. A clear understanding of exactly what the question requires will help you to focus on those parts of the passage in which the relevant points can be found.

When you are reading a question, you may find it useful to underline the **key words** in the question. For example, look at this summary question that was set on the passage 'A Whale of a Time in Oz!' (page 8).

> Read carefully the passage 'A Whale of a Time in Oz!' and then summarise what it tells us about the behaviour of Southern Right Whales and why they were considered to be so suitable for hunting.

From your skimming of this question, you will pick up that the passage is about Southern Right Whales. The key words to underline as part of your scanning process are the instruction *summarise* and then the specific details on which you are to focus: *behaviour* and *why they were so suitable for hunting*.

Skim, scan and select

Now we can look at how skimming and scanning work when reading the passage itself.

1   **Skim the text.** You will notice that there is a **title**, followed by a **smaller title** (**sub-heading**). There is also a **photograph** with a **caption**, and a **sub-heading** two-thirds of the way through the article. These all contain details which can be easily taken in when you first skim/scan the page. They give you a quick, overall view of the subject of the text and the writer's attitude towards the subject. It is important that you make use of clues of this sort when you set out to read the passage.

2   **Scan the text.** Pick out details relevant to the question which you now have firmly fixed in your mind.

3   **Select the points you intend to use.** By scanning you weed out those passages which are not relevant to your purpose.

For this question you are being asked to identify **facts** about the whales and about why they were hunted. It is important that you understand the distinction between facts and opinions. **Facts** are objective details which can be supported by evidence. **Opinions** are subjective views held by the writer and cannot, therefore, be proved as being either right or wrong. Some examination questions may ask you to separate facts from opinions to show that you can distinguish between them. Other types of question may simply ask you to identify one or the other. Look again at the question on this passage (at the top of the page). It asks only for factual details. You should, therefore, include only those in your answer. Having a clear understanding of this difference will make it easier to eliminate irrelevant opinions from your summary.

With these guidelines in mind, we will now look at the passage.

A WHALE OF A TIME IN OZ!

In search of the Southern Right Whale 'down under'.

Helen Highwater

A Southern Right Whale and calf

The first few paragraphs set the scene. Although you will be taking the details in as useful background information, you will also be aware that the Southern Right Whale does not receive a mention until the third paragraph. If you are reading actively, you will immediately notice this and be alert for further information which is going to follow.

As you read through the third and fourth paragraphs, it is likely that you will be asking yourself questions such as 'What do these details tell us about the whales' behaviour?', 'What was it about their behaviour which made them so easy to hunt?', and so on.

Getting there wasn't easy. First there was a 500 kilometre flight from Adelaide on a tiny plane shaped like a toothpaste tube. Then once we'd landed we met up with Gary White, our expedition leader, and his jeep. 200 kilometres along the Eyre Highway we entered the treeless Nullarbor Plain, a semi-desert populated mainly by Aborigines.

Our destination was the head of the Great Australian Bight, where we were to spend two days watching whales. On the way Gary told us what we wanted to know:

'Sadly, over 25,000 whales had been killed before whaling ceased in 1930. By this time Southern Right Whales were virtually extinct. They were known as "Right" whales because they were right for hunting in small land-based boats. They came close inshore, floated when killed, and had thick blubber, which produced the valuable whale oil when it was boiled down. This meant that the poor whales were hunted down in vast numbers by money-making shipowners.

'Right Whales feed on small creatures at or near the surface, gently swimming along with their mouths half open, allowing the sea water to flow in. The water is pushed back out with their tongues, leaving the food behind. Thankfully, they are now a protected species and numbers have risen to nearly 800.'

This was a dismal tale but it had a happy ending – the whales were now safe from murderous whale hunters.

As you move on through the passage, you will find that it alternates between giving facts about the whales' behaviour and details about the scenery and the writer's personal response to seeing the whales as they frolic in the water. The details of the scenery and the writer's opinions may make the passage interesting but you should be skimming over them as they are not details specifically connected to the questions which you are asking yourself.

Two hours before sunset we arrived at our destination. The crumbling limestone cliffs dropped sheer into the deep blue of the bay. It was August, the height of the whales' breeding season. Every three years the whales come from their home waters in the Antarctic to their Australian breeding grounds. Mature females weigh 80 tonnes. The females do not eat at all until they return to the Antarctic. By this time they will have lost 20 tonnes in weight.

As the sun began to set behind us we looked out, but saw . . . nothing. Then boom! Right in front of us the sea erupted as a huge whale burst from the surface, thrusting its body out of the water and smashing down with a noise like a cannon firing. Again and again it surged from the sea, a majestic and thrilling sight.

After a meal under the stars we talked some more. Gary told us that large numbers of female whales and their calves had been in the bay the previous week. The calves are six metres long at birth and they grow to three times that length.

'This was Nature at its finest, awesome and strangely moving.'

Our final day began early. We packed up our camp, walked to the cliff edge and were amazed! I counted 24 whales. Swimming parallel to the shore, very close in, was a long procession of mothers and their calves. They floated past on the surface. Some swam side by side, others lazily rolled over each other as they moved slowly along. They were enormous. As they expelled the air from their blow-holes, great spouts of misty waters shot upwards. This was Nature at its finest, awesome and strangely moving. We were silent watchers of a primeval, wonderful sight. How can people hunt such beautiful and truly amazing creatures?

All too soon we had to go. In October the whales would return home too, home to the Antarctic. We said little. We'd been stunned by the size of Australia, climbed Ayers Rock and followed the tourist trail. These would become distant memories, but our two days whale-watching would remain alive in our hearts for ever.

In general, the language in which the passage is written is not difficult to understand and can be read quite easily by an average candidate. The vocabulary, for the most part, does not consist of long and complicated words. However, in the last-but-one paragraph the writer uses some more complicated sentences.

Here, both the sentence structures and the vocabulary are more complicated. It is a good idea to slow down your skim reading at this point and stop to consider exactly what the words mean. Do these sentences contain information relevant to the question? If they do, then you need to consider how best to put the information into your own words to show the examiner that you have understood (lifting the sentences as they stand and transferring them directly into your answer will be a sure sign to the examiner that you do **not** understand them!).

Even if your understanding of the vocabulary used in these sentences is not entirely secure, your awareness of what the question is actually requiring you to look for should convince you that these are references to the writer's feelings or opinions. They do not have a great deal to do with the whales themselves, apart from telling us how impressive they are, which is a point made elsewhere in the passage anyway. You can safely pass over them and continue to read the passage. It will not then take you long to finish, as the remaining sentences may be of general interest in helping us to understand the writer's feelings but are not relevant to the material for which you are searching.

As you can see from this example, **selection of details** in your reading is vitally important to working under examination conditions. You must have a clear idea of what you are looking for and then focus on finding it and ignoring irrelevant comment or detail (which examiners refer to as **distractors**). The more swiftly you can select the facts and opinions that you actually need to answer the questions, the more time you will have for expressing your understanding of them as clearly as you can to the examiner. Writing your answer will be dealt with in more detail in Chapters 2 (pages 25–35) and 5 (pages 100–102).

The reading you will be required to do in the examination will not always consist of non-fiction, factual material. Sometimes it will involve an extract from a short story or novel, such as the passage about Boy Blue at the end of Chapter 2 (page 36).

Remember: concentration and alertness help to make you a good reader. The more you practise your reading skills, the better your examination performance is likely to be.

■ Practise your active reading skills

Here are some examples of the different types of reading passage which you may be given in the examination. Practise reading through them and see how easily you can grasp their meaning. Remember to try to focus on what seem to be their main concerns as you read.

Exercise 1

The extract opposite is a straightforward piece of informative writing.

■ Its intention is to explain something to you, and when you are reading it you are likely to be scanning it for useful facts and details.

■ Unlike the passage about spotting whales in Australia, it does not contain any photographs or sub-headings which may help to convey the writer's meaning. You will, therefore, need to think carefully about the meaning as you read through it. Try to identify the main points of the author's argument and separate them from the examples he gives to illustrate them.

Tip A useful tip when reading this type of writing is to assume that each new paragraph deals with an important new point. If you can identify what we call the **topic sentence** in each paragraph, you will have found a good 'hook' on which to hang your understanding. For example, in the third paragraph of this passage the opening sentence is clearly the topic sentence. It states the main point of the paragraph and then the following sentences develop this point. Spotting the topic sentences helps you to keep a tight control over your understanding of a writer's argument.

Man is, pre-eminently, the animal who communicates, but until little more than a hundred years ago his thoughts could travel abroad no more swiftly than the sailing ship or the running horse.

The great change began when lightning itself became a messenger for mankind. At first, the electric telegraph was regarded as a superfluous novelty, but within a single lifetime engineers had spun a cocoon of copper wires around the world. In 1886 was laid the first successful Atlantic cable. From that moment, Europe and America were only seconds, and no longer days apart. However, even when the telephone was invented in 1876 it was not possible to *speak* across the Atlantic; the early submarine cables could carry only telegraph messages. They were too sluggish to respond to the hundredfold-more-rapid vibrations of the human voice. Although a transatlantic telephone service was opened in 1927, it depended entirely on radio, which meant that even at the best of times conversations were liable to fadings and cracklings, and to eerie, Outer Space whistles and wails.

The first transatlantic telephone cable went into service in 1956. As a result of the vastly improved service, there was an immediate jump in the number of calls between Europe and America. More cables had to be laid – first across the Atlantic and later across the still wider expanses of the Pacific.

By the dawn of the Space Age, therefore, the problem of inter-continental telephone calls had been solved – but it had been solved so successfully that it had raised yet more problems. The cables could carry only a limited number of conversations, and it seemed unlikely that they could keep up with the rising demand. Moreover, just as the Victorian cables could not cope with the telephone, so the submarine cables of the 1950s were unable to deal with the latest miracle, television – and for very similar reasons. The electric signals involved in the transmission of TV pictures were a thousand times too complex to be handled by a cable. A new breakthrough was needed and the satellites provided it in the nick of time.

From *Voice Across the Sea*, by Arthur C. Clarke, Harper and Row, 1958

Exercise 2

The passage on page 12 is taken from a newspaper article and contains some graphical and layout features which are typical of this type of writing. When you practise reading this article, focus on trying to get a clear picture of what actually happened to Tony Bullimore, since in order to make the article more immediate and dramatic, the writer has not described the events in a strictly logical sequence.

'Thank God . . . it's a miracle'

The thud of a fist and Briton is saved from cruel seas

Report by Ian Burrell

THE RESCUE

It was the thud of a fist on the hull of Tony Bullimore's overturned yacht that told him he was not going to die.

The British yachtsman had spent four days and four nights in an air-pocket inside his capsized yacht, praying that he would be saved. 'I started shouting, "I'm coming, I'm coming",' he said. 'It took a few seconds to get from one end of the boat to the other. Then I took a few deep breaths and I dived out.'

It was the culmination of one of the most dramatic sea rescues of all time. Mr Bullimore had been stranded more than 1,500 miles from the Australian coast and 900 miles from Antarctica. The key to Tony Bullimore's incredible feat of endurance was an ability to remain calm and methodical in his thinking despite the most appalling circumstances.

THE ORDEAL

Trapped in darkness, with freezing waters lapping at his feet and buffeted by 60ft waves, he will have known only too well that he was more than 1,000 miles from the nearest land.

Faced with the danger of being dragged down with the boat, most people would have been tempted to try and jump clear.

Mr Bullimore's sense of calm, developed from years of solo yachting, taught him otherwise. He stayed with the yacht and quickly took stock of the few straws available for him to cling on to.

Yesterday he described the horrific conditions that he had endured.

'Two-thirds of the hull filled with water. There was a hole in the bottom of the hull, in fact really at the top, where one of the windows had come out. This caused water to be sucked in and out at a colossal rate, causing a kind of Niagara Falls, but upside down.

> 'This chap is not an ordinary person like you or me.'

'I had to find myself a spot as high up as possible and put nets around it so that I could crawl in there and lash myself in to get out of the water and to get away from everything.'

Dr Howard Oakley, of the Institute of Naval Medicine, said keeping a clear head and a sense of order were vital. Once he had decided to stay with the yacht, Mr Bullimore's priorities were to activate the distress beacon transmitter and to ensure he was getting enough air. Perched in a makeshift hammock, Mr Bullimore was alone with his thoughts, with nothing visible to focus on. This is the kind of situation that makes people motion sick.

Yet the discomfort of sea-sickness could not break Mr Bullimore's remarkable spirit.

'This chap is not an ordinary person, like you or me,' said a clinical psychologist, Eileen Kennedy.

'The kind of person who takes part in a solo yacht race welcomes challenge and risk.'

THE SURVIVOR

The yachtsman said that during the 'horrific, traumatic experience' he was 'hanging on in there and believing something would happen and just fighting.'

Through four days of darkness and solitude, he depended on 'sheer determination, a little water, a little chocolate' to sustain him.

> 'It was just determination, a little water, a little chocolate . . . hanging on in there.'

But even Mr Bullimore was at his endurance limit.

'I only just made it. Because of weather conditions, I was deteriorating at a reasonable rate,' he said. 'When I knew that the rescue was actually going to happen, I felt ecstatic.'

Adapted from an article in The Independent, 1998

Applying your reading skills

In this chapter we are going to look at some techniques which are specific to the core paper. Section 1 concentrates on multiple-choice testing and Section 2 explains short-answer questions and structured questions. In both sections we have looked very closely at particular examples so that you can see exactly how they work and how you can help yourself to achieve high marks.

Section 1 *Multiple-choice testing*

Reading comprehension tests include a number of different techniques to assess your ability to read with understanding. One of these techniques is multiple-choice testing. It is used in Paper 1, the core paper. Multiple-choice tests:

- draw on different parts of the stimulus material to make sure you have covered the ground
- are an efficient way of testing understanding of a wide range of material in a short period of time
- test reading exclusively – almost nothing has to be written in order to answer the question.

What do multiple-choice questions look like?

You are presented with a reading text and a series of questions. Each question starts with a **stem**, which is the first part of a sentence. Then there are four phrases from which you choose the one correct 'ending' to complete the sentence, according to what you have understood from the reading text. Examiners call the three wrong answers **distractors**, while the right answer is called the **key**.

Example 1

There can't be many high streets in Europe where you can reach out of your car window and pluck an orange from a tree. You turn it disbelievingly in your hand: it must be plastic, part of some costly, surreal tourism campaign. But you peel the orange – and eat it. And as you continue on your way through the town of Plasencia, in northern Extremadura, and drive east along the valley of La Vera, oranges on trees become commonplace.

Oranges on the trees in Plasencia are

A very close to the roads   B on the east side
C made of plastic   D tied on for the tourists

Each of the possible answers picks up a word or idea from the stimulus – in this example, we have underlined the words or ideas linked to each possible answer (they won't be underlined in the exam!). However, only one answer makes a sentence that is a true representation of something conveyed by the text – this is A, which matches the fact that the orange trees are so close to the road that you can pick the oranges from your car.

■ How do multiple-choice questions work?

When examiners set multiple-choice questions, they always follow four important rules. Knowing these rules will help you to work out the right answer!

Rule 1 : The language of the stem must be clear.

Rule 2 : Only one thing may be tested at a time.

These are simple, commonsense rules and are designed to make the question as fair as possible.

Rule 3 : What is asked must be **factual** so that the one right answer can be found by **objective, logical thinking;** opinion cannot be asked for in multiple-choice testing.

Rule 3 is useful to know when you are tackling a multiple-choice question. For instance, look at the following example (it is **not** from a real exam!).

Example 2

Modern Spain is full of routes like this one, dreamed up by excitable tourist authorities. Red and white signs on rocks point the way, renewed annually by a group of local climbers who meet every November to walk the route. Goatbells tinkle, and the sound of running water is everywhere. Continuous rustlings indicate the presence of lizards in the undergrowth. The route rises through oak and chestnut woods for several kilometres before veering left and entering the Garganta de los Infiernos: Hell's Gorge.

Would you enjoy following the tourist route to Hell's Gorge?

A No, because I don't like lizards.
B No, because it is too steep a climb.
C Yes, because you can climb the trees in the woods.
D Yes, because you can refresh yourself in the streams.

This invented question breaks Rule 3 – it's impossible to say what the one **correct** answer is because you are being asked for your opinion. You might be terrified of lizards, in which case you might pick that possibility. You might be terrified of heights and the thought of climbing a tree might be horrific. Who knows? You will not find a question like this on an exam paper.

Tip Remember that you will never be asked your personal opinion in a multiple-choice question – so don't choose your answer on this basis!

In the following example you can find the right answer by thinking logically.

Example 3

A drive around Extremadura can also be a sad experience, because you often see abandoned villages where the young have moved to the cities in search of better times. But there is no sign of this in La Vera. The future, as encapsulated in such sights as a laden donkey tied to a post outside a petrol station, looks bright. The highest point of the road, and the scenic high spot of the journey, is the Yeguas Pass. The view west, out over La Vera, is stunning: an immense patchwork quilted with white villages, plumes of rising smoke and small white explosions of cherry trees in bloom.

The young people of the region have

A left after explosions burnt down their houses
B left their donkeys tied to posts
C moved to the towns for a better life
D left with their belongings loaded on donkeys

A picks up the idea of 'explosions' and smoke rising, but what is being described is a peaceful scene. **B** picks up the fact of the donkeys tied up but suggests an incorrect reason. **C** picks up the point that the young have moved to the towns 'in search of better times'. **D** picks up the idea that the donkeys are 'laden' but again gives a wrong reason for this. The correct answer is **C**.

Rule 4: All the answers should be believable so it is essential to refer to the text itself in order to choose the right one.

Look again at the examples above, and you will see that each of the possible answers makes a reasonably believable sentence, even if one of them is pretty unlikely. It's only by looking at the text that you can distinguish 'possible' answers from the right answer, or key.

Tips   **1** The IGCSE core paper uses a series of six multiple-choice questions in the first part of the paper. Do not assume that there will be a pattern in the correct answers. It is unlikely, but possible, that the correct answers to the six questions are AAAAAA.
2 Look at the question as well as the answers! One danger with multiple-choice questions is that you can be so busy concentrating on the A–D choices that you forget that the stem itself is equally important. It's not just a matter of 'which thing is mentioned' – probably all of them are! The crucial question to ask yourself is '**Which answer goes with the question to make a true statement?**'. Think about this and the rules above as you work through the exercises on the following pages.

■ Practise answering multiple-choice questions

Exercise 1

We have written some notes to help you through this first exercise. From Exercise 2 onwards, you will be on your own.

Our second view of the *Titanic* was breathtaking. As we glided across the bottom, out of the darkness loomed the vertical knife-edge of the bow – the great ship towered above us and suddenly it seemed to be coming right at us, about to run our little submarine down. Gently we brought the sub closer until we could see the bow more clearly. It was buried more than sixty feet in bottom mud. Both anchors still hung in place.

Rivers of rust covered the side of the ship, some of it running the full length of the exposed vertical hull plating and pouring out over the bottom sediment where it formed great ponds as much as thirty to forty feet across. The blood of the great ship lay in pools on the ocean floor. Then, as we rose in slow motion up the ghostly wall of the port bow, our running lights reflected off the still unbroken glass of the portholes in a way that made me think of eyes gleaming in the dark. In places, the rust about them formed eyelashes, sometimes tears: as though the *Titanic* were weeping over her fate. Near the upper railing – still largely intact – reddish-brown stalactites of rust, the result of rust-eating bacteria, hung down as much as several feet, looking like long icicles. I subsequently dubbed them 'rusticles', a name which seems to have stuck.

These rust features turned out to be very fragile. If touched by 'Alvin' (that was the name we called our sub), or dislodged by the thrust from one of our propellers, they disappeared in a cloud of smoke. And once the foamy crust had been knocked away, the steel beneath appeared almost perfectly preserved, only slightly pitted.

Carefully I counted the portholes aft from the anchor to locate the position where the ship's name should be, but I could see nothing.

Alvin rose farther, cleared the railing forward of No. 1 hatch, and we manoeuvred in over the *Titanic*'s mighty forward deck. All at once I was forcibly struck by the sheer size of everything: giant bollards, the huge links of the anchor chains, and even bigger shiny bronze-topped capstans. Until now the ship for me had been somehow ghostly, distant, incorporeal. Now it was very close, very real.

I strained to get a look at the deck's wooden planking just four feet below us. Then my heart dropped. Gone was any hope of finding much *Titanic* woodwork intact, her beauty unblemished by the years. Except for a few fragments here and there, the wood was replaced by thousands upon thousands of small, white, hollow calcareous tubes one or two inches in length – the protective home of wood-boring molluscs.

I began to wonder whether the metal sub-deck would support us when Alvin made her first landing.

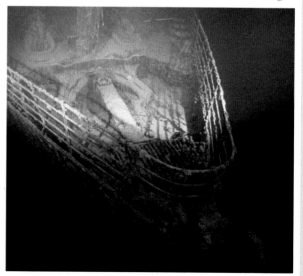

From *The Discovery of the Titanic*, Robert Ballard, Orion, 1995

1 The great wreck was

   A anchored to the sea floor
   B buried deep in the mud
   C standing on its bow
   D travelling across the sea-bed

In question 1, each answer picks up an idea from the first paragraph.
A: the anchors are mentioned in the text but they are hanging – the ship is not anchored, so **A** is wrong.
C: the bow is mentioned, but the ship can't be standing on its bow because the bow is visible to the writer, so **C** is wrong.
D: the fact that the great wreck 'seemed' to be coming towards them is mentioned, but of course it is not the ship that is moving but the submarine, so **D** is wrong. To spot this you have to remember to think about the whole sentence – it is the ship that is mentioned in the question, not the submarine!
The only answer that fits with the question to give a clearly true sentence is **B**, because the text states that the ship was buried deep in the mud.

2 The ship was covered in

   A bacteria
   B blood
   C icicles
   D rust

In question 2, each of the suggested answers picks up a word from the second or third paragraph.
Is the answer **A**? There is a reference to rust-eating bacteria in the text, but look again at the **question** – the text doesn't say that the ship was covered in bacteria, so **A** doesn't match with the question to make a true statement, and it is wrong.
How about **B**? In the text there is a reference to blood – 'the blood of the great ship' – but this is only an image of the rust, used to give a sinister impression. The ship was not really covered in blood, so **B** is wrong.
C may look tempting because the text mentions icicles and if the *Titanic* hit an iceberg it could perhaps be covered in icicles. But the idea of icicles is only an image to tell us what the ship looked like – it was not literally covered in icicles, so **C** is wrong.
What the ship was actually covered in was rust, so **D** is the right answer.

3 The portholes of the wrecked ship had

   A become pitted
   B glass in them
   C lights in them
   D rusted away

For question 3, again it's important to think about the whole sentence that you are making when you consider each answer – it is about the portholes, not just the ship in general. So look for evidence for each of the possible sentences in the text, watching out for a reference to the portholes. You'll find 'the still unbroken glass of the portholes' and you don't have to look any further – the answer must be **B**. If you want to be sure, check where in the passage the other ideas come from and work out why they are wrong.

4 They were steering the little submarine

   A across the forward deck
   B around the anchor
   C down through the hatch
   D through one of the portholes

Analyse question 4 in the same way as question 3. The correct answer is **A** and you will find in the text clear evidence for the sentence, 'They were steering the little submarine across the forward deck'. Match the other three answers with the question and work out why they can't be right.

Now try questions 5 and 6 on your own!

5 The woodwork of the ship was

   A eaten away
   B in long planks
   C rotted away
   D well preserved

6 The men in the submarine were

   A afraid they would see ghosts
   B crying when they saw the ship
   C excited by what they saw
   D hit by a bollard

Exercise 2

Nearly one-fourth of the world's known mammal species are threatened with extinction according to a recent study compiled by the IUCN (World Conservation Union). This suggests that earlier estimates of the number of endangered species must have been too low.

The latest update in a series known as the Red List, the report is the most comprehensive evaluation of globally threatened animals ever compiled, and the first to assess all known mammal species.

Until now, birds were the only group fully assessed. With 11% of all bird species facing the threat of extinction and 70% experiencing population declines, scientists had relied largely on the status of birds as an indicator of the level of threat to all terrestrial life forms.

The number of mammals on the Red List – a shocking 1096 of the 4630 known species – has spurred calls for an intensified international focus on biodiversity loss. The report also found that nearly one-third of all 275 primate species are at risk, almost three times the number of previous estimates.

The new survey was compiled using a revised set of criteria, which the authors described as more objective than those used in

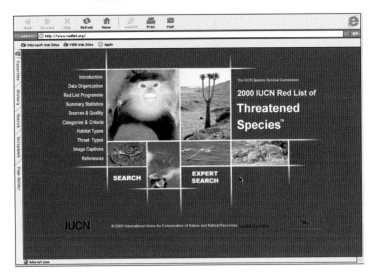

previous estimates, to determine the threat of extinction. The Red List recognises three distinct categories of risk: of the 1096 species of mammals considered threatened, 169 are listed as 'critically endangered', 315 as 'endangered', and 612 as 'vulnerable'. Each classification is largely determined by the rate of a species' population decline over the past 10 years, as well as the number of surviving adults and the stability of habitat.

George Rabb, chair of the IUCN species survival commission which compiled the list, said that the report should serve as a 'red flag', focusing attention on the most significant factor threatening the survival of species: the destruction of habitat brought about by human population growth and economic development.

Other contributing factors, he said, include pollution, overharvesting, and the introduction of foreign species. At current rates of decline, biologists fear that many mammals with niches or habitat needs that conflict with human development may soon come to depend on the tinkering hand of wildlife management and captive breeding – unable to exist without human intervention.

From The Worldwatch Institute, www.worldwatch.org, IUCN Red List, www.redlist.org

1 The number of mammals threatened with extinction is

    A a quarter
    B low
    C 11%
    D 4630

2 Previous reports only

    A reported mainly on birds
    B reported mainly on mammals
    C reported on 11% of species
    D reported on 70% of species

3 The number of mammal species likely to disappear is

  A one-third
  B 275
  C 1096
  D 4630

4 Endangered species are identified by

  A being kept in stables
  B being put on the Red List
  C changing the rules
  D waving a red flag

5 The most important reason for the decline in animal species is

  A animals are being harvested for humans to eat
  B animals are imported from one country to another
  C humans are destroying the places where animals live
  D humans are polluting the atmosphere, stopping animals breathing

6 In the future many mammals will exist only by

  A being bred in sanctuaries or zoos
  B being sent to foreign lands
  C fighting human beings
  D living with people as pets

Exercise 3

A late summer evening, walking back home. Whoosh! A jogger runs by. Arms clenched in concentration, heart pumping and adrenaline flowing. Turn a corner and I nearly hit another one. He apologises. Like the first, he doesn't appear to be enjoying his hobby. Or is he? There's a pained expression on his face, but then maybe that's the point – no pain, no gain. You sense this is something they simply MUST do.

Ever since the 'Get Britain Fit' campaigns of the 1970s, there has been a strong emphasis on health, exercise and participation in sport in general. According to Mintel, 8.3 million adults in the UK now use gyms or fitness centres. However this rise has seen the emergence of a new kind of obsession and the dawn of the fitness addict. There's every possibility that you might

know one – or even become one yourself.

Take Julia, a telephone engineer from Bristol, for example. She started aerobics classes simply 'to do something about myself. It was

a pure vanity thing,' she says.

But it soon became an obsession.

'It quickly developed from twice a week to four times. On a Tuesday I'd do a step class from six to seven, wait 20 minutes and do another aerobics class. Then come home and collapse.'

At its peak Julia was going six times a week. 'I did actually feel healthy,' she explains, 'but I did notice if I missed a day I'd get really crabby.'

Then came the physical effects. 'I started to get cramps and aches and pains. I'd stretch in the morning, feel my hamstring pull and I'd be crippled, walking round the bathroom trying to pull my hamstring out.'

It was also affecting her social life. 'I had started to lose some of the relationships with the friends I had, because of all the time I was exercising. It dominated my life all the time,' she admits.

Julia knew it was time to slow down when she began to get constant pains in her legs, because of the continual high impact exercise, and even now, years later, she has some permanent physical problems which have resulted from this time in her life. 'I've still got loads of bumps on my legs and I've also got a back problem which my chiropractor has confirmed is linked to this period.'

How do people such as Julia find themselves in this situation – and are they really damaging their health in their efforts to get fit? Surely doing too much exercise is preferable to slobbing about? 'I'd definitely say that as addictions go, it's nowhere near as bad as alcohol,' says one academic who has studied this area, Professor Hannah Steinberg of Middlesex University. 'On the whole it is still pretty rare but it is growing.'

On one level, exercise addiction is simply a question of body chemistry, of releasing endorphins, the pleasure receptors in the human brain. Says Professor Steinberg: 'They are released into the bloodstream in times of great exertion, like exercise. It may be that the "high" people get is like one opiate addicts get.' Endorphins also act as a natural painkiller, so if you train very hard and get injured, you tend not to notice it and continue.

For Julia, exercise was her way of staying in control. 'If your life is spinning out of control, exercise is one thing to cling on to. It gave me

something to focus on, something to channel my energies into.'

This issue of 'control' is where exercise addiction and the eating disorders anorexia and bulimia can merge. For one exercise addict, Beth, a Bristol student, the two went hand in hand. Beth started exercising regularly in sixth form, in an effort to 'lose weight and look thinner'. 'I'd be doing aerobics, exercise bikes and swimming at school, and running out of school. At its peak I was running three miles a day and doing half an hour of sit-ups after that. On top of that I wasn't eating properly. Looking back, I think I definitely had an eating disorder at that time,' she explains. 'I desperately wanted to be thinner. I suppose everyone has this image of wanting to be a perfect size 10. You're told that you can't lose weight without exercise, so you don't eat and you exercise a lot. You think you're doing it right, but you're not.'

Jim McKenna, a lecturer at Bristol University's Sport, Exercise and Health Sciences faculty, has seen many examples of so-called exercise dependency. 'The evidence is that more women than men are involved – but then the guys don't tend to want to admit to it,' he says. Exercise addiction is often coupled with an eating disorder that can lead to a loss of menstrual function in women, which in turn can cause calcium loss from the bones and may lead to osteoporosis.

'Men,' explains Jim McKenna, 'will gradually become infertile when they fall below a certain percentage level of body fat. You

become catabolic; that's when your body starts breaking itself down to provide the nutrients you need to give yourself energy – you're eating yourself up because of the amount of exercise and you're starving because you can't find time to eat.'

Another downside to exercise dependency is that the warning signs are hard to spot. Its victims are nowhere near as obvious as alcoholics. 'Runners seem to be particularly affected by this,' explains McKenna. 'Light, wiry types who can run and run don't get warning signs, because they are built to do that kind of activity. Training is a great mask.'

While fitness dependents have their own reasons for pursuing their obsession, at the bottom must lie the social pressures of the 1990s. In Western society, whilst we are taught to be good consumers, there is an increasing emphasis on not consuming too much, on staying thin and looking healthy. Both sexes are bombarded with these sorts of aspirational images. All well and good if you're that size anyway, but men and women come in all shapes and sizes and forcing yourself to be something you're not seems to be counter-productive. 'There does seem to be a "body beautiful" thing that people seem to be obsessed with,' suggests Julia, 'rather than exercising for health's sake.'

And advice for anyone who knows of someone in this state? 'You can't MAKE anyone else give it up if they don't want to,' says McKenna, 'but there is a need to gradually reduce training and to do it right.' ■

Adapted by authors

1 Joggers

    A are a danger to pedestrians
    B have to keep stopping to apologise
    C look as if they are in pain
    D punch people as they go along

2 When she was most obsessed Julia trained

    A twice a week
    B four times a week
    C six times a week
    D seven times a week

3 Julia reduced her exercising because

    A her doctor told her to
    B her social life was not good
    C she felt healthy enough
    D she had problems with her health

4 People exercise hard because it

    A becomes an addiction
    B purifies the blood
    C stops them drinking alcohol
    D stops them getting injured

5 Beth exercised

    A to cure her eating illness
    B so she could get into sports teams
    C so she could lose weight
    D so she could stop her bones becoming weaker

6 Society says

    A exercise and be healthy
    B exercise and be thin
    C exercise to reduce the birth rate
    D exercise to avoid becoming an alcoholic

Exercise 4

After the great rain of 1939, the rainfall declined noticeably in each successive year. In 1940, the slight fall was of no consequence because our major worry was that the accumulation of growth on the land would produce serious bushfires. These did occur on land quite close to us, but my father's foresight in getting cattle to eat down the high grass preserved Coorain from that danger.

In 1941, the only rain of the year was a damp cold rain with high wind which came during the lambing season in May and June and carried off many ewes and their newborn lambs. After that there were no significant rainfalls for five years. The unfolding of a drought of these dimensions has a slow and inexorable quality. The weather perpetually holds out hope. Storm clouds gather. Thunder rolls by. But nothing happens. Each year as the season for rain approaches, people begin to look hopefully up at the sky. It mocks them with a few showers, barely enough to lay the dust. That is all.

It takes a long time for a carefully managed grazing property to decline, but three years without rain will do it. Once the disaster begins, it unfolds swiftly. So it was with us.

My father and I would set out to work on horseback as usual, but instead of our customary cheerful and wide-ranging conversations he would be silent. As we looked at sheep, or tried to assess the pasture left in a particular paddock, he would swear softly, looking over the fence to a neighbour's property, already eaten out and beginning to blow sand.

Each time he said, 'If it doesn't rain, it will bury this feed in a few weeks.' It was true and I could think of nothing consoling to say.

His usual high spirits declined with the state of the land, until the terrible day when many of our own sheep were lost because of a sudden cold rain and wind when they had too little food in their stomachs. By 1942 it was apparent that the drought could be serious.

Shortly afterwards, the first terrible dust storm arrived boiling out of the central Australian desert. One sweltering late afternoon in March, I walked out to collect wood for the stove. Glancing towards the west, I saw a terrifying sight. A vast boiling cloud was mounting in the sky, black and sulphurous yellow at the heart, varying shades of ochre red at the edges. Where I stood, the air was utterly still, but the writhing cloud was approaching silently and with great speed. Suddenly I noticed that there were no birds to be seen or heard. All had taken shelter. I called my mother. We watched helplessly. Always one for action, she turned swiftly, went indoors and began to close windows. Outside I collected the buckets, rakes, shovels and other implements that could blow away or smash a window if hurled against one by the boiling wind. Within the hour, my father arrived home. He and my mother sat on the back step not in their usual restful contemplation, but silenced instead by dread.

A dust storm usually lasts days, blotting out the sun, launching banshee winds day and night. It is dangerous to stray far from shelter, because the sand and grit lodge in one's eyes, and a visibility often reduced to a few feet can make one completely disorientated. Animals which become exhausted and lie down are often sanded over and smothered. There is nothing anyone can do but stay inside, waiting for the calm after the storm. Inside, it is stifling. Every window must be closed against the dust, which seeps relentlessly through the slightest crack. Meals are gritty and sleep elusive. Rising in the morning, one sees a perfect outline of one's body, an after image of white where the dust has not collected on the sheets.

As the winds seared our land, they took away the dry herbage, piled it against the fences, and then slowly began to silt over the debris. It was three days before we could venture out, days of almost

unendurable tension. The crashing of the boughs of trees against our roof and the sharp roar as a nearly empty rainwater tank blew off its stand and rolled away, triggered my father's recurring nightmares of France, so that when he did fall into a fitful slumber it would be to awake screaming. It was usually I who woke him from his nightmares. I, the child in the family, would waken and attempt to soothe a frantic adult.

When we emerged, there were several feet of sand piled up against the windbreak to my mother's garden; the contours of new sandhills were beginning to form in places where the dust eddied and collected. There was no question that there were also many more bare patches where the remains of dry grass and herbage had lifted and blown away.

It was always a miracle to me that animals could endure so much. As we checked the property, there were dead sheep in every paddock to be sure, but fewer than I'd feared. My spirits began to rise and I kept telling my father the damage was not too bad. 'That was only the first storm,' he said bleakly. He had seen it all before and knew what was to come.

From *The Road from Coorain: An Australian Memoir*, by Jill Ker Conway, Vintage, 1992

1 There was most rain in

   A 1939
   B 1940
   C 1941
   D 1946

2 The sheep died because

   A they ate the sand
   B they starved to death
   C they were taken by neighbours
   D they were too weak to resist illness

3 The writer called her mother because

   A she couldn't find the birds
   B she had collected all the wood
   C she was frightened of what she could see
   D it was getting cloudy

4 The dust storm lasted for

   A a day and a night
   B a number of days
   C until the sun went down
   D until they woke up

5 The father's experience in the First World War

   A gave him nightmares
   B happened when he was a child
   C meant he became very tense
   D meant he had seen sand storms before

6 After the storm

   A all the sheep were dead
   B only the paddocks were damaged
   C some of the sheep were dead
   D they didn't find much damage

Section 2 *Short-answer and structured questions*

In the Reading and Directed Writing paper, questions will be set to test your understanding of a piece of text printed on the question paper. The essential thing is to make sure the examiner can see how well you have understood the text. This will often mean expressing your understanding by using your own words, as will be explained below.

The questions are of two different types: short-answer questions and structured questions. **Short-answer questions** are straightforward and – as you would expect – require brief factual answers to show simply that you have understood a particular piece of information in the text. Your answer must include the information which is set out in the examiner's 'mark scheme' – a document guiding him/her on how to award marks for a paper.

A **structured question** is effectively a series of short-answer questions, but the final question in the series is likely to be more open-ended, asking you to analyse what you have read and express a personal response to the text.

▨ Understanding what you have read

This is sometimes referred to as **interpreting** what you have read and is a basic comprehension skill. It involves, of course, not only reading the passage carefully but the questions on it as well. You can find advice about this in Chapter 1 (pages 6–10).

When you read a passage set for a comprehension exercise, you must try to ensure that you understand it well enough to be able to select all the details that are relevant to the question you are answering. For some of the more straightforward questions, all you will have to do is list the details. (Question 1 in the examples later in this chapter – see page 30 – is this type of question.) Although these questions seem simple it is important that you answer them carefully: the examiner cannot know that you have understood a question unless your answer demonstrates your understanding.

▨ Applying your understanding

The more demanding questions will expect you not simply to interpret the text but also to **apply** the information. This may well involve using it in a new situation. For example, you may read a passage describing the sights of a large city and then be asked to imagine that you have just arrived in the city for the first time. You have to write a letter home describing your impressions of the city. In order to do this well, you must:

- **select the relevant information** from the passage
- then **apply it to the context** in which you are required to write.

More complex questions require you to **bring together various pieces of information** from different parts of the text(s) that you have read. Putting these key pieces of information together will produce a new version of the text. This skill is called **synthesis**. An example of a question requiring synthesis is Question 4 on page 30. Synthesis is, of course, particularly important in summary-type questions where you have to identify the key points from the text(s) and put them together in your own, shorter version.

■ Achieving exam success

The secret to success with short-answer and structured questions lies in the way you *read* the passages. You should ensure that you spend enough time understanding the passage as fully as you can, before you begin to write. Remember that when you are reading you are looking to select relevant details. It is best to take it in stages.

Step 1: Read the whole passage once

Read through the passage from beginning to end, at normal reading speed. This will help to fix the whole passage in your mind and enable you to gain a general, overall understanding of it. Do not worry too much at this stage about the occasional difficult word whose meaning is not clear; it is gaining the **overview** of the passage that is important.

Step 2: Read the question

The next step is to read through all the questions that you will have to answer on the passage so that when you re-read the passage you will know what to look out for.

Step 3: Read the passage again

This second reading of the passage is of absolute importance. You must attempt to gain as complete an understanding of the passage as you possibly can. Do not just look at the words; think carefully about what they mean in context, and, in particular, think about those sections on which the questions are focused. It may help to underline or ring key points in the text so that you can find them quickly when you are writing your answers. If you have a clear understanding of both the passage and the questions, you are well on your way to success in this part of the examination.

Step 4: Answer the questions

Try to put yourself in the position of the examiner who is reading your answer. Remember: he/she will only have what you have written on your answer paper as evidence of how well you have understood what you have read. He/she will not know what has gone on in your mind to produce the answers that you have written. It is, therefore, of the utmost importance that what you have written provides the most complete and focused evidence of what you have understood that you can possibly give.

- Make sure the details you select are relevant to the question.
- Write your answers clearly without irrelevant comments.
- Use your own words when asked to explain details or vocabulary from the passage and make your explanation as full as possible, to demonstrate your understanding. If you are asked to explain the meaning of a word such as 'exciting', an answer that reads 'something that makes you feel excited' cannot be rewarded. However, a definition such as 'something that you find stimulating or thrilling' would score full marks.

More complex questions may require you to interpret and apply the material that you have read and, possibly, to extract different points from different sections to produce a complete answer. There are two main points to remember here.

- The more marks there are available for a question, the more points you will need to identify for your answer.
- Include *all* the details that you consider to be relevant.

You might think that some of these are too obvious to be worth including, but unless you write them down on your answer paper, the examiners will not have the evidence they need to be convinced that *you* have understood them.

Different types of reading comprehension passage

The comprehension passages will be factual, imaginative, descriptive or argumentative writing. The types of question set are likely to vary, depending upon the type of passage you are given.

Factual texts

If the passage is an informative, non-fiction piece, it is likely that the questions will ask you to identify specific points and details. Most probably, the order of the questions will follow the order of the passage – that is, the answers to the earlier questions will be found in the first part of the passage, and so on. However, you should look out for those more complicated questions which require you to select details from more than one part of the passage to produce a complete answer. Such questions will usually carry high marks and so can be easily identified. When answering these more complicated questions, you must ensure that you select your details carefully and focus precisely on what the question asks you to do. Unnecessary irrelevance will only confuse an examiner. Remember, careful reading of the question is just as important as careful reading of the passage.

Imaginative or autobiographical texts

If the extract is taken from a piece of fiction or autobiography, then it is probable that there will be a wider range of questions. The earlier questions may still be factually based (e.g. *From your reading of the passage, what have you discovered was the occupation of the main character?*) In this type of question the answer will be either right or wrong and you should be able to check it quite easily. However, the more demanding questions may ask you to use interpretation skills to arrive at the answer (e.g. *From your reading of the passage, what have you learned about the personality of the main character?*) The answers to this type of question are less straightforward to find and you must search the text for clues. The examiners will not be expecting a right or wrong answer to this sort of question; instead they will be looking for evidence that you have understood the details of the passage and can apply this to produce a consistent interpretation of the question.

In conclusion, it is important that you approach the comprehension section of the paper methodically. Careful reading of the passage and the questions is essential, and clearly written, detailed answers to the questions are required. Do not try to shortcut this approach; remember, the examiner can only give you credit for what you have written on the paper. If a point has been omitted, no matter how simple it may seem and how easily you may have understood it, if it is not in your answer the examiner will not know that you have been aware of it.

■ Examples of reading comprehension work

We will now look at how this advice applies in practice. First, read the passage 'After the Bombs, The Human Cost'. It describes the work of an organisation called Feed the Children which brings help to people suffering from the effects of the war in Bosnia in the early 1990s. After this, you will find some questions and some suggested ways of answering them. Finally, we have included some answers given by candidates in the examination, with comments on them made by the examiner.

Example 1

After the Bombs, The Human Cost

The old lady had spent the entire winter in a tiny cellar in Gorazde amid filth and damp and a tumble of cardboard boxes, with no light, nowhere to sit, a little wood-stove in the adjoining cellar, and a waterless sink. How had she survived the bitter weather?

The man who had taken me to visit her was Oliver Burch of the charity Feed the Children. The old lady was one of his 'beneficiaries'; one of nineteen Croats left in the Muslim enclave. He provides her with food and blankets and warm clothes. And visits. This one brought a smile to her toothless old face.

'Why can't you move her?' I asked. 'Not our job,' Oliver said. 'Housing is down to the local social services, and they're amiable, lazy, well-meaning, and totally overwhelmed.' Seeing my newly arrived and still shockable face, he added kindly, 'You haven't seen anything yet.'

I'd had time to get used to one thing before coming to Gorazde – ruined buildings. After a week, it was the undamaged ones that looked strange. I could soon tell the difference between war damage, and homes deliberately brought down with dynamite, or burnt out. These were somehow worse than the shell-holed ones because to destroy homes on purpose seemed so vindictive and senseless.

Oliver came to Bosnia from Britain four years ago as a volunteer. With his Muslim wife, Nerma, he now runs the charity's Gorazde operation. He worked in a bakery in Mostar when he first arrived, and this is where he met Nerma. They made bread together through some of the worst of the war, and now live with their baby daughter, Medina, in a tiny flat in a private house which smells very strongly of cabbage and unflushable toilets.

They have a private generator for lights only; all water has to be fetched, and showers are of the bucket-and-scoop variety. A wood-stove serves for cooking and heating. I slept in the house next door, in a bedroom so cold my landlady used it as a fridge for butter and milk, and wrote my journal by candlelight.

I had no complaints, especially after being taken to 'The Balkans', one of a number of collection centres in Gorazde for Muslim refugees who were chased from their homes by the Serbs. The centres are ex-hotels, schools and blocks of flats, broken-down and shell-damaged warrens of little rooms leading off filthy, unlit corridors. Each room houses a family. One family had two rooms, but there were sixteen of them, four generations, including the oldest daughter, her husband and one-year-old twins, who'd moved back for the winter because it had been too cold where they were living.

These rooms, not to mention the communal toilets on each floor, are, for the most part, almost indescribably squalid. Wood-burning stoves make the walls black; the floors are uncleanable (one woman told me that more than anything she wanted a broom); river-washed clothes are strung on indoor lines. Around the walls are heaps of pitiful possessions housed in makeshift shelving or boxes. Sometimes the boxes in which aid is delivered turn out as useful as the contents – to make tables, stools, storage units, and for carrying water or bathing babies.

I felt awkward in my role as observer before these poor women who have been living like this, some of them, for four years. But they welcomed us with smiles, strong, freshly ground coffee, and something to eat; they posed willingly for photographs and children crawled into Nerma's lap.

Feed the Children is their lifeline. Oliver is not only their immediate source of food; they trust him to ensure that their food parcels reach them intact. But there are hiccups. Oliver can't deliver every item himself; he has to delegate, and those to whom this honour falls sometimes prove untrustworthy. He finds this out by doing frequent spot-checks. When he finds 'irregularities' (a tin of meat mysteriously missing from each parcel, lists containing names of families no longer there) he simply stops deliveries of food to that area.

Next day, someone will approach Oliver in the street. 'Do you have to stop giving us our food?' 'Not at all,' he replies blandly. 'You just need to choose a new delegate, one you can trust to keep our rules.' A new rep is chosen and things get under way again.

© Lynne Reid Banks, Children's Aid Direct, 1996

> **1** State one fact mentioned in the second paragraph which is a reason why the old lady was able to survive the winter. (1 mark)

This is a question requiring straightforward interpretation and you are told exactly where to find the answer so you know you don't need to include information from anywhere else. A correct answer would be something similar to: 'The charity gave her food, blankets and clothes.'

> **2** What two things, according to the passage, led to the buildings being damaged? (2 marks)

Again, this requires simple interpretation, although you need to reword the original statement to demonstrate your understanding. A good answer, earning the two marks, could be: 'Some were ruined by the shells used in the fighting and others were destroyed or burnt down on purpose.'

> **3** What was Oliver's occupation when he first arrived in Mostar? (1 mark)

This is another straightforward piece of interpretation and the answer is 'He was a baker' or 'He worked in a bakery'.

> **4** What do we learn from the passage about the writer's opinion of the women living in 'The Balkans'? (3 marks)

This requires a little more selection and synthesis of material from different points in the text. Find the first reference to 'The Balkans' (paragraph seven, first line) and then select only those details related to the characters of the women. The following answer includes all the points needed and expresses them in a way which proves that the reader has understood the relevant text and the question. It would score the three marks. 'The women were friendly, generous and good-natured. They were not shy as they happily posed for photographs and despite their squalid conditions they tried hard to keep their apartments as clean and tidy as possible.'

As you can see from this example, you need to turn some of the narrative into more general points (for example, 'they posed willingly for the photographs' tells us that they were not in any way shy). The final statement (about keeping their apartments clean and tidy) needs to be inferred from the information given in paragraph eight.

> **5** What problems does Oliver face through not being able to deliver the food himself? (3 marks)

The answer to this question is to be found in the last two paragraphs. However, you need to select your information carefully and also make sure that you explain the difficult words like 'delegate' clearly. A good answer, scoring all three marks, would be: 'There are too many items for Oliver to deliver them all himself and so he has to rely on other people to do it for him. These people are not always honest and may try to keep some of the food for themselves. Oliver, therefore, has to keep a careful check on those who work for him.'

Examples of candidates' answers to comprehension questions

Now we are going to compare the way three different candidates answered some of the questions on the same reading passage, 'After the Bombs, The Human Cost'. Some of the errors they made have been highlighted.

> **6** Why has the old lady not been moved into a better house? (3 marks)

The allocation of three marks to this question suggests that it is necessary to identify three specific details.

Candidate A's response:

Key
■ Errors of expression
Spelling/punctuation errors

The old lady didn't move into a better house because a house where she live is down to the local social services and no money to services herself.

Examiner's comment: This answer did not gain any marks as it does not provide any reason which is given in the passage. There is a hint that the writer understands that the failure to move the old lady had something to do with the local social services but the reference is only general and needs more detailed explanation. The limitations of the writer's expression also prevent the reader gaining a clear understanding of what is being said.

> **Note:** In the examples throughout the book the original spellings, punctuation and style have been retained. Examiners are as much concerned with rewarding positive merits of style, vocabulary and so on as with identifying errors. For this reason, it is unlikely that any examiner would mark up every error made and the marking reflects this principle.

Candidate B's response:

Oliver Burch of the charity Feed, wasn't allowed to move the old lady because that job should be done by the social services. The problem was that services were very lazy and won't do anything.

Examiner's comment: This answer is a little better than Candidate A's. It also refers to the social services with a specific reason being included in the final paragraph. However, the candidate stops here and is unable or unwilling to go beyond this one point — probably he/she did not take any notice of the fact that the question is worth three marks. The answer gained one mark.

Candidate C's response:

The old lady has not been moved into a better house because the local social services, which is suppose to provided houses, are lazy, well-meaning and totally in a chaos.

Examiner's comment: This is a better answer than the other two. The passage has been understood and there is a clear attempt to use own words to show understanding — in this case, 'totally in a chaos' has been used to explain being over-stretched or too busy. This answer scored two marks. There is a further point which could have been made but it requires the use of inference: paragraph four suggests that there may not be enough secure buildings remaining to provide homes for all the people who need them.

> **7** Explain three things that Oliver does to help the people of Gorazde.
> (3 marks)

Candidate A's response:

Oliver provides them with food, blankets and warm clothes. He also gave them with smiles to all the people who stay after the bombs. He also help people for their place to live (ruined buildings). He stops deliveries of food to that area.

Examiner's comment: This answer scored two marks as it mentions that Oliver provides food and blankets for the people in the area. It does not mention that he is in charge of aid in Gorazde (this is exactly the sort of point it is easy to omit, as many candidates assume that it is so obvious that it does not need to be made!) The candidate also fails to mention clearly that Oliver visits the people in the area.

Candidate B's response:

Oliver is charged to provide source of food, ensure that the food parcels reach the people intact, and up to the moment he was the delegate in which people trusted to keep the rules.

Examiner's comment: This response also fails to focus clearly on the question and mentions only the detail about providing food; the rest of the answer lacks specific details. It scored only one mark.

Candidate C's response:

Oliver provides his 'beneficiaries' food, blankets, warm clothes and visits them. He provides food parcels to 'The Balkans' through delegates, and he also does frequent spot-checks to ensures that delegates are keeping to the rules created by the Feed The Children.

Examiner's comment: This answer gains all three available marks in its first sentence. The points are precisely selected and the answer shows a clear understanding. Although the second sentence is not strictly necessary it helps to reinforce the answer and shows that the candidate has understood the point about Oliver being in charge of aid.

8 Make a list of four words which best describe the rooms where people are living in Gorazde. (4 marks)

Candidate A's response:

Poor area
Sad room
Speces room

Examiner's comment: This answer lacks any precise details from the original passage and reveals that the writer's understanding of both the question and passage is extremely limited. It scored no marks.

Candidate B's response:

Very cold bedrooms
Furniture is replaced by boxes
Little rooms with too much people in them
At night a candlelight is all the light they can have (because there are not enough power generators)

Examiner's comment: Candidate B identifies that the rooms were cold and small but makes one irrelevant statement (if the answer had been 'there is very limited, inadequate furniture' then it would have been correct). Although the final statement implies an understanding that the rooms are dark, it is too long-winded and imprecise to be rewarded. The question asks for only **four** words and the writer appears to have forgotten this. However, the answer shows sufficient understanding to be awarded two marks.

Candidate C's response:

> The rooms where people in Gorazde lives are small, smells, unhygenic and unorganised.

Examiner's comment: This again shows a direct and concise response and quickly scores three marks. However, there is no evidence in the passage of the rooms being 'unorganised' and it may be that in attempting to use his/her own words the writer has failed to show a clear understanding of the 'overcrowded' point.

> **9** If you had been to Gorazde with the writer, what do you think your chief memories would have been? Describe **two** different memories and explain why each was important to you. (4 marks)

This is a more complex task worth four marks. The candidates must show some ability to think themselves into a role, identify two distinct memories and give convincing reasons for choosing them.

Candidate A's response:

> I think if I had been to Gorazde with the winter my chief memories would have been ... so please with the peoples who live in that area because all the house were destroyed or burnt out. People are no clothes to make them get warm and no food to eat. Some people no where to live so they have to find somewhere to live. It's might a little room but have to stay with ten people. The house also had a very strong smell of cabbage and unflushable toilets. It's become this problem because there are no water to supply. It was important to me because I can felt how are they like.

Examiner's comment: This answer has obvious limitations of written expression, although the first half does reveal an understanding of the plight of the people. There is a direct and convincing reference to the smell of the houses and some attempt to justify it. This question does not have a mark-per-point mark scheme and enough partial points have been made to achieve a mark of two.

Candidate B's response:

I would never forget the kindness in which people received us. Though the misery they had, they welcomed us with smiles and something to eat, I will never forget that special moment. In fact they were very humble and cheerful people. And the other thing I would never forget, is the way how people lived in Gorazde, really is very terrible.

Examiner's comment: Candidate B identifies the kindness of the people and the harsh state of their lives. The answer is well focused and quite clearly expressed but the reasoning is not fully convincing. It was awarded a mark of three.

Candidate C's response:

If I had been to Gorazde with the writer, my chief memories would have been the conditions of the people and the greeting which the women in 'the Balkans' gave to us. The conditions of the people in Gorazde is important to me because by observing the severe condions of the people I could understand the disastorous effect of war and develop and spread anti-war feelings among people. Also I could take actions and gather support from other people in order to improve the situation in Gorazda by rising money, goods or food. The way in which the women in 'the Balkans' greeted me would be very important to me because I noticed the warm hearted feeling people can still hold although they are in a miserable situation. Also it showed me the strength and courage which people have inside them.

Examiner's comment: Candidate C fully understands the requirements of the question. His/her answer clearly states the two memories in the first sentence. This is followed by well-developed and convincing reasons – in fact, there are more than enough explanations for both points. This answer well deserved the full four marks.

Practise answering reading comprehension questions

Exercise 1

You will probably find the following extract easier to understand than some of the more informative writing you have already looked at in Chapter 1 and the earlier part of Chapter 2. Be careful, therefore, that you do not fall into the trap of reading it passively. It is important that you continue to **concentrate on extracting the meaning** as fully as possible. With this type of writing you are not looking just to identify relevant facts but also, for example, to indicate an understanding of the motives and personalities of the characters described. Think about this as you answer the questions which follow the passage.

Read this extract from a story about Boy Blue. He wants everyone to know how good he is at catching the big crabs that are stranded on the shore. This time he goes too far and in the latter part of the story he has to be rescued by fishermen.

Catching things gave us little boys a great thrill. Boy Blue wanted to catch the crabs as a kind of triumph. He looked like a big crab crawling on all fours, and he made us laugh with the shift and shake of his slouching movements.

The crabs dropped their eyes and remained still. It was always very difficult to tell what they would do. Sometimes they would scamper wildly if you were a mile away, and at other times they would crouch and bundle themselves together the nearer you approached. Boy Blue lay flat in the sand with his hands stretched out full length. The crabs were trying to make a way into the sand. They had seen him but there was no great hurry in escaping. They could appear and disappear while you waited and watched. His hands had them covered but there was no contact. The difficulties had only started.

When you were catching crabs with bare hands you required great skill. You had to place your thumb and index finger somewhere between the body and the claws of the crab. That was very tricky, since the crabs' claws were free like revolving chairs. They could spin in all directions, and the crabs raised and dropped them to make any angle. Hundreds of boys were squeezed in their efforts to trap the crabs barehanded. If you missed the grip, or gripped a minute too soon the claws had clinched you. And they cut like blades. You had to know your job. You had to be a crab catcher, as we would say.

Boy Blue considered that he was a master at the art. He had caught several in his time. The art had become a practised routine. He lay flat with his hands pressed on the crabs' backs. He was trying to gather two of them up together. His thumb had found the spot between the claw and the body of the crab. The crabs were still but buckled tight; so that it was difficult to strengthen the grip. Sometimes they seemed to understand the game. They remained still and stiffly buckled, and when you least expected the claws flashed like edged weapons.

The waves came up and the sand slid back. It seemed they would escape. Boy Blue had missed his grip. The wave came again and the sand sloped. Boy Blue slid back and the crabs were free. He propelled his feet in the sand in an attempt to heave himself forward. His weight pressed down. The wave receded and the sand shifted sharply. He came to a kneeling position and the sand slipped deeper. The crabs were safe. He threw his hand up and stood. The sand shifted under his feet and the waves hastening to the shore lashed him face downward. The salt stung his eyes and he groped his way to his feet. Another wave heaved and he tottered. The crabs! The crabs had disappeared.

We couldn't understand what was happening. Boy Blue was laughing. It made us frightened the way he laughed. A wave wrenched him and now he was actually in the sea. We shivered, dumb. A wave pushed him up, and another completing the somersault pushed him down. He screamed and we screamed too. He was out of sight and we screamed with all the strength of our lungs.

From *In the Castle of my Skin*, by George C. Lamming, Longman, 1979

1 Why did Boy Blue like to catch crabs? (1 mark)

2 What **two** things are crabs most likely to do when they are aware that someone is trying to catch them? (4 marks)

3 What is the greatest danger faced by someone trying to catch crabs with their bare hands? (2 marks)

4 Describe in detail Boy Blue's technique for catching crabs. (4 marks)
5 In your own words state clearly what happened to Boy Blue after he missed his grip on the crabs. (4 marks)

Exercise 2

Read carefully the passage entitled *Leela's Friend* and then answer all the questions which follow.

Leela's Friend

The young boy Sidda was hanging about the gate at a moment when Mr. Sivasanker was standing in the front veranda of his house, brooding over the servant problem.

'Sir, do you want a servant?' Sidda asked.

'Come in,' said Mr. Sivasanker. As Sidda opened the gate and came in, Mr. Sivasanker looked at him hard and said to himself, 'Doesn't seem to be a bad sort . . . At any rate, the fellow looks tidy.'

'Where were you before?' he asked.

Sidda said, 'In a bungalow there,' and indicated a vague somewhere, 'in the doctor's house.'

'What is his name?'

'I don't know, master,' Sidda said. 'He lives near the market.'

'Why did they send you away?'

'They left the town, master,' Sidda said, giving the stock reply.

Mr. Sivasanker was unable to make up his mind. He called his wife. She looked at Sidda and said, 'He doesn't seem to me worse than the others we have had.' Leela, their five-year-old daughter, came out and gave a cry of joy. 'Oh, Father!' she said, 'I like him. Don't send him away. Let us keep him in our house.' And that decided it.

Sidda was given two meals a day and four rupees a month, in return for which he washed clothes, tended the garden, ran errands, chopped wood and looked after Leela.

'Sidda, come and play!' Leela would cry, and Sidda had to drop any work he might be doing and run to her, as she stood in front of the garden with a red ball in her hand. His company made her extremely happy. She flung the ball at him and he flung it back. And then she said, 'Now throw the ball into the sky.' Sidda clutched the ball, closed his eyes for a second and threw the ball up. When the ball came down again, he said, 'Now this has touched the moon. Come. You see here a little bit of the moon sticking.' Leela keenly examined the ball for traces of the moon and said, 'I don't see it.'

'You must be very quick about it,' said Sidda, 'because it all will evaporate and go back to the moon. Now hurry up . . .' He covered the ball tightly with his fingers and allowed her to peep through a little gap.

'Ah, yes,' said Leela. 'I see the moon, but is the moon very wet?'

'Certainly, it is,' Sidda said.

'What is in the sky, Sidda?'

▶▶

'God,' he said.

'If we stand on the roof and stretch our arm, can we touch the sky?'

'Not if we stand on the roof here,' he said. 'But if you stand on a coconut tree you can touch the sky.'

'Have you done it?' asked Leela.

'Yes, many times,' said Sidda. 'Whenever there is a big moon, I climb a coconut tree and touch it.'

'Does the moon know you?'

'Yes, very well. Now come with me. I will show you something nice.' They were standing near a rose plant. He said, pointing, 'You see the moon here, don't you?'

'Yes.'

'Now come with me,' he said, and took her back to the yard. He stopped near the well and pointed up. The moon was there, too. Leela clapped her hands and screamed in wonder, 'The moon is here! It was there! How has that happened?'

'I have asked it to follow us about.'

Leela ran in and told her mother, 'Sidda knows the moon.' At dusk he took Leela in and she held a class for him. She had a box filled with catalogues, illustrated books and stumps of pencils. It gave her great joy to play the teacher to Sidda. She made him squat on the floor with a pencil between his fingers and a catalogue in front of him. She had another pencil and commanded, 'Now write.' And he had to try and copy whatever she wrote in the pages of her catalogue. She knew two or three letters of the alphabet and could draw a kind of cat and crow. But none of these Sidda could copy, even remotely. She said, examining his effort, 'Is this how I have drawn the crow? Is this how I have drawn the *B*?' She pitied him and redoubled her efforts to teach him. But that good fellow, though an adept at controlling the moon, was utterly incapable of plying the pencil. Consequently, it looked as though Leela would keep him there, pinned to his seat, until his stiff, inflexible wrist cracked. He sought relief by saying, 'I think your mother is calling you in to dinner.' Leela would drop the pencil and run out of the room, and the school hour would end.

From *Malgudi's Days*, by R.K. Narayan, Penguin, 1994

1 Describe, in your own words, Mr. Sivasanker's initial response to the boy, Sidda. (2 marks)

2 Explain, using your own words, the phrase *giving the stock reply* in line 13. (1 mark)

3 What do you learn about the character and attitudes of Leela from the episode with Sidda and the ball? (3 marks)

4 Describe, as fully as you can, Leela's attitude towards Sidda as revealed in the passage. (4 marks)

5 In your own words describe the character of Sidda as fully as you can. You should comment on what you know about his history as well as describing his relationships with the other characters in the passage. (10 marks)

Remember to support your answers with quotations from and references to the passage when appropriate.

Exercise 3

Read carefully the passage entitled *The new school* and answer all the questions which follow.

The new school

A young girl named Esther goes to a new school in Russia when her family are exiled from Poland, in 1941.

The morning I was to go to school for the first time, I woke up in a blackness as mysterious as the heart of a dark forest, the sounds nearby its strange beat. But the howl of a wolf way out in the country gave me my bearings.

I took up my little notebook, and a small stub of pencil, my only academic possessions. How long would they last? How small could I write?

I quickly got dressed, as warmly as I could, although deep winter had not yet arrived. I pulled a sweater over my thin little blouse, and struggled into my black leather shoes, which were not only pinching but which were beginning to crack from the wet and the mud, and endless drying in front of our little stove. On went my one and only coat. I was ready to go.

Mother had to be at the bakery early that day and so, clutching my notebook and pencil, I went to school alone. It never occurred to me that for a child to walk alone down a deserted Siberian road, so obviously a stranger, required some courage. I was too busy trying to rehearse the Russian alphabet I would need to know in my new school.

In room number five, a few children in caps and coats were seated at their desks watching the teacher write on the blackboard. She turned when I came in and looked at me so severely my heart sank.

'You must be Esther Rudomin. From Poland. Your Russian will be poor.' It was as if she was reading from a dossier that would determine some sort of punishment. 'It will be my task to see that you improve it. My name is Raisa Nikitovna. Go to the last desk of the third row and sit down.'

Without another word, she picked up a book, and called out a page number. Everyone had a book but me. The feeling must have been something like being the only soldier without a gun. I leaned towards the girl next to me and asked if I might share her book. She grudgingly agreed. She was a very pretty girl with short blonde hair, and eyes the special blue of northern countries. I asked her name, but she told me to be quiet; there was absolutely no talking allowed in class.

My first lesson in school in Siberia was memorable for being a chilly one. It was not only the Russian author's meaning that evaded me, lost as it was in a sea of strange letters formed in the Russian alphabet, but so did the book itself – literally. My classmate somehow managed to keep slipping it out of my field of vision, which forced me to strain, squirm, and nudge her to bring the book closer. Naturally, I had barely read the first paragraph when Raisa Nikitovna began to quiz the class. To my horror, one question was directed at me. As I began to answer in my halting Russian, all the children turned to stare at me.

When the lesson was finished, Raisa Nikitovna introduced me to the class: 'This is Esther Rudomin, who comes from Poland. As you can tell, she does not know Russian well and she will have to work hard to catch up. She will share her books with Svetlana. Stand up, Svetlana.' Svetlana turned out to be the pretty little girl sitting next to me; the prospect of *sharing* with her was not heartening. The more attention I got in class, the more she sulked. I sensed that Svetlana wanted to be the queen bee and that I had become her natural enemy. This was confirmed when I asked if I might come to her house and study with her. The answer was a sharp 'No!' I would be allowed to go there to fetch books when she had quite finished with them, but otherwise I could jolly well trot home and study alone.

At the end of my first day at school, I went home and collapsed on the sofa. Out of the confusion of the day, three giants emerged to be slain: Svetlana, Raisa Nikitovna, and the Russian alphabet.

From *The Endless Steppe*, by Esther Hautzig, Puffin, 1993

1 What were Esther's greatest worries about going to her new school?
(3 marks)

2 Describe, in your own words, the way Esther was treated and what her feelings were when she first met her new teacher. (3 marks)

3 What were the problems Esther encountered when she tried to read the book? (3 marks)

4 Explain, in your own words, the meaning of the phrase *my halting Russian*. (paragraph eight) (1 mark)

5 Imagine you are Esther. Write your diary entry describing your first day at the school and describe your feelings about the events which happened. (10 marks)

Remember to support your answers with quotations from and references to the passage when appropriate.

Ans 2 – When the teacher - Raisa Nikitovna saw her with this serious, grave and severe look ~~made~~ Esther's heart skip a beat. She assumed her Russian to be feeble and ordered her to perch on her seat. Esther thought the teacher was giving her a harsh punishment. She thought that the teacher was too strict.

Becoming a better writer

This chapter gives you some key guidelines and principles about writing which are relevant to any kind of writing task. Whatever piece of writing you try, you need to **think about its purpose** and decide what effect this has on your writing style. There are two key questions to ask yourself:

- **What is it for?** In other words, what kind of writing piece is it (it could be anything from a fantasy story to a business letter) and what do you want to say? You need to be able to **use different styles for different purposes**.
- **Who is it for?** Who are the readers for this piece of writing? You need to be able to **use different styles for different audiences**.

Even when we think about just one kind of writing task – a letter – the style will need to be different depending on who the letter is for (a relative? a newspaper? a friend?) When you write an article you need to think about your readers: if it is for a group of young people, for instance, you need to think about how to make it clear and interesting for them, not just about what information you want to include.

Different styles for different purposes

Writing to inform or explain

This kind of writing is factual and the important thing is for it to be as clear as possible, whether you are explaining a situation, an activity or an interest, or providing some instructions for carrying out a task. Make sure your writing is **focused and objective, clear and systematic**.

Be focused and objective

Your purpose is to make the information clear to your readers, not to give them your own opinion on the subject, so stick closely to the subject and don't be tempted to add comments of your own.

Be clear and systematic

The point of an explanation is that it should be simpler and clearer than the original. Here are some techniques to help you achieve this.

- Use vocabulary that is easy to understand.
- Be careful not simply to repeat chunks of the original text; instead, find simpler ways to express the same ideas so that you are genuinely explaining them.
- Use sentences that are not too long or complicated.
- Make sure your punctuation is accurate and helpful so that readers can easily see their way from one point to the next.
- Use a new paragraph for every main point that you make: start the paragraph with a 'topic sentence' to tell your reader what the paragraph will be about and use the rest of the paragraph to develop the point.

Example of informative writing

SPORTS INJURIES

Sports-related injuries occur when sportsmen and women either fail to warm up properly, over-train, use incorrect equipment or adopt a faulty technique. Injuries may also follow an accident or foul play. Injuries to soft tissues, including muscles and tendons, are very common and lead to pain and various degrees of immobility. Fortunately, many sports-related injuries can be prevented by observing a few simple measures such as warming up and cooling down properly, using the proper equipment and correct techniques.

COMMON SPORTS INJURIES

Ankle Sprain

Ankle Sprain: caused by tearing the ligament fibres that support the ankle when the foot turns over onto its outer edge. An ankle sprain may occur in many different types of sport, but it is commonly associated with badminton, football, squash and tennis.

Pulled Hamstring

Pulled Hamstring: caused by tearing the muscle fibre at the back of the thigh as a result of overstretching. A pulled hamstring often occurs while sprinting or kicking a ball.

Torn Cartilage

Torn Cartilage: caused by a sudden twisting movement while the knee is bent and subject to the full weight of the body. Footballers, rugby players and skiers are particularly prone to cartilage trouble.

Tendonitis

Tendonitis: inflammation of a tendon at the back of the heel. Various causes include long-distance running shoes (wearing new running shoes, wearing running shoes that do not support the heel) and change of normal running surface.

Tenosynovitis

Tenosynovitis (inflammation of tendon linings): commonly occurs in the wrist, caused by the overuse of muscles. Any racket sport may lead participants to use a vulnerable, powerful grip, e.g. rowing and weightlifting. Contributory factors include using the wrong size handle or a faulty technique when gripping the racket, oar or bar.

This piece of informative writing is in the form of a leaflet. Points are made under clear headings. In a continuous piece of writing such headings would not be necessary, but here they aid understanding.

Technical terms for injuries are explained in straightforward vocabulary.

Shin Splints

Shin Splints: caused by strained tendons or muscles in the front of the lower leg when walking or running. This results in pain around the shin area that eases off when resting. Shin splints are associated with unusual or abnormal foot posture.

Bruises

Bruises (contusions): Bruises occur when an injury causes bleeding from blood capillaries beneath the skin. This leads to discoloration under the surface. Bruises arise following a blunt blow such as a punch or kick and may appear hours, or even days after an injury.

Blisters

Blisters form on skin that has been damaged by friction or heat. Tissue fluid leaks into the affected area forming a 'bubble'. Never deliberately burst a blister as this may lead to infection. Should the blister break, cover it with a dry, non-stick dressing. Otherwise, leave a blister to heal on its own and cover with a special protective blister plaster.

From UniChem Pharmacies

Sentences tend to be short, each dealing with a single point.

Here each section is separated by a heading, but note that the colon is used to good effect to clarify.

Each paragraph begins with a topic sentence and the rest of the paragraph elaborates, giving examples to illustrate.

Writing to argue or persuade

This kind of writing needs to be **convincing and logical**. Here are some useful techniques.

- Decide **what** you want to persuade your reader to believe. Which viewpoint are you going to put forward?
- Make 'for and against' lists: one list of the facts and ideas from the text which support your viewpoint, and another list of those which do not. NB You can change your chosen viewpoint at this planning stage, but don't change it as you are writing!
- State your chosen viewpoint simply at the beginning.
- For each main point that you make to support your viewpoint, **give evidence and examples** to back up your case – **use the text!**
- **Be balanced** – your argument will be at its most convincing if you make points for both sides but prove that your own chosen viewpoint is the better one. Use your 'for and against' lists.
- Use paragraphs to help you make your points clearly. Start a new paragraph for each main point that you make and use the rest of the paragraph to give your evidence. This will mean that your paragraphs are of roughly similar lengths.
- Use persuasive phrases such as: 'It seems clear to me that . . .'; 'The text shows that . . .'; 'This example indicates that . . .'.
- Use linking phrases to move between the two sides of the argument, such as: 'Nevertheless, . . .'; 'On the other hand, . . .'.

- Rhetorical questions are a good way to get your reader on your side: these are questions which have an obvious answer, and the answer supports your point of view! For example, if you were arguing against animal experiments, you could ask: 'Would you like your own pets to have shampoo squirted into their eyes?' If you were arguing in favour of animal experiments, you could ask: 'Your little brother is dangerously ill – would you rather he had drugs whose safety had been tested on animals, or no drugs?'
- Finish by restating your viewpoint, perhaps saying also that although you can see the other point of view, you are convinced that yours is the right one.

Example of persuasive writing

Apples and Pears

Jay Rayner

Some recent scientific research has indicated that being overweight may not be as serious a health problem as it was once thought to be. The journalist Jay Rayner, himself a heavy person, investigated this issue. Some of his findings are printed below.

According to research conducted by, among others, Kay-Tee Khaw, Professor of Gerontology at Cambridge University, excess body fat is only really a problem when it's in your abdominal cavity, blanketing the vital organs. Laid there it's far more likely to cause health complications like heart disease or diabetes.

To assess it you need to find out if the waist measurement, taken at the level of your navel, is bigger than the measurement of your hips. If your hips are larger than your waist then you are classed as pear-shaped, and there's probably far less to worry about. Fat around your thighs and bottom is only likely to slow you down rather than kill you. It is worth noting that women, the real diet fanatics in Britain, are naturally pear-shaped; indeed it may come as something of a relief to know that, using the waist–hip measurement, the vast majority of women who are officially classed as overweight have nothing to worry about at all.

If, however, all the weight is on your stomach, you are apple-shaped. You'll see any number of apples in the saloon bars the length and breadth of the country, their beer bellies propped up on the tables. That's when there is cause for concern.

'Certainly if two patients are of similar weight,' Professor Khaw says, 'I would put more pressure on the person with the high waist–hip ratio to try and lose weight.'

This article is taking a different view from the normal one – the normal view is that anyone who is overweight is in dreadful trouble. This article is persuading the reader that being overweight is not necessarily a problem.

The article is clearly paragraphed. Each paragraph takes us a little further forward in the argument.

Quotations from experts give the argument authority. Note that in the first paragraph Kay-Tee Khaw's full title is given, which gives the whole argument more importance and authenticity.

But there are a growing number of academics who are prepared to be even more reassuring. Dr Tom Sanders is Professor of Nutrition at King's College London and co-author of the deliciously titled book **You Don't Have To Diet,** which has to make him a good bloke from the kick-off. His argument comes in two revelatory parts. Firstly, he says, 95 per cent of diets don't really work. Stick to boiled eggs and cabbage for three weeks, chew celery stalks and swallow milk shakes with the consistency of wet concrete and you may well lose weight, but it will probably be in the form of water and muscle rather than fat. What's more it will all go back on again very quickly. The only people to gain from diets are the people flogging them to you.

The second part of his argument is even more intoxicating. It is this: most overweight people do not even have a problem. 'The health risks of obesity have been greatly exaggerated,' he says. 'It does depend on age. The longer you are fat the greater the risk, because weight does go on as you get older. But it's a small risk compared to that of, say, smoking. I would argue that if giving up smoking made you put on a stone in weight it's still healthier to give up smoking.'

'Most experts do not regard obesity on its own as an independent risk factor for heart disease, in the absence of raised blood pressure, raised blood cholesterol or diabetes.' And just because you are overweight doesn't mean your cholesterol levels will be through the ceiling; skinny people have just as much likelihood of having arteries swimming with liquid fat. One statistic is very revealing: while the incidence of obesity has doubled, the rate of heart disease has dropped by over 30 per cent. If obesity really was such a major factor in causing heart disease, we should have expected to see more of it rather than less.

'Put simply,' Professor Sanders says, 'we've taken eating, a perfectly normal physiological activity, and turned it into a problem.' This is not a prescription for just letting yourself go. You should keep a steady weight – rather than letting your weight yo-yo – and take some exercise: becoming vastly obese is not something to get neurotic about.

Indeed, beyond a certain age it's a positive boon to be overweight. 'Skinny people of between 50 and 55 have a higher mortality rate. The older you get, being underweight becomes a greater risk to health than being overweight.' With more flesh on your bones, you have a greater chance of surviving the illnesses that strike in later years.

From *The Mail on Sunday*, 1997

Note how You Don't Have To Diet is picked out in bold. This pulls you up short.

Note the use of vocabulary:
- *'flogging' (which sounds more critical than 'selling')*
- *'intoxicating' – the idea that overweight people can get drunk with joy at what is being said.*

Note the links at the beginnings of sentences which take you on:
- *If, however, . . .*
- *But there are a growing number of . . .*
- *The second part of his argument . . .*
- *'Put simply,' Professor Sanders says . . .*

Writing imaginatively to entertain your readers

If you are writing an imaginative piece – narrating a story, for example – you will not have to structure your piece in the same logical, argued way as for an informative or persuasive piece. However, it is still important that your writing has a clear structure. Perhaps most importantly, you need to know how your story will end before you start (see the section on planning on pages 52–54). You might want your ending to be a surprise to your readers, but it shouldn't be a surprise to you! The beginning is important, too. For a story you can either:

- start by setting the scene – this is fine, but don't give too much time/space to it, keep it to one short paragraph
- go straight into the story, for example with a line of dialogue.

A good piece of imaginative writing is **varied and inventive**. Here are some ideas on how to make sure your skills in this area are clear to the examiner!

Be varied and inventive

- Use some words which are abstract and colourful.

- Use descriptive vocabulary: adjectives, adverbs.

- Use images, for example, 'she grinned like a crocodile'.

- Use exclamations and/or words that convey their meaning through sound (these might be dramatic, for example, 'Thud!' or 'Crash!'; they might just be well-chosen words that convey the exact sound you have in mind, for example, 'tinkling', 'rustled').

- Your paragraphs should vary in length. An occasional very short paragraph can make a strong impact. Some paragraphs might even be just one word long, such as 'Help!'

- Your sentences should also vary in length – this is a good way to have an effect on your reader's feelings. For example, if you have just been setting a frightening scene, a short sentence such as 'We waited.' or even just 'Silence.' can be very effective.

Example of imaginative writing

Flight

A short story by Doris Lessing

Note the image that is created at the beginning – 'The sunlight broke on their grey breasts into small rainbows.'

Above the old man's head was the dovecote, a tall wire-netted shelf on stilts, full of strutting, preening birds. The sunlight broke on their grey breasts into small rainbows. His ears were lulled by their crooning, his hands stretched up towards his favourite, a homing pigeon, a young plump-bodied bird which stood still when it saw him and cocked a shrewd bright eye.

'Pretty, pretty, pretty,' he said, as he grasped the bird and drew it down, feeling the cold coral claws tighten around his finger. Content, he rested the bird lightly on his chest, and leaned against a tree, gazing out beyond the dovecote into the landscape of a late afternoon. In folds and hollows of sunlight and shade, the dark red soil, which was broken into great dusty clods, stretched wide to a tall horizon. Trees marked the course of the valley; a stream of rich green grass the road.

You will see that the paragraphs are of varied lengths, some of them very short.

His eyes travelled homewards along this road until he saw his grand-daughter swinging on the gate underneath a frangipani tree. Her hair fell down her back in a wave of sunlight, and her long bare legs repeated the angles of the frangipani stems, bare, shining-brown stems among patterns of pale blossoms.

She was gazing past the pink flowers, past the railway cottage where they lived, along the road to the village.

Metaphor is used to enhance the description effectively – 'Her hair fell down her back in a wave of sunlight'.

His mood shifted. He deliberately held out his wrist for the bird to take flight, and caught it again at the moment it spread its wings. He felt the plump shape strive and strain under his fingers; and, in a sudden access of troubled spite, shut the bird into a small box and fastened the bolt. 'Now you stay there,' he muttered; and turned his back on the shelf of birds. He moved warily along the hedge, stalking his grand-daughter, who was now looped over the gate, her head loose on her arms, singing. The light happy sound mingled with the crooning of the birds, and his anger mounted.

▶▶

'Hey!' he shouted; saw her jump, look back, and abandon the gate. Her eyes veiled themselves, and she said in a pert neutral voice: 'Hullo, Grandad.' Politely she moved towards him, after a lingering backward glance at the road.

'Waiting for Steven, hey?' he said, his fingers curling like claws into his palm.

'Any objection?' she asked lightly, refusing to look at him.

He confronted her, his eyes narrowed, shoulders hunched, tight in a hard knot of pain which included the preening birds, the sunlight, the flowers. He said: 'Think you're old enough to go courting, hey?'

The girl tossed her head at the old-fashioned phrase and sulked. 'Oh, Grandad!'

'Think you want to leave home, hey? Think you can go running around the fields at night?'

Her smile made him see her, as he had every evening of this warm end-of-summer month, swinging hand in hand along the road to the village with that red-handed, red-throated, violent-bodied youth, the son of the postmaster. Misery went to his head and he shouted angrily: 'I'll tell your mother!'

'Tell away!' she said, laughing, and went back to the gate.

He heard her singing, for him to hear:

'I've got you under my skin,
I've got you deep in the heart of . . .'

'Rubbish,' he shouted. 'Rubbish. Impudent little bit of rubbish!'

Growling under his breath he turned towards the dovecote, which was his refuge from the house he shared with his daughter and her husband and their children. But now the house would be empty. Gone all the young girls with their laughter and their squabbling and their teasing. He would be left, uncherished and alone, with that square-fronted, calm-eyed woman, his daughter.

He stooped, muttering, before the dovecote, resenting the absorbed cooing birds.

From the gate the girl shouted: 'Go and tell! Go on, what are you waiting for?'

Obstinately he made his way to the house, with quick, pathetic persistent glances of appeal back at her. But she never looked around. Her defiant but anxious young body stung him into love and repentance. He stopped. 'But I never meant . . .' he muttered, waiting for her to turn and run to him. 'I didn't mean . . .'

She did not turn. She had forgotten him. Along the road came the young man Steven, with something in his hand. A present for her? The old man stiffened as he watched the gate swing back, and the couple embrace. In the brittle shadows of the frangipani tree his grand-daughter, his darling, lay in the arms of the postmaster's son, and her hair flowed back over his shoulder.

'I see you!' shouted the old man spitefully. They did not move. He stumped into the little whitewashed house, hearing the wooden veranda creak angrily under his feet. His daughter was sewing in the front room, threading a needle held to the light.

He stopped again, looking back into the garden. The couple were now sauntering among the bushes, laughing. As he watched he saw the girl escape from the youth with a sudden mischievous movement, and run off through the flowers with him in pursuit. He heard shouts, laughter, a scream, silence.

'But it's not like that at all,' he muttered miserably. 'It's not like that. Why can't you see? Running and giggling, and kissing and kissing. You'll come to something quite different.'

▶▶

He looked at his daughter with sardonic hatred, hating himself. They were caught and finished, both of them, but the girl was still running free.

'Can't you *see*?' he demanded of his invisible grand-daughter, who was at that moment lying in the thick green grass with the postmaster's son.

His daughter looked at him and her eyebrows went up in tired forbearance.

'Put your birds to bed?' she asked, humouring him.

'Lucy,' he said urgently. 'Lucy . . .'

'Well what is it now?'

'She's in the garden with Steven.'

'Now you just sit down and have your tea.'

He stumped his feet alternately, thump, thump, on the hollow wooden floor and shouted: 'She'll marry him. I'm telling you, she'll be marrying him next!'

His daughter rose swiftly, brought him a cup, set him a plate.

'I don't want any tea. I don't want it, I tell you.'

'Now, now,' she crooned. 'What's wrong with it? Why not?'

'She's eighteen. Eighteen!'

'I was married at seventeen and I never regretted it.'

'Liar,' he said. 'Liar. Then you should regret it. Why do you make your girls marry? It's you who do it. What do you do it for? Why?'

'The other three have done fine. They've three fine husbands. Why not Alice?'

'She's the last,' he mourned. 'Can't we keep her a bit longer?'

'Come, now, dad. She'll be down the road, that's all. She'll be here every day to see you.'

'But it's not the same.' He thought of the other three girls, transformed inside a few months from charming petulant spoiled children into serious young matrons.

'You never did like it when we married?' she said. 'Why not? Every time, it's the same. When I got married you made me feel like it was something wrong. And my girls the same. You get them all crying and miserable the way you go on. Leave Alice alone. She's happy.' She sighed, letting her eyes linger on the sun-lit garden. 'She'll marry next month. There's no reason to wait.'

'You've said they can marry?' he said incredulously.

'Yes, dad, why not?' she said coldly, and took up her sewing.

His eyes stung, and he went out on to the veranda. Wet spread down over his chin and he took out a handkerchief and mopped his whole face. The garden was empty.

From around a corner came the young couple; but their faces were no longer set against him. On the wrist of the postmaster's son balanced a young pigeon, the light gleaming on its breast.

'For me?' said the old man, letting the drops shake off his chin. 'For me?'

'Do you like it?' The girl grabbed his hand and swung on it. 'It's for you, Grandad. Steven brought it for you.' They hung about him, affectionate, concerned, trying to charm away his wet eyes and his misery. They took his arms and directed him to the shelf of birds, one on each side, enclosing him, petting him, saying wordlessly that nothing would be changed, nothing could change, and that they would be with him always. The bird was proof of it, they said, from their lying happy eyes, as they thrust it on him. 'There, Grandad, it's yours. It's for you.'

There is creation of sound through the use of short words and repetition – 'He stumped his feet alternately, thump, thump, on the hollow wooden floor'.

▶▶

They watched him as he held it on his wrist, stroking its soft, sun-warmed back, watching the wings lift and balance.

'You must shut it up for a bit,' said the girl intimately. 'Until it knows this is its home.'

'Teach your grandmother to suck eggs,' growled the old man.

Released by his half-deliberate anger, they fell back, laughing at him. 'We're glad you like it.' They moved off, now serious and full of purpose, to the gate, where they hung, backs to him, talking quietly. More than anything could, their grown-up seriousness shut him out, making him alone; also, it quietened him, took the sting out of their tumbling like puppies on the grass. They had forgotten him again. Well, so they should, the old man reassured himself, feeling his throat clotted with tears, his lips trembling. He held the new bird to his face, for the caress of its silken feathers. Then he shut it in a box and took out his favourite.

'*Now* you can go,' he said aloud. He held it poised, ready for flight, while he looked down the garden towards the boy and the girl. Then, clenched in the pain of loss, he lifted the bird on his wrist, and watched it soar. A whirr and a spatter of wings, and a cloud of birds rose into the evening from the dovecote.

At the gate Alice and Steven forgot their talk and watched the birds.

On the veranda, that woman, his daughter, stood gazing, her eyes shaded with a hand that still held her sewing.

It seemed to the old man that the whole afternoon had stilled to watch his gesture of self-command, that even the leaves of the trees had stopped shaking.

Dry-eyed and calm, he let his hands fall to his sides and stood erect, staring up into the sky.

The cloud of shining silver birds flew up and up, with a shrill cleaving of wings, over the dark ploughed land and the darker belts of trees and the bright folds of grass, until they floated high in the sunlight, like a cloud of motes of dust.

They wheeled in a wide circle, tilting their wings so there was flash after flash of light, and one after another they dropped from the sunshine of the upper sky to shadow, one after another, returning to the shadowed earth over trees and grass and field, returning to the valley and the shelter of night.

The garden was all a fluster and a flurry of returning birds. Then silence, and the sky was empty.

The old man turned, slowly, taking his time; he lifted his eyes to smile proudly down the garden at his grand-daughter. She was staring at him. She did not smile. She was wide-eyed, and pale in the cold shadow, and he saw the tears run shivering off her face.

From *The Habit of Loving*, by Doris Lessing,
Flamingo, 1993

Decide for yourself how effectively the end of the story works and what the link is between the grandfather, grand-daughter and the pigeons.

■ Different styles for different audiences

Who are you writing for?

Now that we have looked at the purpose of your writing, or **what** you are writing for, it's important also to think about your **audience**, or **who you are writing for**. The IGCSE syllabus requires you to: 'show a sense of audience and an awareness of register and style in both formal and informal situations'.

When you are writing in an exam, in one sense your audience is always one adult – the examiner. However, sometimes for a particular writing task you will also be required to consider another specific audience, for example:

children

a school newspaper

your headteacher

a member of your local community council

It is important to think about your audience and how it should affect the way you write.

- If you are writing for children, the vocabulary you use must be simple, the sentences must be fairly short and they certainly must not be complex.
- If you are writing for your headteacher or to a member of your local community council, then it is appropriate to explore your subject in a more complex or sophisticated way, and to feel free to use more difficult or technical vocabulary.

Don't ever start your piece of writing without asking yourself the question 'Who am I writing for?' If your writing shows that you are aware of your audience, you will gain higher marks.

■ Planning your writing

Structuring a piece of writing

The way in which you structure a piece of writing depends on the purpose of the piece and the audience it is being written for.

A structure is likely to go wrong if you don't plan the whole piece of writing before you start. Most importantly, you must know what the end is going to be. If you are writing an argumentative or informative piece, you need to be clear how you are going to balance the argument with points for or against, or how you are going to give one piece of information more prominence than another. If you are writing an imaginative piece, you need to know how you are going to introduce characters and how you are going to describe them, how you are going to create atmosphere and setting, how the plot is going to develop and how your ending is going to work.

On page 58 you will find some comments about paragraphing. Paragraphing is always important but the way you use paragraphs depends on the purpose of your writing. For instance, an argumentative piece will normally be divided into paragraphs of roughly equal length, as an argument has to have a clear and balanced structure. In an imaginative piece the length of the paragraphs will probably be more varied, as the different elements of the narrative will have different degrees of importance.

Generally speaking, the structure should always have the following three parts:

■ introduction: in a factual piece, this should state **briefly** what the theme of the piece is and – if appropriate – what opinion you are putting forward on this theme; in an imaginative piece, you may choose to set the scene or to go for a more dramatic/immediate start
■ main body of explanation/argument/narrative
■ conclusion/story ending.

Practical ways to plan your writing

English examiners say that it is quite obvious that a lot of candidates do not plan their writing. This matters, because well-planned writing will almost always score more highly than writing that has not been planned. Whether you are doing a piece of writing in response to a text you have read (see Chapter 4) or a piece of continuous writing for an essay or coursework assignment (see Chapter 6), it is essential that you plan what you are going to write. There are various methods you can use. **Spider diagrams** and **lists**, as explained in the following pages, are two possibilities, but you may find another method that works better for you.

Spider diagrams

Stage 1

■ Write your topic in the middle of the page and around it write down all the things that you might write about.

■ At this stage, don't stop to think too much – just write down any relevant ideas that come to mind.

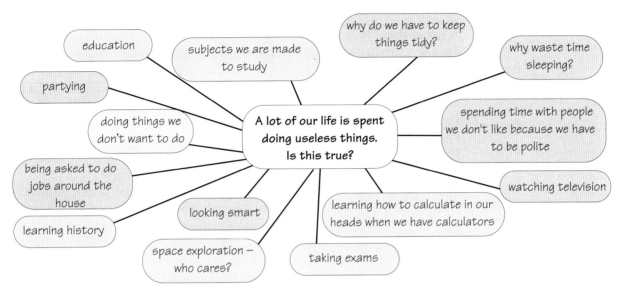

Stage 2

■ The next stage is to decide if there are things that need to be discarded, and how to order the points that are being kept.

– There are a number of points about education (linked by pink lines).

– There are a number of points about personal life (linked by blue lines).

– The idea about space exploration is probably going to be discarded.

■ Number the points to give them an order; each numbered point will be a paragraph or part of a paragraph in your essay.

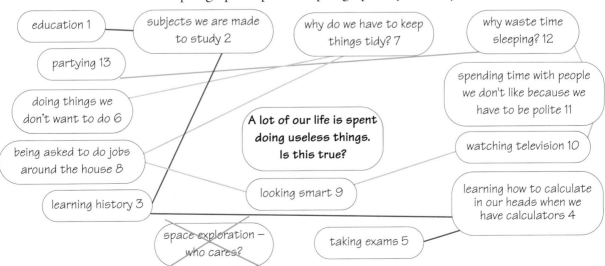

Tips
1 At this stage, don't be afraid to cross things out.
2 If you find that two of your ideas are closely linked, you should probably combine them.
3 Remember that it is not just a case of putting one side of the argument – the points being made need to be answered.

Stage 3
The order of the essay now looks like this:

A lot of our life is spent doing useless things. Is this true?

Para 1 General statement about importance of education (1)
Para 2 However – subjects we are made to study are a waste of time (2). Why learn history? (3) Why bother to learn to do calculations in our heads – calculators! (4)
Para 3 Why do examinations in subjects which are of no importance? (5)
Para 4 General statement about doing things we don't want to do (6)
Para 5 Being pestered to keep our rooms tidy (7)
Doing jobs around the house we don't want to (8)
Being made to look smart when we want to be comfortable (9)
Para 6 We watch television when we can't think of anything else to do (10)
We spend time with people we don't like (perhaps relatives) because we have to (11)
Para 7 Why can't someone invent something which means we don't have to waste time sleeping? (12)
What we want to do is party (13)
Para 8 Conclusion
What is important in life? What is unimportant?

This might not be how your plan would look in terms of content and ideas. However, it shows you how you might go about planning.

Why not take the title and do your own plan? You could then go on to write the essay.

Lists

Instead of a spider plan, you may prefer simply to put things down in a list. With this method, it's important to look carefully at the whole list again **before you start to write**.

- Don't be afraid to change the order of your points.
- Don't automatically think your first ideas are the best: check through the list and discard/replace some points if you have second thoughts.

However you choose to plan, the crucial point is this: **don't be afraid to spend time on planning!** If you have an hour to do a piece of writing, you should spend fifteen minutes planning it. One of the reasons people don't plan is because they panic about not having enough time. Look on the positive side: if you have a very clear plan in front of you, you don't have to waste time worrying about what to put next, so you will write much faster and more efficiently.

■ Improving your writing

Always keep in mind what the examiner is looking for when he/she is marking any piece of writing, whether it is a summary, a piece of directed writing or a piece of coursework. The IGCSE English syllabus states that you should be able to:

- exercise control of the appropriate grammatical structures, and
- demonstrate an awareness of the conventions of paragraphing, sentence structure, punctuation and spelling.

Using Standard English

Languages vary. Each language differs according to the particular area where it is being spoken, and a language as widespread as English has many different variations and versions. There are two main kinds of variation:

- accents, which are simply variations in the way the language is pronounced
- dialects, which are more significant variations, each with its own words and expressions.

The accent and dialect spoken in an area are often an important part of that area's identity. It is a mistake to say that any particular dialect of the language is 'wrong' although, in practice, people compare other dialects of English to the form that has come to be known as Standard English.

The term 'Standard English' is the form of English that is agreed to be generally accepted for written English, and it is the form of the language taught to students learning English. Your written work for IGCSE should therefore be almost entirely Standard English. This means following some generally recognised 'Standard English' rules about:

- punctuation
- spelling (although US spelling is not penalised in IGCSE)
- paragraphing
- sentence structure.

While written English – for learning purposes, at least – should conform to Standard English, the same does not apply to speech. It would be impossible, for example, to speak in complete sentences all the time – and where are the paragraphs? In speech, language is much less planned and more natural. So, when you are writing for your IGCSE English, don't write as you speak *unless* you are writing down some words that were spoken or are meant to be spoken, for example:

- when you are quoting someone
- when you are writing direct speech
- when you are writing a script.

Spelling

Some people not only convince themselves that they can't spell but think that, because they can't spell, everything they write is a failure.

The first point to make is that spelling is not the most important thing in the world. If it is a problem for you, look at ways in which you can deal with it. Lack of confidence can make a problem seem worse than it really is. There is no such person as a perfect speller. Everyone makes mistakes from time to time. However, some key strategies can help to improve your spelling, as explained below.

How to improve your spelling

- **Look at words**. People who read a lot see words and absorb them. If you come across a word that you find difficult, pause for a moment and look at it. Look at the shape of the word. After a while you will find that you recognise the word more easily and you can automatically think of its shape.
- **Draw up a list of common words.** Some words occur more frequently in your writing than others. Draw up a list of these words and spend a few minutes each day or every other day reading the list, covering it up and practising writing the words.
- **Learn some spelling rules.** Although there are a lot of words that break rules, nevertheless you can learn rules about spelling which are helpful. 'I before E except after C' for example, helps you spell correctly a whole variety of words that have this letter combination. Get hold of a book on spelling and look up the rules. Don't try to learn them all at once; just try to learn one or two at a time.
- **Say words out loud rather than just staring at the paper**. It won't always mean that you spell them correctly but, if you write down what you hear, the chances are that the word will be recognisable and it might jog your memory.
- **Use a dictionary to check your spelling rather than as the first step**. Don't be discouraged if you can't find the word straight away. Remember, for instance, that some words, such as 'know' and 'gnome', have silent first letters.
- **Make sure you copy out names correctly.** If you are doing a piece of directed writing and there are proper names in the stimulus material, or if you are responding to a piece of literature, there is no excuse for getting the spelling of names of people or places wrong.
- **Remember that vocabulary is more important than spelling**. Don't let uncertainty about spelling frighten you away from using challenging and interesting vocabulary. It is better to use interesting vocabulary with the occasional spelling error than to 'dumb down' your writing, using only very simple words that you know you can spell.
- **Most importantly, remember to check through what you have written**. One of the things to check is your spelling. You will probably not correct everything, but increasingly you will find that you can spot your own mistakes.

Punctuation

The first question you should ask yourself when you are thinking about punctuation is, 'What is it for?' Punctuation is all about making life easier for the reader. In particular, it indicates to the reader where he or she needs to pause. There are four punctuation marks that indicate a pause and each indicates a different length of pause.

■ The shortest is the **comma**. A comma allows you to group words within a longer sentence so that the reader can see the idea developing. If you can, read what you have written out loud. You will find that you naturally pause, and each time you do, put a comma.

■ The longest pause is a **full stop**. You put full stops at the ends of sentences. They indicate that the point is complete and finished. Remember that you can't turn simple sentences into more complex ones just by putting commas instead of full stops. However short the sentence, once the idea is complete put in a full stop.

■ In some ways the **semi-colon** is the most difficult of the pause marks to use. When you are reading, look out for semi-colons to see where writers have used them. Read through this chapter and you will see that we have used semi-colons in several places. If you write a sentence in two balanced halves, and you want to keep the ideas of the two halves together rather than separating them into two sentences, use a semi-colon. The pause is a little longer than a comma and, by using it, you will be saying to the reader 'This is one idea which has two halves'.

■ The last of these four pause marks is the **colon**. You use a colon most frequently to introduce a list of items. It allows a substantial pause before the list but it doesn't separate everything completely, as a full stop would. (You start a list with a colon and then often use a semi-colon or a comma between the different items on the list.)

Other punctuation marks have specific jobs to do and we will mention two of them here.

■ A **question mark** is a specialised full stop – in fact, part of it *is* a full stop. It is used at the end of a sentence that is in the form of a question. It is a signal to the reader that a question has been asked and that either the next sentence will be in the form of an answer or the reader will be required to think out the answer for him/herself.

■ The **exclamation mark** is also used in place of a full stop. It is used at the ends of very short sentences, sometimes one-word sentences, where the writer wants to draw attention to something or pull the reader up short.

You must also know how to punctuate direct speech.

■ You put speech marks round the words that are actually spoken.

■ Other punctuation marks, such as full stops, commas and question marks, go inside the speech marks.

■ Every time speech shifts from one speaker to another, you start a new line.

Remember those three points and you won't go far wrong. Don't forget that the purpose of punctuation is to help the reader. Write a paragraph with no punctuation at all and see how difficult it is to read. If you read it aloud, you will notice that you naturally put the punctuation in.

Using paragraphs

- A paragraph is a collection of sentences that go together to make a section of a piece of writing. The sentences are all about the same idea.
- The paragraph normally begins with a topic sentence which tells you what the paragraph is going to be about. The other sentences then develop the ideas.
- You could say that paragraphing is a sort of punctuation. A sentence is a group of words that go together to make a sensible whole; a paragraph is a group of sentences that do the same thing.

Make sure not only that you use paragraphs, but that you use them correctly. Sometimes it's easy to forget about paragraphing when you are writing quickly in the exam and concentrating on what you want to say. It's important to read through your work to make sure that:

- you have started a new paragraph often enough
- you have started the new paragraphs in sensible places.

Example of clear paragraphing

The short article opposite is written in five paragraphs. You will see that each paragraph develops a different point.

Elsewhere we have talked about structure. Clearly the paragraphing has given this short article a very good structure.

Tip If the piece you are writing is for a leaflet, advert or pamphlet or is some other kind of publicity material, then you will need to use other devices as well as, or instead of, paragraphs, to divide your text into 'bite-sized' chunks that are quick and easy to follow. For example, you might use:

- several short sub-headings, or
- bullet points, like the ones being used here!

Putting the boot in

by Marcella Moray Araujo

The first paragraph deals with the sadness of the situation. You will also see that it begins with a sentence which immediately catches your attention.

The second paragraph is about the action the school has had to take.

The third paragraph deals with a national view.

The fourth paragraph talks of progress.

The final paragraph returns to the situation in general.

We all know football can make grown men cry. But the world's most popular game is reducing even small girls to tears. Zara Robins, 12, was selected to join 10 boys on her school team. So successful was the team that one sour defeated school complained to the Football Association. The FA contacted the school and enforced Rule No. 37: no mixed football in schools after the age of 11.

Although staff and other pupils supported Robins, the headmaster had no option but to remove her from the team, or lose the school's league points. Robins herself said she would rather see her side go through and, like all true heroes, took the suspension like a man. When her mother contacted the FA, she was told that Rule No. 37 was introduced to promote women's football. Girls will never learn to play well, the FA declared, while they are intimidated and bullied by boys on the football pitch.

There is a general agreement in the UK that boys are naturally better at football. This should come as no surprise – we only ever see men playing it on TV. For skilled female players, girls-only football is not challenging enough: it's slower and the style is not the same. Perhaps more importantly, not all schools provide opportunities for all-girl teams to train. Three years ago 35 per cent of schools had girls' teams. While the FA talks up the importance of women's football it may still be some time before school teams get the chance to play and train regularly.

There are signs of progress, but although girls can now use local club facilities, the clubs are not yet signing girls. It is still very hard for the few girls who are good to find an outlet for their talent.

The idea behind Rule No. 37 is that, at or about 11 years of age, boys become physically stronger and faster than girls and, therefore, if paired with girls in competitive sports, the risk of injury for the girls is higher. On the other hand, both little boys and grown men are frequently injured as well, and girls play hockey, which is both tough and fast. The only trouble with football is that girls simply don't play it enough.

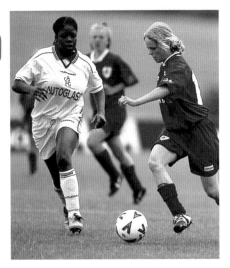

**Adapted from *The Guardian*,
14 September, 1994**

Tenses

Quite often students get tenses confused, swapping from present tense to past tense and back again, especially in stories. When you are writing, think carefully about the tense you are writing in – if you are writing in the present tense, then stick to it. You might want to flash back occasionally to remind your reader of something in the past, but make sure that you come back to the present after the flashback. If you are writing in the past, then stick with the past tense.

Controlling and choosing language

Your ability to control and choose how you use language is also important. You can demonstrate your ability by:

- using a variety of sentence structures to produce different effects
- using a variety of vocabulary which is appropriate for what you are writing.

The examiner will also be looking for evidence of your ability to:

- construct an argument
- order a short story
- write persuasively.

The evidence for this will often be in the way you organise and develop your writing.

Last but not least . . .

Make sure your handwriting can be read easily. If the examiner can read only one word in three, he or she will gain only a partial understanding of what you are trying to say. Try to see it from the examiners' point of view – they can only mark what they can read!

Tip If you are the sort of person whose brain works faster than your pen, then when writing an exam essay it may be a good idea to concentrate on writing neatly. The effort involved in doing this helps to slow down your thought processes, giving you time to organise and express your ideas clearly.

4 | Applying your writing skills

There are three situations in which you may be producing a piece of writing as part of IGCSE English:

- as a directed writing task, in response to a reading passage – for example, writing a summary
- as an essay task
- as one of the items for your coursework folder.

The syllabus states that you should be able to:

- understand and convey information
- understand, order and present facts, ideas and opinions
- evaluate information and select what is relevant to specific purposes
- articulate (clearly convey to your reader) experience
- express what is felt and what is imagined
- communicate effectively and appropriately.

Chapter 5 of this book concentrates on the skills you need for successful summary writing, and Chapter 6 gives some advice about continuous writing – essays and coursework pieces. In this chapter, we shall look at some of the specific forms of 'directed writing' you may be asked to produce in Papers 1 and 2. 'Directed' writing means that you are given a very clear framework for your writing. You will be given some material to read and the writing task will be very closely linked to this. So, for instance, you might be given some information to read and asked to write a letter which draws on the material you have read. This could be a letter of complaint to a company or a letter to a newspaper or magazine.

Letters are only one of a number of possible writing frameworks. We shall look at the following possibilities in this chapter:

- a speech
- a dialogue or conversation
- a letter
- a report
- a persuasive article
- a continuation of a story
- a leaflet.

Writing a speech

When you are writing a speech, whether it is for directed writing or for coursework, there are two very important things to remember.

1   A speech is a means of communicating with an audience – possibly quite a large audience – and you want to be sure that they all understand what you are saying. To help with this, think of more than one way of making the same point and build these into your speech. This is a key feature of a successful speech – listen out for it next time you hear someone speaking to an audience.

2   Whatever you are talking about in a speech, you want to make sure that your audience is agreeing with you as you go along. **Rhetorical questions** – questions that have an obvious, expected answer that supports the point you want to make – can help to get the audience 'on your side'. For example: 'Do we really want to see a rise in crime in our village?' or 'Is it right that children should have to work in these conditions?'

In a directed writing task, the instructions for your speech will indicate who your audience is. Think carefully about whom you are addressing. For example, if you are asked to write a speech for a young audience, you will be free to use informal language which might not be appropriate for an adult audience.

Example 1

Read the extract on pages 63–64, taken from *From Pole to Pole* by Michael Palin, then answer the following question.

> Imagine you have talked to Ivan, the schoolmaster. You decide that you want to do something to help his pupils and have arranged a meeting for parents and students in your own school. You must make a persuasive speech at the meeting.
>
> Use information from the passage and write your speech. You may add ideas of your own.

This task, which is taken from Paper 1 of an IGCSE exam, poses several problems.

- You are being put in a specific situation and what you write should show some understanding both of the situation and the role you have to play in it.
- You are asked to write the words of a *speech* which is intended to *persuade* your audience. You must, therefore, make what you write sound like a speech, while ensuring that you write in acceptable Standard English (see page 55). You must also concentrate on sounding persuasive.
- You must show that you have understood the ideas and content of the original passage and can make good use of them.
- As well as keeping the main ideas of the passage in mind, you are also expected to add relevant and appropriate ideas of your own.

Careful thought and planning are necessary. You must keep the task clearly focused in your mind at all times. Try to do this as you read the text.

We head north and west from Kiev, making for the town of Narodichi. It's 60 km due west of Chernobyl, two of whose reactors, our guide reminds us, are still operational. The Ukrainian Parliament has voted unanimously to close them down. The Soviet government has refused. The Ukrainians claim 8000 died as a result of the accident. The official Soviet figure is 32.

We are passing through woodlands of pine and oak scrub interspersed with harvested fields and cherry and almond orchards. An army convoy of 40 trucks passes, heading south. After a while the woodland gives way to a wide and fertile agricultural plain. The first indication that this abundance is tainted comes as quite a shock. It's a sign, set in brambles and long grass, which reads, 'Warning: It is forbidden for cattle to graze, and for anybody to gather mushrooms, strawberries and medicinal herbs'.

We stop here and put on our yellow badges, which register radiation levels, and which will be sent back to England for analysis after our three-hour visit. Armed with these and a radiation detector, we enter Narodichi where people have lived with radiation for over five years. It's a neat, proud little town with a chestnut-lined main street and a silver-painted Lenin in front of the party headquarters. In a year's time there will be no one here.

In the municipal gardens the grass is uncut but a fountain still plays. There are several memorials. One is a scorched tree with a cross on it – local people think that the forest protected them from the worst of the blast. Beside the tree are three large boulders, one of which commemorates four villages and 548 people evacuated in 1986, another 15 villages and 3264 people evacuated in 1990. Twenty-two more villages and a further 11,000 people will be going in 1991. An inscription reads: 'In memory of the villages and human destinies of the Narodichi region burnt down by radiation.'

One of the most polluted areas is the children's playground, with 13 to 17 times normal radiation levels. The red metal chairs hang down from the roundabout and blue steel boats swing gently in the breeze, but no one is allowed to play here any more.

Ivan, the local schoolmaster, is short and podgy and his face is an unhealthy grey. There were 10,000 children in the region, he tells me, now there are 3000. Two of his pupils pass by on bicycles and he grabs them and introduces us. The boys, just back from a Pioneer camp in Poland, look bored, and reply in monosyllables, which Ivan translates thus: 'The children send fraternal greetings to children throughout the United Kingdom'. He smiles proudly and a little desperately. I ask if the children's work has been affected by their proximity to Chernobyl. He sighs and nods.

'There is not a single healthy child here.'

►►

As we drive out of Narodichi, Ivan talks proudly of the history of his town, interspersing this with casually chilling present-day observations.

'This is the bridge over the Oush river. It is an area of the highest pollution.'

We come to the village of Nozdrishche, which was evacuated last year. There are no ruins, there is no devastation or destruction. Wooden cottages with painted window-frames stand in their orderly rows. Flowers are in bloom and grasshoppers dart around in lush overgrown gardens. It is a hot, soft, gentle summer's day. Yet scientists who have visited the area say it could be 700 years before this place comes back to life. It is hard to know what to believe, for whatever curse lies over these villages is the more frightening for being invisible. It is how one has heard the countryside would be after a nuclear war – benign, smiling, deadly.

A year's exposure to the weather has not yet dissipated a faint smell of disinfectant in a small, deserted maternity hospital. A poster on the wall depicts the American space shuttle spinning round the earth, with the single word 'Nyet!' beneath. There is a book on breastfeeding, its leaves nibbled by mice, an examination chair, medical records still in files, and a portrait of Lenin which has fallen out of its frame and lies in a corner beneath a scattering of glass slides and syringes. Conscious of the limited time we have been advised to spend here we move on through the village. I catch sight of two figures down a lane to one side of the main street. One is a very old lady, whose name is Heema, and the other her nephew. Heema is 90 years old and has refused to be moved from the village. She says she has been moved five times since the disaster and now she is too old and ill. Her one wish is to die in the house in which she was born, but that is now cordoned off with barbed wire, so she will remain here with her daughter. They are the only inhabitants of Nozdrishche.

Further along the road, at the village of Novoye Sharno, the radiation detector bleeps for the first time.

'Pay attention, please,' says Ivan, 'the radiation is very high here.'

This is one of the villages evacuated in 1986, immediately after the explosion and fire, and the village shop is now almost submerged in the undergrowth. Inside it is a mess of broken shelves, abandoned goods, smashed bottles.

'There was a panic here,' our guide explains, unnecessarily.

We drive back through Narodichi, where, as in Novoye Sharno and Nozdrishche and over 40 villages in this region alone, the grass will soon grow around doors that will never be opened again, and anyone who comes here will be informed of the dangers and the risks which those who lived here were not told about until it was too late.

From *From Pole to Pole* by Michael Palin,
BBC Consumer Publishing (Books), 1995

Now study a sample response. The examiner's comments are in blue.

Example of a candidate's response

The audience is directly addressed at the start and the phrase 'Parents and students' is repeated effectively later.

There is plenty of evidence that the content of the original passage has been clearly understood ('it may have looked normal . . .' indicates that the candidate has clearly appreciated Michael Palin's response to his surroundings).

Parents and students, I'm sure you have heard of the destruction in Ukraine after their terrible nuclear accident. I here to tell you that we all should pitch in to help mostly the children of the worst affected areas of the country. I have been to Ukraine and met the people; it may have looked normal, but the radiation has done too much damage beyond mention.

Most of the children don't have any classes because of the destruction and disruption the nuclear accident. The children in numerous villages are still smiling, because they really don't know the damage caused.

Parents and students, we can write to these children, maybe this will make them see a better tomorrow. We can send them pictures of thing here in our country, and we could also introduce the pen-pal service, where a student from here writes to a student in Ukraine. When the situation improves their we can introduce a student exchange programme

Key

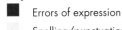

■ Errors of expression
  Spelling/punctuation
  errors

There is a definite attempt to build on the original content and to include his/her own ideas, for example the suggestion of offering support to students in the Ukraine, although perhaps at this stage a pen-pal service is not the most practical idea!

The ideas and the content of the answer are also underdeveloped with the result that the writer has not fully demonstrated his/her persuasion skills. For example, the idea of the pen-pal scheme is stated without much explanation. A better answer would have linked it more effectively to the comments about the plight of the children. In fact, the writer could have made much better use of details from the original passage in his/her attempts to persuade the audience to feel sympathy for the people of the area.

On first impression, this is quite a good answer. There is a convincing 'speech' style. Nevertheless, the answer has some limitations; there are errors of expression which will prevent it being placed in the highest bands.

The answer communicates well, but the limitations of the content and expression would limit it to a mark in the **grade** D range.

Example 2

Here is a similar task from Paper 2, based on two texts on the theme of child labour. One is from *Children of the Indifferent God* and the other is from *Les Misérables*. Here is the question, followed by the texts.

> You are very keen that your school friends should understand the horrors of child labour. You have been given permission to organise a meeting in school to address them on this topic.
>
> Write your opening speech. Use ideas from **both** passages.

Children of the Indifferent God

Child labour would be eradicated in India if only the laws against it were implemented, suggests Anjana Maitra-Sinha.

Child labour has been defined as 'any work which interferes with the child's full physical development, opportunities for the desirable minimum of education, or needed recreation'. India has the second largest child population in the world, 145 million. It also has the largest number of child labourers in the world, 6.22 per cent of the national workforce. Estimates of the figure range from 13.59 to 17.36 million, most of whom are under 14 years of age. There are over 100,000 child workers in New Delhi alone.

Children mainly find employment as domestic helps and in factories, mills, small tea and snack shops and construction sites. According to a recent UNICEF report, every third house in India has a working child and every fourth Indian under the age of 15 is employed. Child labourers are often paid very little for long hours of labour. Sometimes they are not paid at all.

The recent argument over the employment of children in the carpet industry has resulted in a ban on Indian carpet exports in many countries. The sharp eyes and nimble fingers of children make them invaluable for the carpet industry, a big foreign exchange earner which employs over 300,000 children.

Persuaded into the jobs by false promises of high pay, most of these children work in terrible conditions, with low wages and poor food and shelter. They fall prey to various diseases. The wool fluff which circulates in the tiny, ill-ventilated rooms which serve as carpet factories results in many breathing problems.

At festivals, firecrackers worth millions and made in the small factories in the town of Sivakasi go up in flames all over India. Most of these fireworks are produced by children. Sivakasi is notorious as the 'child labour capital of the world'. Over 250,000 children work in its 350 factories, most of which are licensed to operate. The town is in a relatively barren area and its small factories are the main source of income for its people.

A special feature of Sivakasi is that more girls figure on its employment rolls than boys. Girls in fact outnumber boys in the ratio 3:1. There are two reasons for this. First, girls have more nimble fingers.

Second, many families send the sons to school and keep the daughters away from education.

Other industries which employ children on a large scale are those manufacturing locks, glass and bangles. It is estimated over 1.5 million children work in glass, carpet and lock factories in Uttar Pradesh.

The little children are exposed to many health hazards. Contract labourers working in brick kilns develop lung diseases. Mica and other chemicals found in glass bangle manufacturing are also harmful.

Sivakasi, with its inflammable products, is infamous for its fatal accidents. An explosion in July 1991 claimed 39 lives and injured dozens more. Other afflictions of its child labourers are anaemia, night blindness, myopia and breathing problems.

After 14 to 16 hours of daily mental and physical pressure, child labourers cannot but have a stunted development. They often grow up to become criminals.

There are comprehensive laws in India with regard to child labour. For instance Article 39 of the Constitution offers specific protection to children.

The Factories Act (1948) prohibits the employment of children under 18 in factories.

The policy for children adopted in August 1974 recognised the nation's children as a supremely important asset. The national policy on child labour formulated in 1988 suggested children employed as part of the family be treated differently from those outside the family structure.

A national action plan for children was approved by the Union cabinet in June 1992. It adopted international standards for 'child survival, development and protection'.

The Child Labour Action and Support Programme sponsored by the International Labour Organisation is being finalised to supplement government efforts. The University Grants Commission has been urged to be liberal in granting financial assistance to universities wishing to set up child labour study groups.

A former president of India explained the term 'child labour' in two phrases: first as 'an economic practice' and second as 'a social evil'. The first signifies employment of children in gainful occupation with a view to adding to the family income. The second, a broader aspect, takes into account the dangers children are exposed to and the resultant denial of opportunities for development.

The chief reason for child labour is, of course, the abysmal poverty of the people. Extra hands to supplement the family income are always welcome. Another reason is illiteracy among children.

The rapid pace of urbanisation – 109 million Indians lived in cities in 1971 as compared to 217 million 20 years later – is also responsible for the growth of child labour. Other factors include ignorance and the erosion of social, cultural and moral values.

Though the problem has spread its tentacles deep into India's social fabric, it is not insurmountable. Coordination of health, nutrition and educational programmes and involvement of non-governmental organisations could fight child labour effectively. The media can contribute by increasing public awareness.

Adapted from

The CalcuttaTelegraph, 30 March 1993

This passage is adapted from *Les Misérables*, a novel written in the nineteenth century by Victor Hugo. Cosette's mother is paying the Thénardiers to look after her but they treat her like a slave.

Cosette existed between the two of them, subject to pressure from either side like a creature that is at once ground between mill-stones and torn apart by pincers. Each had his own way of treating her. The blows she received came from the woman; the fact that she went barefoot in winter was due to the man. She ran upstairs and down, washed, swept, scrubbed and polished, drudged and gasped for breath, carried heavy burdens and performed arduous tasks, small though she was. There was no mercy to be expected from either mistress or master. The inn was a trap in which she was caught and held, her state of servitude the very pattern of oppression, herself the fly trembling and powerless in a spider's web.

The child endured and said nothing; but what goes on in the souls of those helpless creatures, newly arrived from God, when they find themselves thus flung naked into the world of men?

Four new travellers had arrived and Cosette was a prey to gloomy misgivings. Although she was only eight, her life had been so hard that she viewed the world already with an old woman's eyes. Her face was bruised by a blow from Mme Thénardier, which caused that lady to remark, 'She looks a sight with that black eye'.

She was thinking as she sat under the table that the night was very dark, and that the jugs and pitchers in the bedrooms of the new arrivals had had to be filled, so that there was no more water in the house. There was some reassurance in the fact that not much water was drunk in the tavern. They had no lack of thirsty customers, but it was a thirst calling for wine, not water. Nevertheless she was given cause to tremble. Mme Thénardier lifted the lid of a cooking pot bubbling on the stove, then seized a glass and went over to the water-butt, while the little girl watched her in alarm. Only a thin trickle came when she turned the tap, half-filling the glass, and she exclaimed, 'Bother! We're out of water.'

There was a moment of silence while Cosette held her breath.

'Don't worry,' said Thénardier, looking at the half-filled glass. 'That'll be enough.'

Cosette went on with her work, but her heart was thumping. She counted the minutes as they dragged by, praying for it to be tomorrow morning. Every now and then a customer would put his head outside and say, 'It's black as pitch. You'd need to be a cat to get about without a lantern on a night like this,' and she would tremble afresh.

Then a traveller who was stopping in the house came into the general room and said angrily:

'My horse hasn't been watered.'

'Indeed it has,' said Mme Thénardier.

'I tell you it hasn't, mistress,' the man said.

Cosette scrambled out from under the table.

'But he has, monsieur. I took him water myself, a whole bucketful, and I talked to him.'

This was not true. Cosette was lying.

'No higher than my knee and lies like a trooper!' the traveller cried. 'I tell you he hasn't, my girl. I know it for sure. When he's thirsty he snorts in a particular way.'

Cosette stuck to her guns, speaking in a voice so stifled with terror as to be scarcely audible.

'All the same, he has.'

'Look,' said the man angrily, 'there's not much in watering a horse, is there? Why not just do it?

Cosette dived back under the table.

'Well, that's right,' said Mme Thénardier. 'If the horse hasn't been watered it ought to be. Where's the girl got to now?' She peered under the table and saw her crouched at the far end, almost under the drinkers' feet. 'Come out of there, you!'

Cosette crept out again.

'Now, Miss good-for-nothing, go and water that horse.'

'But, Madame,' said Cosette faintly, 'there's no water left.'

Mme Thénardier's answer was to fling open the street door.

'Then go and get some,' she said.

Disconsolately Cosette fetched an empty bucket from a corner of the hearth. It was larger than herself, large enough for her to have sat in it. Mme Thénardier turned back to her stove and dipping in a wooden spoon tasted the contents of the pot.

'Plenty of water in the spring,' she muttered. 'No trouble at all. I think this could have done without the onions.'

She went over to a drawer in which she kept small change and other oddments.

'Here, Miss Toad,' she said. 'Here's a fifteen-sou piece. While you're about it you can get a large loaf at the baker's.'

Cosette took the coin without a word and put it carefully in the pocket of her apron. Then, with the bucket in her hand, she stood hesitating in the doorway, as though hoping someone would rescue her.

'Get a move on,' cried Mme Thénardier.

Cosette went out and the door closed behind her.

From *Les Misérables* by Victor Hugo

As you can see, this is very similar to the task in Paper 1 and the same principles apply to writing this speech. There are three key points to notice:

- There is an additional complication here which is that you must include ideas from **both** passages. This makes it all the more important to plan your answer – don't get so involved in the first passage that you neglect the other one, or you will have thrown some marks away.
- The question refers specifically to the *horrors* of child labour and says that you are keen to get this across to your audience. So, you must ensure that your speech is sufficiently convincing to influence the feelings of your listeners.
- Notice who your audience is – your school friends. So although the topic is a serious one, the setting is not entirely formal, and the audience is partly familiar to you. This will have an effect on the style and tone of your speech.

Now study a sample response. The examiner's comments are in blue.

Example of a candidate's response

The second paragraph shows the writer has successfully picked up relevant details from the first passage and applied them effectively for his/her own purpose.

Boys and girls of _ School, I thank you for attending this meeting. For those of you that do not know me my name is John and I would like to address you on the topic of child labour.

How would you feel if you had to get up at 6 o'clock tomorrow morning, work 16 hours in a hot Brick factory with little or no rest for 30 cents?

I can see on many of your faces, the horror of it. 30 cents for a days work. But my friends this happens all over the world.

India has the second largest child population in the world and it also has the largest number of child labourers in the world. That is around 14 to 17 million children working for a living, most of them under the age of 14. None of them have part-time jobs like you may have, they work in factories, mills and construction sites. getting paid very little or not at all.

Apart from a few slips, the language is accurate. There is a convincing 'speech' style. The audience is directly involved by statements such as, 'These were all children younger than many of you sitting out there.'

These children most of whom can not read or write, and have had no education, are subjected to physical and mental abuse in many cases. They are also exposed to many health hazards. In July 1991 a factory in Sivasaki in India claimed 39 lives and injured dozens more. These were all children younger than many of you sitting out there. Other affliction of child labourers are anaemia, night blindness, myopia, lung disease and breathing problems.

After working 14 to 16 hours of hard labour with daily mental and physical pressure many children traumatized and often grow up to become criminals.

There is some reference to the second passage, but it is less well developed. For example, although the writer refers to conditions in the nineteenth century, it is done in a very limited way with little specific detail.

In the 19th century children in our country were subjected to such conditions as India has today. Children were beaten and starved and made to work harder than any of us could ever imagine.

We should think ourselves lucky, this country has laws against child labour, we are entitled to a proper education, many children are not. Just remember when you get up for school tomorrow morning, children in many other countries have been up hours before us, working in terrible conditions, dangerous conditions, with no education for less money than a packet of sweets.

There is no doubt that the candidate has understood the task and has used the material in the passages to produce an effective argument against child labour which would produce a positive response from an audience. There is, in fact, a clever attempt to relate directly to the imagined audience by referring to their own experience, which shows that the writer has fully understood the role that he/she is expected to play. ('None of them have part time jobs like you may have.')

This is clearly expressed, direct and well structured. It makes good use of ideas from the first passage, which have been well selected and intelligently absorbed into the writer's argument.

However, despite these many good points, the ideas have not been sufficiently developed (4th paragraph) or imaginatively used. For example, the references to the physical problems (myopia, etc.) tend to be no more than straight listing of points; a better answer would have built them more effectively into the writer's argument. The limited reference to the second passage is also a weakness with this answer and, despite its many good points, it was not quite of the standard for an A so was awarded a grade B.

Practise writing a speech

Exercise 1

Now try an example from another paper. Note that the question identifies your audience very specifically – a group of parents. Before you start and as you plan your writing, think carefully about how this fact might affect what you say and how you say it.

> Imagine that you are a member of a safety organisation and that you have been asked to give a brief talk to a group of parents about the dangers of residential swimming pools.
>
> Use details from the following article and write your speech in about a page to a page and a half.

Protecting children from pool accidents

A child's risk of drowning is much greater than most people realise, especially in residential pools.

Pools are great fun, terrific for cooling down on a hot day and for getting aerobic exercise. But they are also a responsibility. As residential pools have proliferated, so, unfortunately, has the opportunity for tragedy.

While in recent years there has been a decline in drownings among teenage boys in the United States, most of whom succumb in natural bodies of water, there has been no comparable drop in drowning deaths among young children, most of whom succumb in pools – usually the family's pool.

A child's risk of drowning is much greater than most people realise.

Children under the age of five are 14 times as likely to die in a pool as in a motor vehicle. Of those who survive near-drownings, many are permanently brain damaged.

Yet, while the vast majority of parents take care to secure their young children in car seats, far fewer take comparable precautions around pools.

Instead of adopting proven safety measures to prevent pool accidents, too many parents, grandparents and others who have residential pools rely on things like admonitions about not going near the pool alone, the false security of swimming lessons and flotation devices for toddlers, and their sincere but often misguided belief that they will watch closely and constantly when a child is in or near the pool.

A study revealed telling circumstances surrounding the pool-related deaths of young children. Two-thirds occurred in the family pool and one-third in pools owned by friends or relatives.

Nearly half the children were last seen in the house and nearly a quarter were last seen in the yard or on the porch or patio; no one knew the youngsters had gone near the pool.

Only about one-third of the children were in or around the pool just before drowning.

Finally, more than three-fourths of the children had been seen five minutes or less before being missed and subsequently found in the pool.

The lessons to be learned from these statistics include the facts that drowning accidents happen very quickly, in familiar surroundings and during very short lapses in supervision.

There are no cries for help to alert caretakers that a small child is in trouble in the water. The only effective protection is to ensure that children cannot get near a pool without being accompanied by a responsible and trained caretaker whose attention is not distracted by phone calls, door bells, reading matter or the care of other children who are not in the pool.

Adopting proven safety measures is a better alternative to the false security of swimming lessons and flotation devices.

While many communities have safety regulations governing residential pools, it is the pool owner's responsibility to follow them. Regardless of local laws, to minimise the risk of pool accidents every owner should adopt these minimal safety standards:

■ Fence it in. A fence or comparable barrier completely surrounding the pool is the best preventive, reducing the risk of pool drownings by about 70 per cent, an Australian study showed. It is just as important to fence in an above-ground pool as an in-ground pool, since a small child can easily climb the ladder and fall into the water.

■ Cover it.

■ Remain vigilant. Children in or near pools must be watched constantly by a responsible and well-informed caretaker.

A moment's lapse can spell disaster. Never assume that a child who has taken swimming lessons or is using a flotation device can safely be left unattended, even just to answer the door.

For added security when the caretaker is not nearby in the water, children who are not good swimmers could wear properly fitted flotation vests, which keep their heads above water.

■ Prepare for emergencies. In addition to the standard ladders or steps to help people climb out of pools, there should be a circular buoy on a rope, a long-handled hook and a rescue ladder at the poolside.

A poolside telephone with emergency phone numbers posted next to it is both a convenience and a critical safety feature.

Anyone in charge of children playing in or near water should be trained in cardiopulmonary resuscitation and be prepared to use it the moment a child is pulled from the water.

Waiting for emergency personnel to arrive can doom a nearly-drowned child.

■ Observe other safety measures. Keep toys like tricycles and balls away from pools. Do not permit horseplay in the water. Children should not be allowed to dunk each other, push each other into the water or yell in jest for help. Mark the pool's deep end and, preferably, use a floating pool rope to denote where the water would be above the children's chins. Never permit diving at the shallow end or from the sides of the pool or into an above-ground pool.

From *The New Straits Times*, 5 July 1994

Safe as Houses?

Every year many children aged five and under are killed because of accidents in the home, and large numbers need hospital treatment. How can you make your child, grandchild or any young visitor safer in your home?

In the kitchen

The main types of injury in the kitchen are burns and scalds, often caused by children pulling kettles full of boiling water over themselves or tipping up pans on the cooker. Other hazards include cups and teapots full of hot drinks, hot oven doors, and hot irons. Children can also be at risk from slippery kitchen floors and from household chemicals.

In the bathroom

Children can be scalded by bath water which is too hot, and they can also drown in the bath – even in only a few inches of water. Some children often like to investigate toilets, which can be unhygienic or even unsafe if some cleaning products have been used.

Slamming doors

When children are playing together it's very easy for hands or fingers to get caught in doors. Few of these injuries are serious but they're all very painful.

Falls down stairs

The under-twos are most at risk on the stairs because they try to crawl or walk up or down them before they're really ready to. Additional risks are caused by toys or other objects left on the stairs, loose carpet or poor lighting.

Falls from windows

As soon as a child is mobile, low windows, or windows with climbable objects in front of them, become a major hazard, especially on upper floors.

Fires and matches

Fire is the most common cause of accidental death in the home for children. Around half these deaths are thought to be due to children playing with matches.

Medicines and chemicals

Some houses may contain a selection of medicines and household chemicals which can be very dangerous if swallowed by small children.

Near the house

Children are also at risk near the house – particularly if they're unsupervised. Keep garages and sheds containing tools locked and take the same care with chemicals as you would in the house.

Exercise 2

Try to answer the following question based on the text Safe as Houses?.
Again, the question identifies your audience – a group of ten-year-olds.
Take this into account as you plan your talk.

There has been an increase in accidents involving young children at home.

Your teacher has given you a speaking assignment. It is to talk to a small
class of ten-year-olds on the subject of keeping younger brothers and sisters
safe at home. The talk is sub-titled 'How you can help'. She has given you the
sheet 'Safe as Houses?' to start you off.
  Write what you would say.

■ You do not have to use all the material and you must not copy sentences
  from it.
■ You might wish to include questions and comments from your ten-year-old
  audience.

Additional exercises

1 You have to make a speech to your class about an issue that you believe
  in passionately. Here are some possibilities:

  ■ You are a vegetarian and you want everyone to stop eating meat.
  ■ You want people to be more environmentally conscious.
  ■ You don't see the point of school uniform and you want it abolished.

  Whatever your chosen topic, write the speech you would make to your class.
2 An important group of visitors is coming to your school and you have
  been chosen to make the welcoming speech. Decide what you would say
  and write your speech.
3 Think yourself into the future. You have decided that you are going to try
  to get yourself elected to your country's national parliament. You have
  ideas about what should be done to benefit your country. Here are some
  possibilities:

  ■ You believe that things would improve economically if there were better
    communications and you want to advocate a road-building programme.
  ■ You believe that farmers should be encouraged more as they are the
    backbone of the country and are the only people who can provide food
    for the poor.
  ■ You believe that the country should scale down its armed forces because
    they are costing far too much and the country should follow peaceful
    policies anyway.

  You will almost certainly have some ideas of your own to use as well as, or
  instead of, any of these. Write the words of a speech which you would
  make to the people you want to vote for you.

■ Writing a dialogue or conversation

If you are asked to write a dialogue or conversation you might be given a clear indication of how to set it out, but sometimes the decision will be left to you. When you are left with a choice, there are three possibilities.

1 You could set it out as **a playscript** with the names of the speakers on the left-hand side of the page and the words that they speak on the right. This is the easiest method for any conversation. If you want to give a 'direction' about how the person speaks, put it very briefly in brackets after his/her name.

James (brightly) *It will be all right on the night.*

Esmerelda (discouragingly) *You always say that.*

2 You might write it out as **a conversation** using speech marks:

'It will be all right on the night,' he said brightly.

If you choose this style, you must put the words that are actually spoken inside speech marks. Remember as well that every time you shift from one speaker to another you must start a new line.

'It will be all right on the night,' he said brightly.
'You always say that,' responded Esmerelda discouragingly.

3 The third way you might deal with the task is to write it in what is called **reported speech:**

He commented that it would be all right on the night, but she responded discouragingly that he always said that.

Tip   If you choose method 2 or method 3, try to use a wide range of words as alternatives to 'said', to make your writing more interesting (as in the above example). Here are some possibilities:

exclaimed	shouted	whispered	answered	retorted	suggested
replied	whined	muttered	questioned	laughed	queried
sneered	called				

Example of a script-writing task

In the example that follows you would be expected to take your information from the main article, the accompanying diagrams and, perhaps, the captions which relate to the diagrams. You would also be expected to use some ideas of your own.

Once again, you are required to put yourself into a role and to write your answer as speech. However, the register (language and tone) you use for a conversation should be considerably different from that used for the formal speech we looked at on pages 61–65. It is also important that you select points from the material which would be suitable for each of the speakers in the conversation.

Imagine that you are working in a research laboratory investigating the harmful effects of noise. You have some neighbours who are worried that their children enjoy playing music very loudly. They come to you for advice.

Write a script of your conversation. Write between 25 and 35 lines.

Noise

Excessive noise can have a serious effect on health, and is associated with stress and anxiety. Very loud noise causes physical damage to the delicate structures in the ear, and may result in deafness.

Noise is a form of pollution which can be merely irritating, or cause physical or emotional damage. For some people, the sound of music played very loudly is annoying, while others revel in it. Similarly, it may be enjoyable for some to drive a motor bike, while other people find the noise anti-social.

Long-term exposure to loud noise can bring about stress which has physical signs such as an increase in oxygen consumption and heart rate, possibly leading to effects on the heart and circulation. Tiredness, irritability and sleep disturbances may also occur.

The physical effects of noise on the ears can be serious. Prolonged, loud noise causes physical discomfort; it actually 'hurts the ears'. And if it is too loud or goes on for too long, it, at first, causes temporary hearing loss, then deafness, due to permanent damage to the delicate mechanism of the inner ear. Rock musicians performing in front of very powerful speakers frequently have permanent hearing damage.

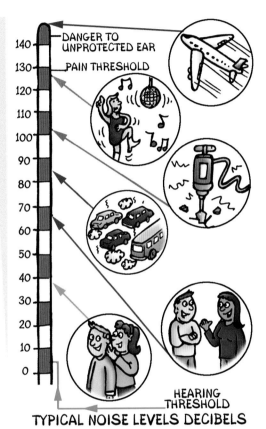

TYPICAL NOISE LEVELS DECIBELS

If used at too high a volume, personal stereos can cause severe hearing loss. Although the speakers are so tiny that they can even be fitted inside the ear, the sound they produce is directed straight down the ear canal and can cause damage if the volume is turned up too high.

Don't underestimate the harmful effects of noise. It is the form of pollution which has the most immediate effect on people. It can cause severe stress.

From *The Environment and Health*, by Brian Ward, Franklin Watts, and *Wake Up to What You Can Do for the Environment*, DETR 1989

Example of a candidate's response

The stage directions are not directly relevant to the answer.

Although the opening speeches may be useful as scene-setting, they do not really contribute much to the answer as a whole.

> There is a knock at the door Mark gets up from his chair placing some paper work on the table. On answering the door he finds it is Jason and Carole from next door, a middle age couple with conserned looks on their faces.)
>
> Mark (opening the door)   Hello again, how are you both?
>
> Jason   Very well thanks, and you?
>
> Mark (opening the door a little wider)   Work, work, work, that's all it seems to be these days. Would you like to come in?

Carole   We don't really want to bother you, if you are busy. We can come back another time. We have just got a couple of question to ask you, a bit silly really. (looking slightly embarrassed and going red)

Mark   No, come in what's on your mind

(Jason and Carole come into the hall and hold each others hand)

Once the writer starts to deal with the relevant points about noise it becomes clear that he/she has understood the text and selected important points from it sensibly.

Jason   I remembered from the last time we spoke that you were investigating the harmful effects of noise. We just wanted some advise that's all. (looking at Carole)

Mark   I will see what I can do for you. Whats the problem.

Jason   It's the children really, they play their music far to loud and we are worried about the effects. Its driving us crazy.

The candidate's expression reveals some limitations; the material is, in places, still very close to its original leaflet format ('Tiredness, irritability and lack of sleep can occur') and there is an overall sameness about the sentence structures which does not provide a convincing speech register.

Mark   Well long term exposure to noise can bring about stress, which we have found can bring about physical signs. Tiredness, irritability and lack of sleep can occur. Are they showing any of these signs?

Carole (Looking at Jason)   No not that I'm awair of.

Mark   How loud do they play it?

Jason   Much louder than they need to, anyone would think they are deaf.

Mark   Physical effects on the ear are serious to. If it goes on to loud for to long, it can cause tempory hearing loss and then deafness due to perminant damage to the inner ear.

One of the most positive features of this answer is the way in which it manipulates the material for its own purposes. For example, the writer takes the opportunity to mention a personal stereo in order to include a further range of points.

Carole   That's it, no more loud music. We will get them a personel stereo.

Mark   I'm afraid thats the worst thing to do, they can cause servere hearing loss, the sound goes direclty into the ear canal and causes damage. The best thing is to get them to turn in right down, to a level where everyone is happy. Noise is a polution, which can cause everyone damage.

Jason   Well thanks for that. We know what to do now, no more loud music, it was driving us mad any way.

(With a smile on their faces they turned and left.)

Key

Spelling/punctuation errors

There are basic errors of spelling ('awair', 'tempory').

This writer has a good understanding of the task and writes a convincing conversation. However, there is some unnecessary padding and some lack of development of ideas. This answer scores a **grade B** but no higher because of the weaknesses listed.

Practise writing a dialogue or conversation

Just occasionally, especially in Part 2 of Paper 2, you may be asked to write a dialogue or conversation. Use the following exercises to help you practise writing these in a script format.

Exercise 1

The following article was printed in *The New Straits Times*.

Imagine you are Mohamad Muzri Mat Sari and you are talking with a group of your friends about the day you fell off the pipe and broke your arm.

Write a page to a page and a half of the dialogue.

Dangerous balancing act to get to and return from school

By C. Navaratnam

STUDENTS living in Kampung Pasir and Taman Datuk Mansor off Jalan Rasah, Seremban, do a balancing act – one which could prove fatal – on their way to school daily.

They have become adept at carrying their bags while balancing themselves to cross a 50-metre pipe about 5m over the Sungai Linggi.

The alternative is to walk two kilometres to school.

Some 60 students of Sekolah Menengah Jalan Loop are forced to use the pipe daily as this is the only way of crossing the river.

On rainy days, when they have to hold an umbrella and balance their bag at the same time, students do a risky 'horse ride' on the pipe which is embarrassing for the girls.

To date, a housewife has died after falling into the river. A student has broken an arm in a similar accident.

Residents have made several appeals to State Assemblymen and Members of Parliament for a bridge across the river.

Now, they can only pray that their children make it safely across the river every time they go to and return from school.

'Yes, promises were made several times especially before the elections but nothing has been done until today. We are really disappointed.' said K. Pannir Selvam, 37, whose son uses the pipe daily.

'I think the authorities will only act when a child falls into the river. I am praying that my son will return home safely from school daily.'

Housewife Tang Chow Har, 40, recalled the day when her best friend fell while crossing the river about 15 years ago. Her body was later found 2km away.

'Her death was a big blow to me,' she said.

Tang said she is prepared to collect funds if the authorities are willing to build a bridge across the river.

►►

'A bridge is essential to us as it will only take us about five minutes to reach the main road by crossing the river. If we have to use the other route, it will take us about 25 minutes,' added Tang.

Fourth-former Nur Balkiesh Sulaiman said she had no choice but to use the pipe to get to school.

'On rainy days, when it's dangerous to walk across, we have to "horse ride" the pipe to get to the other end. It is very embarrassing for us,' she said.

'We have to also bear the heat when we return tired and hungry after school. We are unable to hold an umbrella in one hand and the books in the other while crossing,' said 15-year-old Intan Razuna Mohamad Iqbal.

Fourth-former Mohamad Muzri Mat Sari, 16, recalled the day when he fell off the pipe and broke his arm.

'It was in the morning and while I was half way along the pipeline, I slipped and fell. Thank God I did not fall into the river and I am lucky to be alive,' Mohamad Muzri said.

Several pupils admitted that it was a hazard to cross along the pipeline but preferred doing so instead of walking more than two kilometres to reach the school.

'Of course, my parents would like me to go by bus or use the other route but it is too far. My friends and I are extra cautious while crossing on the pipe,' said Form Two pupil P. Sivaraman.

'We not only have to use the pipe in the morning but also in the afternoon when we go for extramural activities.

'We always make it a point to return before dusk,' added Sivaraman.

From *The New Straits Times*, 8 July, 1994

Exercise 2

Imagine that you are a very keen football fan but your friend prefers playing computer games. Write a conversation with your friend in which you try to persuade him or her to come to a football match with you.

Exercise 3

You overhear a conversation between your mother and your aunt. They are planning a surprise birthday party for a family member. What do they say?

Exercise 4

An important person is visiting your school. You have been chosen to show her round. Write the conversation that you have as you show her round the school.

■ Writing a letter

You may be asked to read some information and write a letter in response. The following are just three examples of the type of letter you might be asked to write:

- a letter of complaint or enquiry to a company

- a letter to a magazine or newspaper, commenting on the material and giving your reaction

- a letter explaining or apologising for a problem.

As with any piece of writing, remember to think about the **audience** and the **purpose**.

1 **Who are you writing to?** This will help you to decide how formal your letter needs to be. If it is a letter to a friend, for instance, it can be in a chatty style and you can use some informal, colloquial language. For example, instead of 'I feel I must express my views on . . .' it would be more appropriate to say 'I must tell you what I thought about . . .'.

2 **What are you writing for?** Is it to complain, to make a request, to apologise, or to defend or attack a particular point of view? The answer to this question will have an effect on how you write. For example, if it is a letter to a company then your points must be clearly ordered and written in a systematic, logical way. One important point: even if your letter is making a complaint about a situation or attacking someone else's opinion, it should never be abusive or rude.

How should your letter be set out?

Although the layout of a letter may not be as important as the content, you should follow certain guidelines. Study the letter layouts for a personal and a formal letter on pages 82–83, and use them appropriately. You must set your letter out neatly; there is never any excuse for an untidy-looking letter.

A personal letter to a friend or relative

Put your address at the top right-hand corner, with the date underneath it.

7 Hillside Close
Anytown
Blankshire
AB1 2YZ

1 November 2002

Dear Claire

_____

_____

_____

_____

_____

_____

_____

_____

_____

_____

_____

_____

_____

_____

Use an informal ending.

With love from

A formal letter

Put your address at the top right-hand corner.

7 Hillside Close
Anytown
Blankshire
AB1 2YZ

Put the name and address of the person you are writing to on the left-hand side of the page.

Mr Brown
Head of Leisure Services
Blankshire Council
Council Offices
Anytown
Blankshire
AB4 6JQ

Put the date below this address.

2 November 2002

If you don't know the name of the person you are writing to, start 'Dear Sir/Madam'.

Dear Mr Brown

_____

_____

_____

_____

_____

_____

_____

_____

_____

_____

If you used the person's name at the start of the letter, end with 'Yours sincerely'.
If you started the letter 'Dear Sir/Madam', end with 'Yours faithfully'.
If you know the person you are writing to quite well, you could end your letter more informally: 'With best wishes', for example.

Yours sincerely

Examples of letters

Read these two letters about a dog that got out of control.

Dear Mrs Arensky,

I would like to apologise for the unfortunate incident that I caused in your mini-market last Thursday. I have talked it over with my parents who have suggested that I write to you to explain how it happened.

I admit that it was my fault in bringing my dog, Kevin, into your shop in the first place. As we approached the meat counter, Kevin recognised an old enemy of his disappearing round the corner. Unfortunately, he has had a lot of trouble with that young man on several occasions. He simply set off with me behind him. When he started to overtake the shoppers, they all looked round, and several collided with each other. Kevin's lead became entangled with someone's legs and the owner of them fell into the pile of eggs which crashed to the floor. People started to slip over, and in no time at all there was total disorder. Kevin eventually caught up with his enemy and bit him in the leg.

Although it was really just an accident, I realise that it is my responsibility to apologise and to offer to pay for the damage. My parents have generously said they will lend me the money which I can pay back over what will probably have to be a very long period of time.

Yours sincerely,

Olga Mishkin

This letter starts off by getting straight to the point.

A development paragraph clearly explains exactly what happened.

The third paragraph neatly rounds off the letter with a return to the opening.

The letter has started with a name and so the ending is correct.

Dear Mrs Arensky,

My parents have made me write this letter though I don't think it's fair. You should blame that man Serge who's always shouting at my Kevin. You can't expect me to stop him chasing him. Kevin's stronger than me anyway and once he sets off nothing will stop him. And you have to admit it is a bit silly to put all those eggs there. They're just asking to be knocked over, aren't they. You see, Kevin was on a long lead and I just held on. I couldn't just let go. I shouted at him too. Anyway half the trouble was your shoppers. They didn't look where they were going. So they bumped into each other. I thought it was funny when one old lady got trapped against the tins of vegetables and they all collapsed on her. I mean you have to laugh, don't you.

Yours,

Olga Mishkin

No paragraphing and the content is not ordered.

The tone of the letter is all wrong – it is not apologetic but it is complaining.

The content of the letter is distorted as Olga tries to shift the blame.

Given that this is a formal letter, the ending is incorrect. It should be 'Yours sincerely'.

Practise writing a letter

Exercise 1

Read the article on pages 79–80 with the headline 'Dangerous balancing act to get to and return from school', then try the following task.

> You are one of the students who has to use the pipe daily to get to and from school.
>
> Write a letter to the authorities asking them to consider building a bridge across the river. Include:
>
> ■ reference to the facts
> ■ reference to the dangers, including reference to accidents that have occurred
> ■ your own feelings as someone who has to use the pipe on rainy days.
>
> Write between a page and a page and a half.

Exercise 2

Study the advertisement; then try the task that follows.

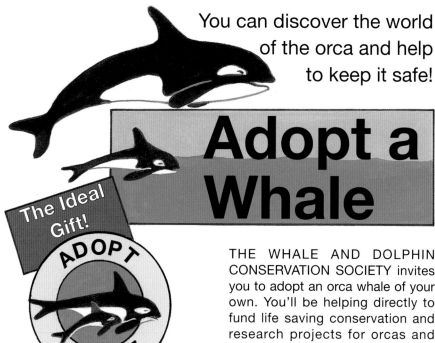

You can discover the world of the orca and help to keep it safe!

Adopt a Whale

The Ideal Gift!

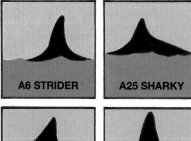

To arrange your adoption, simply select one of the whales detailed and complete an application form.

A6 STRIDER

A25 SHARKY

A42 HOLLY

A5 TOP NOTCH

THE WHALE AND DOLPHIN CONSERVATION SOCIETY invites you to adopt an orca whale of your own. You'll be helping directly to fund life saving conservation and research projects for orcas and other whales and dolphins.

You will receive: an adoption certificate/colour picture of your whale, a window sticker, a welcome letter with lots of information and every six months ORCALOG with updates of your whale. A Friend of the Orcas also receives the video "ORCA, A LESSON IN HARMONY" featuring the wild orcas of British Columbia. A Special Friend of the Orcas receives the regular pack, the video and a full colour orca print! Give Adopt a Whale as a gift and your friend or relative will get a card stating the present is from you.

Adapted from the Whale and Dolphin Conservation Society

Imagine that instead of using the advertisement, the WDCS decides to circulate a letter to all schools persuading them to adopt a whale.

Write the letter.

■ Write about a page and a half allowing for the size of your handwriting.
■ Select material for your letter from the poster but do not try to use everything.
■ Order the parts of your letter carefully, and start and finish it properly.
■ Write in a persuasive tone.
■ Do not copy whole sentences from the poster.

■ Writing a report

The key to writing a successful report is to organise your facts clearly. A report concentrates primarily on information, though it may well be leading to a particular conclusion or opinion.

■ Use headings to make it clear what your main points are: start with one major heading, and use others to divide your writing into short sections.
■ Before you start writing, decide on the headings you want to use and make lists under these headings; this will help to ensure that in your final piece the facts are presented in an organised way.
■ The sections or paragraphs of a report should be shorter than they usually are when you are writing stories or essays. This helps the reader to assess the information quickly.
■ A report is written for a particular readership. Make sure you know who the readership is before you start.

Writing a journalistic report

The key points given above about report-writing also apply to the writing of journalistic (news or magazine) reports. However, journalistic reports have a few special features.

■ They usually start with a headline. Choose one which sets the tone for what comes after – are you reporting a tragic or shocking event, or a funny or surprising event, or are you giving a straightforward account of a recent political decision, for example?
■ A journalistic report often contains transcripts (written records) of interviews, which are reported verbatim (word for word). If you choose to use this technique, you must either use speech marks correctly or turn the interview into reported speech.

Example of a news report

Look at the key features of a news report, highlighted on this article.

This type of article needs a headline.

There is an introductory paragraph which summarises the content.

Paragraphs are short, much shorter than in a piece of continuous writing.

Articles of this type gain enormously from quotations from people involved.

MIRACLE ESCAPE AT BUSY CROSSING

At midday today, a cyclist who lost control of his bicycle narrowly missed death as he swerved round an articulated lorry and a small car. The small car subsequently hit a lamp post but fortunately no-one was injured. Chaos was caused when the lorry shed part of its load.

The incident happened when Inderjit Singh, 32, of 46 Victory Road, found that the brakes on his bicycle had failed. 'I was riding quickly towards the junction and the traffic lights were red. It is all downhill you know. When I applied my brakes, nothing happened. I just went hurtling towards the junction.'

The driver of the lorry, Wing Koh, 45, of 123 Main Street, was moving away from the lights when he saw Inderjit Singh. He said that he had no chance to avoid the cyclist who managed to avoid him by executing a smart manoeuvre. Wing Koh added that as the front of his lorry swooped round, he found himself heading for a small yellow car travelling in the opposite direction.

'a write-off' says visitor

The driver of the car, Rejoice Ntuli, a visitor to our city, was only just able to avoid the cyclist. 'I braked hard,' she said, 'and my car swerved to the right, hitting a lamp post. The car is a write-off, but I think that I am all right.'

The police were called to the scene as traffic was brought to a standstill. The lorry shed part of its load of colourful mechanical toy animals, some of which were set in motion by the accident and caused bystanders much amusement.

no prosecution

An official statement from the police revealed that no-one would be prosecuted as a result of the incident. Inderjit Singh thanked the police for their assistance and said that he was happy to be alive.

Small sub-headings give the reader a quick guide.

Practise writing a report

Exercise 1

Read the following applications for an English teaching post at your school, and answer the question that follows.

Mr A Rahman

b 1970

Educated: O'Brien International College; University of Cambridge (Good Honours degree in Economics).

Teaching Experience:
1993–present: International School of Africa, Assistant teacher for English and Drama, Economics and Geography

Short Courses attended
1993: Drama for Secondary Schools
1993: Introductory Course for English teachers
1995: Teaching poetry to junior secondary pupils

Extracts from References
'Mr Rahman's lessons are original. He believes strongly in pupil talk . . .

He is an excellent tutor, and this often becomes intermixed with his academic work . . . He is kind and finds it difficult to lay the law down firmly . . .

So far his examination results are disappointing but he is about to go on a course in Cambridge to improve them . . .

He can turn his hand to so many subjects. He has helped us out in timetable crises. He is a good colleague.'

Extracts from Letter of Application
'I have really loved my time here, especially the drama and the small poetry group I founded. I have written two short African plays both of which were performed . . .

I love the creative approach, especially using ICT, but my chief interest is in giving the children a love of reading. That is still one of the best experiences they can have.'

Mrs Elizabeth Setton

b 1950

Educated: Enbright Girls' Academy, England; Oxford University (1st Class Honours degree in English Literature, Certificate of Education).

Teaching Experience:
1974–1984: Assistant teacher, Enbright Girls' Academy
1984–1992: Second in English Department, Enbright Girls' Academy
1992–1998: Head of Department, Grimoldby Upper School (mixed)

Other work experience
1998–present: Manager, Hutton's Book Shop

Extracts from References
'Mrs Setton works hard and expects the same of everyone else. She is proud of her results . . .

She is efficient and punctual as clockwork. She arrives and leaves at exactly the same time each day . . .

She always has good advice to give to the rest of the staff . . .

She has enjoyed her time at the book shop. I think she found it a welcome break from classroom stress . . .

Grimoldby Upper School is full of lively, demanding children. On the whole, Mrs Setton coped quite well with the changes from her previous post . . .

No lazy child ever gets away with it!'

Extracts from Letter of Application
'I think what we need is a return to good standards of reading and writing. I think spelling and punctuation are vital; those of my colleagues who insist on children having "fun" are quite mistaken. In the long run, children do not thank them for that. I am very willing to take part in a few out of school activities, though, I must say, my work generates a good deal of marking, and I need time to complete it.'

Your school needs an additional English teacher.

Imagine you are the Director of English at your school. The Principal has asked you whether Mr Rahman or Mrs Setton might be suitable and has given you the information printed above.
　Write a report to the Principal, in which you explain your views.
　You may:
■ prefer one applicant to the other
■ decide that neither is suitable
■ urge the Principal to interview both of them.

You should write between a page and a page and a half.

Exercise 2

Write a report for a teenage magazine on fashion or music, a film, a TV series, or a tour by your favourite singer.

Exercise 3

Write a report on a local music festival.

■ Writing a persuasive article

A persuasive article must be clear and well structured. For example, you might well start with a point, develop it and then return to it in the last sentences to emphasise that it is the important point of the article.

■ A certain amount of bias is likely in a persuasive article. For instance, a report on a football match written for the local newspaper of the home side might be rather different from a report written for the local newspaper of the away side. It might be different in the claims it makes about which individuals played best, who tried hardest, or what the highlights of the match were. However, if an article is too obviously biased, no one will take it seriously, so you have to **include some convincing facts, not just opinions**. The persuasiveness depends on the facts you select and how clearly you present them.
■ Quotations can be used effectively in a persuasive piece, so long as you select those which support the point of view you want to put across.

Look back at the example of a persuasive piece of writing in Chapter 3 (pages 44–45). You will find that it includes plenty of facts and figures, and that these are more convincing than a one-sided argument without supporting evidence would have been. Practise writing a few persuasive articles by trying the exercises opposite.

Practise writing a persuasive article

Exercise 1

On page 12 in Chapter 1 of this book there is an article about a British sailor whose boat overturned, leaving him trapped. Others then had to risk their lives to save him. People have various attitudes towards this sort of incident.

> Write an article in which you try to persuade your readers that people who get into difficulties while taking part in dangerous sports or outdoor activities have only themselves to blame and other people should not risk their own lives to help them.

Exercise 2

> Imagine that your local football team has suffered a heavy defeat. Write a persuasive article for your local newspaper to convince your readers that the team lost only because the referee was biased.

Exercise 3

> Write a persuasive article for a national newspaper on what you consider to be the most important social issue in your country. It might be the plight of old people; it could be that there are not enough resources for education; it could be that part of your country is suffering from a dreadful drought. Or it could be a totally different issue that you choose.

■ Writing a continuation of a story

Another directed writing task which you may be set is to write a continuation of a story. There are a few important points to keep in mind when tackling this type of task.

The examiners will **not** have a list of key points of content that they will expect you to include. *However*, they will expect you to follow certain conventions. The main ones are listed below.

- Remember that whatever you write as a continuation of a story must be relevant to the ideas in the passage you have already read. Occasionally, candidates try to use this type of task as an opportunity to repeat an essay they have written during their course, even though it has very little connection with the subject of the story. Examiners usually spot this and award them very few marks. (Incidentally, this point about relevance applies equally to continuous writing.)

- Your continuation should make use of the pointers contained in the original story and lead towards a conclusion which could convincingly follow on from what you have already read. Try to ensure that the way you write about the characters in the story is consistent with what you already know about them. Read the original story carefully to make sure you pick up any hints that indicate how events are likely to develop.
- Remember to continue the story by using the same narrative conventions as the original. For example, if the original story was written in the first person ('I did', etc.) then your continuation should also be written in the first person. You should also make sure that you use the same tense as that used in the original story.
- As far as possible, you should try to write in a similar style to that of the original. Some attempt to follow the type of sentence structures, adjectives, similes and metaphors used by the author of the original will be seen as a positive feature of your writing.

Example of a continuation of a story

Here is an example of a question requiring you to continue a story. The candidate's response which follows on pages 94–95 will help to clarify some of the points we have made. (All spelling and punctuation mistakes have been corrected in order to allow you to concentrate on the content and style of the story.)

The time when the rains didn't come for three months and the sun was a yellow furnace in the sky was known as the Great Drought in Trinidad. It happened when everyone was expecting the sky to burst open with rain to fill the dry streams and water the parched earth.

But each day was the same; the sun rose early in a blue sky, and all day long the farmers lifted their eyes, wondering what had happened to Parjanya, the rain god. They rested on their hoes and forks and wrung perspiration from their clothes, seeing no hope in labour, terrified by the thought that if no rain fell soon they would lose their crops and livestock and face starvation and death.

In the tiny village of Las Lomas, out in his vegetable garden, Manko licked dry lips and passed a wet sleeve over his dripping face. Somewhere in the field a cow mooed mournfully, sniffing around for a bit of green in the cracked earth. The field was a desolation of drought. The trees were naked and barks peeled off trunks as if they were diseased. When the wind blew, it was heavy and unrelieving, as if the heat had taken all the spirit out of it. But Manko still opened his shirt and turned his chest to it when it passed.

He was a big man, grown brown and burnt from years of working on the land. His arms were bent and he had a crouching position even when he stood upright. When he laughed he showed more tobacco stain than teeth.

But Manko had not laughed for a long time. Bush fires had swept Las Lomas and left the garden plots charred and smoking. Cattle were dropping dead in the heat. There was scarcely any water in the village; the river was dry with scummy mud. But with patience one could collect a bucket of water. Boiled, with a little sugar to make it drinkable, it had to do.

Sometimes, when the children knew that someone had gone to the river for water, they hung about in the village main road waiting with bottles and calabash shells, and they fell upon the water-carrier as soon as he hove in sight.

'Boil the water first before drinking!' was the warning cry. But even so two children were dead and many more were on the sick list, their parents too poor to seek medical aid in the city twenty miles away.

Manko sat in the shade of a mango tree and tried to look on the bright side of things. Such a dry season meant that the land would be good for corn seeds when the rains came. He and his wife Rannie had been working hard and saving money with the hope of sending Sunny, their son, to college in the city.

Rannie told Manko: 'We poor, and we ain't have no education, but is all right, we go get old soon and dead, and what we have to think about is the boy. We must let him have plenty learning and come a big man in Trinidad.'

And Manko, proud of his son, used to boast in the evening, when the villagers got together to talk and smoke, that one day Sunny would be a lawyer or a doctor.

But optimism was difficult now. His livestock was dying out, and the market was glutted with yams. He had a great pile in the yard which he could not sell. Manko took a look at his plot of land and shook his head. There was no sense in working any more today. He took his cutlass and hoe and calabash shell which had a string so he could hold it dangling. He shook it, and realised with burning in his throat that it was empty, though he had left a few mouthfuls in it. He was a fool; he should have known that the heat would dry it up if he took it out in the garden with him. He licked his lips and, shouldering the tools, walked slowly down the winding path which led to his hut.

From *A Drink of Water* by Samuel Selvon

'After another month the rains came.' Continue the story until the moment the rainclouds appear.

■ Make Manko the main character.
■ Use what you have learned about Manko, his family and life in the village.
■ Write between a page and a page and a half.

Candidate's response

Time passed. Every morning Manko awoke and looked hopefully at the sky. The burning sun looked back at him, mockingly.

The pile of yams became smaller. Rannie, Sunny and Manko had eaten them and drunk the boiled dirty water from the river. This was all they had to eat for days.

Rannie had grown weak and become ill. Manko was worried: she was feverish but he had no spare water with which he could bathe her burning forehead.

Manko sat by Rannie's side holding her hand as she lay on the floor of the hut. He felt that his great strength too was fading away. He had not laughed now for many months. He had watched his animals slowly dying from starvation and lack of water to drink. There were very few of them remaining by now. If the rains were to come soon there might be just enough to allow him to rebuild his stock. If the rains did not come he dared not think what would happen. The water in the river was by now no more than a tiny trickle.

Only Sunny kept their spirits alive. The boy lived up to his name. On this day he had gone to the river to find what water he could. Manko talked quietly to Rannie. Soon the rain would come, he told her. All would be well: Sunny would be able to go to college.

'Father, Father, come quickly.'

He heard Sunny shouting outside the hut and rushed out to see what was upsetting him. Rannie struggled to her feet and walked slowly to the door.

'Father, look … look!'

Manko was worried. Had his son hurt himself? He was standing outside the hut pointing at … nothing.

'What is it, Sunny? My old eyes are weak. What can you see?'

'Father, look at the sun.'

Manko screwed up his eyes and peered at the sun. Could it be true? Yes, it was. Slowly, surely, a black cloud was covering the burning, golden ball. The sky had turned from blue to deep grey. Great, heavy clouds were approaching.

'Father, can you see now? The clouds ... they are bringing rain.'

Rannie had joined them now. Manko embraced his wife and his son. The rains were coming. Within minutes, great, heavy drops of water were soaking them to the skin. The ground had turned to mud and already green shoots were beginning to appear.

Manko stood soaked and happy. Now he could plant his corn seeds. Maybe Sunny would be an important man after all.

The writer of this continuation has made a positive attempt to follow the style and content of the original story and to use the suggestions given in the wording of the question. The writer has wisely not attempted to produce too ambitious a story but has concentrated on a single event. Remember that you are working under time restrictions.

The continuation makes some attempt to imitate the sentence structures of the original and shows an awareness of the type of descriptive techniques it uses, in particular, through the ways in which the sun is repeatedly referred to and described. The candidate also tries hard to include details from the original story. For example, he/she brings in references to the dying cattle, the corn seeds and the description of Manko as a tall man who used to laugh a lot. The continuation also shows that the writer has understood the relationship between Manko and Rannie and, in particular, their hopes for Sunny.

The impression given by this piece of writing to the examiner would be a positive one. It may not be the continuation of the story which the author of the original had in mind but what has been written is consistent with what has gone before and is perfectly credible. It is worth a high mark for its content and its attempt to follow the style of the original. A continuation which concluded with a much less happy ending would also have been perfectly acceptable, as long as it showed similar merits of structure, style and content.

Practise writing a continuation of a story

Exercise 1

Read this story and then complete the task that follows.

THE GOLD-LEGGED FROG

by Khamsing Srinawk

The sun blazed as if determined to crisp every living thing in the broad fields. Now and again the tall, straight, isolated *sabang* and *payom* trees let go some of their dirty yellow leaves. He sank exhausted against a tree trunk with his dark blue shirt wet with sweat. The expanse round him expressed total dryness. He stared at the tufts of dull grass and bits of straw spun in a column to the sky. The brown earth sucked up into the air cast a dark pall over everything. A whirlwind. He recalled the old people had told him this was the portent of drought, want, disaster and death, and he was afraid. He was now anxious to get home; he could see the tips of the bamboo thickets surrounding the house far ahead looking like blades of grass. But he hesitated. A moment before reaching the shade of the tree he felt his ears buzz and his eyes blur and knew it meant giddiness and sunstroke. He looked at the soles of his feet blistered from the burning sandy ground and became indescribably angry – angry with the weather capable of such endless torture. In the morning the cold had pierced his bones, but now it was so hot he felt his head would break into bits and pieces. As he remembered the biting cold of the morning, he thought again of his little son.

● ● ● ●

That same morning he and two of his small children went out into the dry paddy fields near the house to look for frogs for the morning meal. The air was so chilly the two children on either side of him shivered as they stopped to look for frogs hiding in the cracks of the parched earth. Each time they saw two bright eyes in a deep crack, they would shout, 'Pa, here's another one. Pa, this crack has two. Gold-legged ones! Hurry, Pa.'

He dashed from place to place as the voices called him, prying up the dry clods with his hoe. He caught some of the frogs immediately, but a few jumped away as soon as he began digging. It was the children's job to chase and pounce on them. Many got away. Some jumped into different fissures obliging him to pry up a new cake of earth. If his luck was good, besides the frog, he would find a land snail or razor clam buried waiting for the rains. He would take these as well.

The air was warming and already he had enough frogs to eat with the morning rice. The sound of drumming, the village chief's call for a meeting, sounded faintly from the village. Vague anger again spilled over as his thoughts returned to that moment. If only he had gone home then the poor child would be all right now. It was really the last crack. As soon as he poked it, the ground broke apart. A fully grown gold-legged frog as big as a thumb leaped past the bigger child. The younger raced after it for about twelve yards when it dodged into the deep hoofprint of a water buffalo. The child groped after it. And then he was shocked almost senseless by the trembling cry of his boy, 'Pa, a snake, a snake bit my hand.'

A cobra spread its hood, hissing. When finally able to act, the father with all his strength brought the handle of his hoe three times down on the back of the serpent leaving its tail twitching. He carried his child and the basket of frogs home without forgetting to tell the other to drag the snake along as well.

On the way back his son cried softly and moaned, beating his chest with his fists and complaining he could not breathe. At home, the father summoned all the faith-healers and herbalists whose names he could think of and the turmoil began.

'Chop up a frog, roast it, and put it on the wound,' a neighbour called out.

When another shouted, 'Give him the toasted liver of the snake to eat,' he hurriedly slit open the snake to look for the liver while his wife sat by crying. The later it got, the bigger the crowd. On hearing the news, all the neighbours attending the village chief's meeting joined the others. One of them told him he had to go to the District Office in town that day because the village chief told them it was the day the government was going to hand out money to those with five or more children, and he was one who had just five. It was a new shock.

'Can't you see my boy's gasping out his life? How can I go?'

'What difference will it make? You've called in a lot of doctors, all of them expert.'

'Go, you fool. It's two hundred baht they're giving. You've never had that much in your life-time. Two hundred!'

'Leave this for a bit,' another added. 'If the boy dies, you'll be out, that's all.'

'I won't go,' he yelled. 'My child can't breathe and you tell me to go. Why can't they give it out some other day? It's true I've never had two hundred baht since I was born, but I'm not going. I'm not going.'

'Jail,' another interjected. 'If you don't go, you simply go to jail. Whoever disobeyed the authorities? If they decide to give, you have to take. If not, jail.'

The word 'jail' repeated like that affected him, but still, he resisted.

'Whatever it is, I said I'm not going. I don't want it. How can I leave him when he's dying?' He raised his voice. 'I'm not going.'

'You go. Don't go against the government. We're subjects.' He turned to find the village chief standing grimly at his side. His voice dried up immediately.

'If I don't go, will it really be jail?' he asked.

'For sure,' the village chief replied sternly. 'Maybe for life.'

That was all there was to it. Dazed, he asked the faithhealers and neighbours to take care of his son and left the house.

From *The Politician and other stories*, by Khamsing Srinawk,
Oxford University Press, 1992

Continue the story, saying what happened after the father visited the District Office and returned home.

- Make the father the focus of your story.
- Use what you have learned about his life, his family and their circumstances.
- Write between a page and a page and a half.

■ Writing a leaflet

When you are writing a leaflet, you must think about the layout and language you need to use. Look at leaflets in doctors' waiting rooms, travel agents, railway and bus stations, and so on. You will find that they have a clear layout, so that your eye is taken straight to the important information. They are also written in simple, straightforward language, so that the information is easy to understand. You will find some more ideas to help you write leaflets on pages 150–151.

Practise writing a leaflet

Exercise 1

Here is an article about a man who lives on the streets of London and sees no way out of his situation.

Just another day for drinking to forget

By David Harrison

SHANE Thomas did not really notice Christmas this year. Home was a doorway in the Strand, London. Bed was a couple of tattered blankets. Christmas lunch was pizza and beans provided by the charity Crisis from a mobile food van outside Waterloo Station.

'I don't believe in Father Christmas,' he said yesterday, back at the mobile van, celebrating Boxing Day with a bowl of corned beef hash. 'Every day's much the same for me.' Shane, 37, has been sleeping on London's streets for 12 years after walking out of his council flat in Kennington when he was unable to pay his bills.

Since then, he has begged, borrowed and stolen to survive. He is bright and articulate, but says he is 'an emotional mess', who has never been able to maintain steady relationships with girlfriends.

Over the years, in doorways and on park benches, drink has tightened its grip. Shane says he is probably an alcoholic.

'When I drink, I drink. It's all there is to get you away from all this. It was freezing over Christmas. If you had to sleep in the sort of places I sleep in every night, you'd hit the bottle too.'

Crisis and other charities are providing the homeless with food and beds in temporary hostels over Christmas, but Shane has stayed away. They can be noisy places and fights sometimes break out, he says.

'I prefer to be on my own.'

He wants a flat of his own again, but as a single man is way down the council's priority list. The private sector? The best references Shane can offer landlords are from other rough sleepers.

'Can you imagine it?' he asks bitterly. 'I certify that Shane Thomas is a model tenant. He always leaves his shop doorway immaculate.' But he doubts that a council flat would solve his problems. 'I have to sort my problems out first, to be sure that I can cope with the responsibility of living in a flat again.' Meanwhile, no address means no job. Shane has not worked since he went on the streets. Before that, he drifted from one low-grade job to another, but says even that work is not available these days.

Shane's problems started early in life. 'I came home from school one day when I was 10 and my mother had left. I was glad to see the back of her, but my father wasn't much better. He beat me all the time.' Shane left home at 15, and survived

by doing work in factories, on building sites and in hotels. He had his flat for four years. 'Then one day I saw this pile of bills. I thought: I can't cope, so I just walked out.' He went abroad, slept rough, came back, did the same here. The homeless culture was enveloping him.

'It's become a way of life. I suppose I want to get out of it. I can't go on like this until I die, can I? But at the moment I can't see any way out. I just have to concentrate on one day at a time, on just surviving.'

From *The Observer*

Crisis and other charities are providing the homeless with food and beds in temporary hostels over Christmas.

> Write a leaflet for the charity Crisis, asking for help for the homeless over Christmas.
>
> You are hoping for donations or practical help. The leaflet is to be delivered to people's homes.
>
> Use the information in the article as the basis for your writing. You may also add ideas of your own.

Exercise 2

The following question refers to the text on swimming pool safety, on pages 72–73. Use this text as a source of information for your leaflet.

> Write a short guide for young children advising them on how they should behave around swimming pools.
>
> ■ You should set your points out clearly.
> ■ Remember who your intended audience is.
>
> Write about a page.

Tip   If you choose to write a travel guide for your coursework folder, you should apply the same techniques as for writing a leaflet.

5

Writing summaries

Writing a summary is one of the main tasks that you will be required to do in the examination. Although it involves writing, it is your **reading** skills that will really determine your success in the summary question, as we'll explain below. It is also important that you keep a clear head when attempting the task.

Summaries come in different forms. You may have to:

- read one lengthy passage and summarise only part of it
- read one passage and write two summaries under different headings
- read two different passages and then combine their points into one focused paragraph.

No matter what form the question takes, the basic principles of summary writing remain the same. What the examiner is looking for is **evidence** that you:

- have **understood** what you have read
- can **select the relevant information**
- can express the information **using your own words** and **in a shorter form** than in the original.

Remember that examiners always play fair; they will not ask you to summarise a passage unless it is possible to do so by using fewer words than were in the original!

Some practical guidelines

Summary writing needs good planning and cannot be rushed. You will probably have to write 150–200 words. The writing itself will not take very long; the most important process is **deciding what to include** – that's why your active reading skills are essential. In the examination you will have about 40 minutes to answer this question. The writing out of your final, neat version should not take more than 10 minutes. You have, therefore, at least 30 minutes to read the passage and write your plan.

Once you have this basic approach clearly in mind, you can begin the task with confidence. Don't panic: remember, all the information you need to include will be in the original passage(s), so all you have to do is identify the really important points.

Step 1: Read the question carefully

This is very important, as it is unlikely that you will be required to summarise the whole of the original passage. The wording of the question will direct you towards the points you should include. For example, the whole passage may be about everyday life in Japan, but you may be asked to summarise only what it tells you about going to school in that country. You must, therefore, keep the wording of the question clearly in mind when reading the passage.

Step 2: Read right through the passage(s) once

This will allow you to gain a good, overall understanding of what the text(s) is (are) about.

Step 3: Identify the information that is relevant

Refresh your memory of what the question asks you to do and then read through the passage(s) again very carefully. At this stage you should underline or highlight on the question paper all the information that is relevant to the question. You must be ruthless. Ignore anything that is not relevant, no matter how interesting you may find it. It may help if you give your summary a title.

Tips
1 There will be some points in the original passage that are harder to find than others – the author may have **implied** them rather than stating them explicitly. You will probably get higher marks if you are able to identify and include these implied points.
2 You can safely **ignore**: illustrations, quotations, long descriptions and strings of adjectives.

Step 4: Make notes in your own words

Now is the time to put pen to paper. You should make rough notes of the points you have identified, **using your own words** as far as possible. Remember, the examiners will not know how well you have understood the passage unless you do this. Try to:

- **paraphrase (rephrase) parts of the text to which you refer**
- use synonyms – words with the same meaning – instead of the exact words from the text.

This will make it very clear to the examiners that you understand what you have read.

Tip
Check that you have made **each point only once**: it's an easy mistake to include three examples of the same point. The author of the original passage is allowed to repeat ideas; you don't have the space to do so.

Step 5: Count the main points

Once you have noted all the main points, count up how many you have identified. If you have identified twenty points and your summary is to be 200 words long, then you will know that you ought to write about ten words for each point.

Tip
One of the main mistakes in summary writing is to use up too many words writing the early points, so the summary becomes top-heavy and unbalanced. Remember that all points should be given equal weighting.

Step 6: Write the summary

Once you have written rough notes in your own words, you should try to write them up as a piece of continuous prose, trying to keep to the required word limit. If your notes are sufficiently detailed, this may only be a fine-tuning job. However, if you are someone who writes sketchy notes, then you may need to produce a rough draft before your final one.

Tip An important word of warning – **do not include:**

- personal opinions
- extra information or explanations
- your own comments or opinions on the points made in the original text(s)
- quotations from the original passage(s).

The examiners do not want to know your personal opinions about the topic; instead, they want to know how well you have understood the original author's viewpoint.

Step 7: Final check

Once you have written your summary, read it through to check that it makes sense; count the number of words you have used, and write the total (honestly!) at the end.

Tip Although it is important to try to keep to the required word limit, don't worry if you exceed it by ten to twenty words; you will not be penalised for this. If you exceed the required word limit by 50 words or more, however, you will probably not reach the highest marks because you will not have shown your ability to select the key points and stick to them, writing concisely. If you write considerably less than the suggested word limit, you will not be penalised for not writing enough, but you will probably have reduced your score by leaving out some important points.

▮ Style matters

For most IGCSE summary questions your written expression is assessed, as well as your ability to identify and summarise relevant points. For Paper 1, up to 5 marks may be awarded for style, in addition to the 15 marks available for selection of the correct points. In Paper 2, 5–10 marks may be for style, which is a significant percentage of the marks available for the question. It is therefore very important that you take care with the quality of your writing, as well as the content. A typical example of a mark scheme used by examiners when assessing your writing style is given opposite. You will notice that the copying of significant chunks of material directly from the passage will not score highly – this is because copying the text does not prove that you have understood it. It is important that your writing convinces the examiner that you have understood the text and can interpret what you read.

Sample mark scheme

Paper 1

Award a mark for style and language out of five, according to the following:

1 mark No real idea of purpose or organisation/serious language faults/heavy lifting/points difficult to distinguish.

2 marks Some idea of purpose and organisation/expression simple with frequent errors/considerable lifting.

3 marks Engagement with the task/some sense of summary/fair expression/some controlled lifting (that is, words and phrases are lifted but it is clear that the candidate understands the material).

4 marks Understanding of task and real engagement/good sense of summary style/generally own words.

5 marks Ability to manipulate the material in good summary style/language accurate and appropriate/assured use of own words.

Paper 2

Marks for style:

1–2 marks Some lack of understanding of relevant points/control of language is poor.

3–4 marks Candidate has answered coherently/relevant points but with little development/competent use of language but errors.

5–6 marks Relevant points are made and there is some development and explanation/language is competent and correct.

7–8 marks Relevant points have been made and developed/understanding is clear and explanation is well expressed and detailed/language is fairly sophisticated and varied.

9–10 marks Good points have been made and developed/understanding is clear and expression is precise/language is correct, sophisticated and varied.

■ Examples of summary work based on a single text

The following passage is taken from Michael Palin's book *From Pole To Pole*. The summary question set on this was:

Imagine that you are Michael Palin visiting the Chernobyl area. In your own words summarise what you see of the effects of the disaster. Describe your reactions and emotions. Your answer should be about 200 words.

We head north and west from Kiev, making for the town of Narodichi. It's 60 km due west of Chernobyl, two of whose reactors, our guide reminds us, are still operational. The Ukrainian Parliament has voted unanimously to close them down. The Soviet government has refused. The Ukrainians claim 8000 died as a result of the accident. The official Soviet figure is 32.

We are passing through woodlands of pine and oak scrub interspersed with harvested fields and cherry and almond orchards. An army convoy of 40 trucks passes, heading south. After a while the woodland gives way to a wide and fertile agricultural plain. The first indication that this abundance is tainted comes as quite a shock. It's a sign, set in brambles and long grass, which reads, 'Warning: It is forbidden for cattle to graze, and for anybody to gather mushrooms, strawberries and medicinal herbs'.

We stop here and put on our yellow badges, which register radiation levels, and which will be sent back to England for analysis after our three-hour visit. Armed with these and a radiation detector, we enter Narodichi where people have lived with radiation for over five years. It's a neat, proud little town with a chestnut-lined main street and a silver-painted Lenin in front of the party headquarters. In a year's time there will be no one here.

In the municipal gardens the grass is uncut but a fountain still plays. There are several memorials. One is a scorched tree with a cross on it – local people think that the forest protected them from the worst of the blast. Beside the tree are three large boulders, one of which commemorates four villages and 548 people evacuated in 1986, another 15 villages and 3264 people evacuated in 1990. Twenty-two more villages and a further 11,000 people will be going in 1991. An inscription reads: 'In memory of the villages and human destinies of the Narodichi region burnt down by radiation.'

One of the most polluted areas is the children's playground, with 13 to 17 times normal radiation levels. The red metal chairs hang down from the roundabout and blue steel boats swing gently in the breeze, but no one is allowed to play here any more.

►►

Ivan, the local schoolmaster, is short and podgy and his face is an unhealthy grey. There were 10,000 children in the region, he tells me, now there are 3000. Two of his pupils pass by on bicycles and he grabs them and introduces us. The boys, just back from a Pioneer camp in Poland, look bored, and reply in monosyllables, which Ivan translates thus: 'The children send fraternal greetings to children throughout the United Kingdom'. He smiles proudly and a little desperately. I ask if the children's work has been affected by their proximity to Chernobyl. He sighs and nods.

'There is not a single healthy child here.'

As we drive out of Narodichi, Ivan talks proudly of the history of his town, interspersing this with casually chilling present-day observations.

'This is the bridge over the Oush river. It is an area of the highest pollution.'

We come to the village of Nozdrishche, which was evacuated last year. There are no ruins, there is no devastation or destruction. Wooden cottages with painted window-frames stand in their orderly rows. Flowers are in bloom and grasshoppers dart around in lush overgrown gardens. It is a hot, soft, gentle summer's day. Yet scientists who have visited the area say it could be 700 years before this place comes back to life. It is hard to know what to believe, for whatever curse lies over these villages is the more frightening for being invisible. It is how one has heard the countryside would be after a nuclear war – benign, smiling, deadly.

A year's exposure to the weather has not yet dissipated a faint smell of disinfectant in a small, deserted maternity hospital. A poster on the wall depicts the American space shuttle spinning round the earth, with the single word 'Nyet!' beneath. There is a book on breastfeeding, its leaves nibbled by mice, an examination chair, medical records still in files, and a portrait of Lenin which has fallen out of its frame and lies in a corner beneath a scattering of glass slides and syringes. Conscious of the limited time we have been advised to spend here we move on through the village. I catch sight of two figures down a lane to one side of the main street. One is a very old lady, whose name is Heema, and the other her nephew. Heema is 90 years old and has refused to be moved from the village. She says she has been moved five times since the disaster and now she is too old and ill. Her one wish is to die in the house in which she was born, but that is now cordoned off with barbed wire, so she will remain here with her daughter. They are the only inhabitants of Nozdrishche.

Further along the road, at the village of Novoye Sharno, the radiation detector bleeps for the first time.

'Pay attention, please,' says Ivan, 'the radiation is very high here.'

This is one of the villages evacuated in 1986, immediately after the explosion and fire, and the village shop is now almost submerged in the undergrowth. Inside it is a mess of broken shelves, abandoned goods, smashed bottles.

'

►►

There was 'a panic here,' our guide explains, unnecessarily.

We drive back through Narodichi, where, as in Novoye Sharno and Nozdrishche and over 40 villages in this region alone, the grass will soon grow around doors that will never be opened again, and anyone who comes here will be informed of the dangers and the risks which those who lived here were not told about until it was too late.

From *From Pole to Pole* by Michael Palin,
BBC Consumer Publishing (Books), 1995

Tip   The question gives a suggested length of 200 words. It asks you to imagine that you are Michael Palin, which means that you should answer it by writing in the first person ('I . . .'). You need to focus on describing what you see (i.e. facts) and on your reactions and emotions. The ringed words in the question are the key words.

Model summary

The passage has been annotated showing where the relevant points occur. The effects have been circled and expressions of reactions and emotions have been underlined. These could be listed as follows:

Facts, i.e. the effects that you see

1 warning sign
2 yellow badges
3 radiation detector
4 scorched tree with the cross on it/memorials
5 inscriptions on the boulders
6 dead playground
7 unhealthy-looking people
8 deserted village
9 deserted hospital
10 old lady, can't go home
11 barbed wire around the house
12 smashed village shop/signs of panic

Reactions/Emotions:

13 Shock, horror
14 depression, sadness
15 sympathy with the schoolmaster
16 helplessness
17 frightened by 'the invisible curse'
18 concern for his own safety

These notes could produce the following final version of the summary:

As we approach Narodichi, I notice with horror the sign ordering people not to pick any vegetables which grow in the area. We put on the badges which check our radiation levels and take the radiation detector with us. The village contains memorials of the disaster – a burnt tree with a cross on it and two inscribed boulders. The children's playground is empty as no one is able to play there any more. I meet Ivan, the local schoolmaster. He looks ill and I feel great sympathy for him and the unhealthy children for whom he is responsible. I am moved by the pride he shows in his town's history as I know that the area is likely to remain polluted for centuries to come. We move on to another empty village; it contains a depressingly deserted hospital. The only people we meet are an old lady and her nephew; she has no desire to move away as they have no future to move to. Their houses are shut off with barbed wire. The village shop is smashed up and unattended. We are aware that our safety is at risk if we stay for too long.

This answer contains 194 words.

Examples of candidates' work

We will now look at how two candidates tackled this task in the exam. The examiner's comments refer to the numbered notes on page 107.

Candidate's response: 1

The answer uses only 165 words, and the first paragraph, which takes up 37 of these words, is unnecessary and irrelevant. This paragraph does not state what has been seen nor does it describe reactions and emotions, so it is not answering the question.

The second paragraph records a clear reaction ('shocked'), and the reference to 'the state of the poor people' being unhealthy shows that point 7 has been understood.

This is followed by a clear reference to point 8 ('evacuated'), but the word has been lifted from the original passage.

I am Michael Palin and I've just returned from a mission, that of travelling from one pole to the other. On my trip I've passed through Russian towns which were bombarded with nuclear bombs during the war.

I was shocked in seeing the state of the poor people. All the children's faces were pale and unhealthy and some areas were evacuated due to radiation. Chernoby was a nice village with many trees and grass but no cultivation could be done due to the radiation.

The forest next to the town was sacred to the local people as they think that it saved them from the worst of the blast. I feel sorry for these people and for the future of living with deseases caused by radiation and most of all for their past which was terrible. Right now

I am glad that the worst has past and wish that something could be done, that maybe proper food and treatment is given to these poor people.

At the end of the second paragraph the writer loses focus on the question and writes what the town was like before the accident; this information is not required.

The next relevant point made is that the writer feels 'sorry' for the people (points 14 ,15). An understanding of point 13 is confirmed by the use of the word 'terrible'.

The final sentence shows a general understanding of Michael Palin's concerns for the people, but lacks specific reference and adds little to what has already been said.

Marks awarded

Only two of twelve facts are mentioned, which means that at the most only two marks can be awarded. The candidate did a little better on the emotions/reactions section: he/she achieved a mark of five for this section as the writing was quite fluent and a few points had been understood. In total, this answer gained seven marks out of the possible twenty. The lack of precise, specific details prevents this answer from scoring more highly.

Candidate's response: 2

The first fact to be noticed is the 'sign' (point 1), and the shock of seeing it is reinforced by the opening sentence of the answer as well as by the reference to the face turning white, which shows an understanding of point 13.

Point 8 is mentioned next (although 'evacuated' is quoted rather than explained); 'devastates' also shows a sympathetic understanding of Michael Palin's emotions (points 13 and 14).

When arriving at Chernobyl, you look upon the woodland which opens out into a wide and fertile agricultural plain. There doesn't seem to be any radiation destruction. Then I see a sign which reads that no cattle is to be grazed here and nothing is to be eaten or taken from this place. My face turns white and my reaction is unexplainable, I can't believe it. We stop and test this area for its radiation levels, it does contain some. As we move on I pass villages where you might expect people, but I am told that the villagers had been evacuated this devastates me, then, women and children had to grab a few belongings and move from their homes.

We neared the children's playground which was one of the most polluted areas. I was dumbfounded and I had no expression on my face, the radiation levels here were 3 times the normal radiation levels. I told to me that there was once 10,000 children in the region and know all the ones which remained were 3,000 which were unhealthy. This sent chills up my spine, innocent children were dead. We passed a bridge which was over the Oush river, this area was highly polluted. Lastly we passed the village of Novoya Sharno, where my radiation detecter went off, the radiation levels were quite high. I can't explain my emotions or reactions, but it made me see how thankful I should be for I'm alive and healthy.

The second paragraph opens with a reference to point 6 (the dead playground), followed by a sentence which shows a clear understanding of his emotions and reactions. Then comes a reference to the unhealthy children (point 7) as well as an implied understanding of 'the invisible curse' (point 17).

The final relevant selected point is a reference to the writer's radiation detector, followed by a statement which adds a further point about emotions/reactions.

Marks awarded

This answer uses 247 words so is within the range set for this question. The writer works through the passage methodically and selects points intelligently. Despite the limited number of 'fact' points, this answer contains sufficient details to be awarded six marks for this section. The appreciation of the range of the writer's feelings is of quite a high level, however, and the mark awarded for this section was eight, making a total of fourteen.

Practise summarising a single text

Now that you have looked at these two answers and are able to study the points included in the model summary, you should be able to write a practice answer to this question. Try to include as many of the points on page 107 as possible, within the required word length.

Read the report 'Nightmare Neighbours' and then summarise:

- the problems caused by neighbours
- the advice given about how to deal with them.

Use your own words. Write between 200 and 250 words in total.

Nightmare Neighbours

A clash with a neighbour can make life hell. And if things turn sour between you and your neighbour, you may not be able to get away from the problem – unless you move house.

For this report, we take the disputes which people have most often with neighbours and explain how to deal with each of them.

Noise next door can drive you mad. It could come from a barking dog or from non-stop, all-night parties. If you can't bear it any longer, contact the Environmental Health Department of your local council. You'll need to prove that the noise stops you from enjoying your property or that it is making you ill. You will need proof, so keep a diary.

Many house and car alarms seem to go off for no reason at any time of the day or night. If this is a problem you can phone either the police or your local Environmental Health Officer. There is a new law which allows them to turn off a car alarm, and to enter premises to disconnect an alarm which keeps going off.

If your neighbours have the builders in, you may have to put up with drills and cement mixers. There is bound to be some disturbance; but if you cannot bear the noise, or it is taking place at night, then you can take them to court to make them stop work. This is called taking out an injunction.

If your neighbour's dog has bitten you, or frightens you, you will want to take action. Contact the local dog warden or the police. A court can order that a dog is muzzled and kept on a lead. If a dog continually enters and fouls your garden, the easiest thing to do is to put up a fence!

The parking place right outside your house is not part of your property. You have no legal right to park there. However, you have a legal right to enter your driveway or garage. Some local councils now operate parking schemes for residents. If your neighbours are always parking so you can't get out, contact the Highways Department of your local council. It is in charge of traffic management and control.

Call the police if you think your neighbour's parking habits are illegal.

If your neighbour fences off some of your land or starts growing plants in what you think is your garden then you have a problem. Arguments over land ownership are hard to solve. They can be sorted out in court but this could cost you a lot of money. You have to decide just how much time and money you are prepared to spend.

Some disputes are about party walls. These are walls built right on the boundary between homes. You and your neighbour are both responsible for these. You have to carry out repairs to your side of the wall. You cannot force your neighbour to repair his side.

If your neighbour's hedge or tree is hanging over your property you can prune it back to the boundary but no further. You are not allowed to take fruit from a neighbour's tree just because the branches hang over your fence.

Many complaints are about neighbours' building extensions. People who wish to build extensions must have planning permission. The council must put up a notice at the site or write to all those who may be affected. You have 21 days to object to the proposal. Put your objection in writing and try to get other people to do so, too.

We hope that the information above will be useful. Good luck!

Adapted from *Which?* magazine

■ Examples of summary work based on two texts

The following summary task is taken from Paper 2 of the IGCSE exam. The texts are on pages 112–115 and the task is on page 116. This is a more demanding task, requiring you to take details from two quite long passages, one factual and one fictional (these are passages you have seen before, in the chapter on reading skills, pages 66–69). Your scanning and selection skills are particularly tested here. No specific word limit is mentioned but the formula to write about a page and a half is typical of this paper.

Note that the task requires you to explain how child labour is *both* 'an economic practice' *and* 'a social evil'. It's important, therefore, for you to think carefully about what these phrases mean, and to prove in your answer that you have understood them.

Referring to both passages, explain how child labour is:
a) an economic practice (how does it affect the money making business)
b) a social evil (the problems that affect the society as a whole).

Text 1

Children of the Indifferent God

(10) economic

Child labour would be eradicated in India if only the laws against it were implemented, suggests Anjana Maitra-Sinha.

Child labour has been defined as 'any work which interferes with the child's full physical development, opportunities for the desirable minimum of education, or needed recreation'. India has the second largest child population in the world, 145 million. It also has the largest number of child labourers in the world, 6.22 per cent of the national workforce. Estimates of the figure range from 13.59 to 17.36 million, most of whom are under 14 years of age. There are over 100,000 child workers in New Delhi alone.

Children mainly find employment as domestic helps and in factories, mills, small tea and snack shops and construction sites. According to a recent UNICEF report, every third house in India has a working child and every fourth Indian under the age of 15 is employed. Child labourers are often paid very little for long hours of labour. Sometimes they are not paid at all.

The recent argument over the employment of children in the carpet industry has resulted in a ban on Indian carpet exports in many countries. The sharp eyes and nimble fingers of children make them invaluable for the carpet industry, a big foreign exchange earner which employs over 300,000 children.

Persuaded into the jobs by false promises of high pay, most of these children work in terrible conditions, with low wages and poor food and shelter. They fall prey to various diseases. The wool fluff which circulates in the tiny, ill-ventilated rooms which serve as carpet factories results in many breathing problems.

At festivals, firecrackers worth millions and made in the small factories in the town of Sivakasi go up in flames all over India. Most of these fireworks are produced by children. Sivakasi is notorious as the 'child labour capital of the world'. Over 250,000 children work in its 350 factories, most of which are licensed to operate. The town is in a relatively barren area and its small factories are the main source of income for its people.

A special feature of Sivakasi is that more girls figure on its employment rolls than boys. Girls in fact outnumber boys in the ratio 3:1. There are two reasons for this. First, girls have more nimble fingers. Second, many families send the sons to school and keep the daughters away from education.

Other industries which employ children on a large scale are those manufacturing locks, glass and bangles. It is estimated over 1.5 million children work in glass, carpet and lock factories in Uttar Pradesh.

The little children are exposed to many health hazards. Contract labourers working in brick kilns develop lung diseases. Mica and other chemicals found in glass bangle manufacturing are also harmful.

Sivakasi, with its inflammable products, is infamous for its fatal accidents. An explosion in July 1991 claimed 39 lives and injured dozens more. Other afflictions of its child labourers are anaemia, night blindness, myopia and breathing problems.

After 14 to 16 hours of daily mental and physical pressure, child labourers cannot but have a stunted development. They often grow up to become criminals.

There are comprehensive laws in India with regard to child labour. For instance Article 39 of the Constitution offers specific protection to children. The Factories Act (1948) prohibits the employment of children under 18 in factories.

The policy for children adopted in August 1974 recognised the nation's children as a supremely important asset. The national policy on child labour formulated in 1988 suggested children employed as part of the family be treated differently from those outside the family structure.

A national action plan for children was approved by the Union cabinet in June 1992. It adopted international standards for 'child survival, development and protection'.

The Child Labour Action and Support Programme sponsored by the International Labour Organisation is being finalised to supplement government efforts. The University Grants Commission has been urged to be liberal in granting financial assistance to universities wishing to set up child labour study groups.

A former president of India explained the term 'child labour' in two phrases: first as 'an economic practice' and second as 'a social evil'. The first signifies employment of children in gainful occupation with a view to adding to the family income. The second, a broader aspect, takes into account the dangers children are exposed to and the resultant denial of opportunities for development.

The chief reason for child labour is, of course, the abysmal poverty of the people. Extra hands to supplement the family income are always welcome. Another reason is illiteracy among children.

The rapid pace of urbanisation – 109 million Indians lived in cities in 1971 as compared to 217 million 20 years later – is also responsible for the growth of child labour. Other factors include ignorance and the erosion of social, cultural and moral values.

Though the problem has spread its tentacles deep into India's social fabric, it is not insurmountable. Coordination of health, nutrition and educational programmes and involvement of non-governmental organisations could fight child labour effectively. The media can contribute by increasing public awareness.

Adapted from
***The Calcutta Telegraph,** 30 March 1993*

Text 2

Cosette existed between the two of them, subject to pressure from either side like a creature that is at once ground between mill-stones and torn apart by pincers. Each had his own way of treating her. The blows she received came from the woman; the fact that she went barefoot in winter was due to the man. She ran upstairs and down, washed, swept, scrubbed and polished, drudged and gasped for breath, carried heavy burdens and performed arduous tasks, small though she was. There was no mercy to be expected from either mistress or master. The inn was a trap in which she was caught and held, her state of servitude the very pattern of oppression, herself the fly trembling and powerless in a spider's web.

The child endured and said nothing; but what goes on in the souls of those helpless creatures, newly arrived from God, when they find themselves thus flung naked into the world of men?

Four new travellers had arrived and Cosette was a prey to gloomy misgivings. Although she was only eight, her life had been so hard that she viewed the world already with an old woman's eyes. Her face was bruised by a blow from Mme Thénardier, which caused that lady to remark, 'She looks a sight with that black eye'.

She was thinking as she sat under the table that the night was very dark, and that the jugs and pitchers in the bedrooms of the new arrivals had had to be filled, so that there was no more water in the house. There was some reassurance in the fact that not much water was drunk in the tavern. They had no lack of thirsty customers, but it was a thirst calling for wine, not water. Nevertheless she was given cause to tremble. Mme Thénardier lifted the lid of a cooking pot bubbling on the stove, then seized a glass and went over to the water-butt, while the little girl watched her in alarm. Only a thin trickle came when she turned the tap, half-filling the glass, and she exclaimed, 'Bother! We're out of water.'

There was a moment of silence while Cosette held her breath.

'Don't worry,' said Thénardier, looking at the half-filled glass. 'That'll be enough.'

Cosette went on with her work, but her heart was thumping. She counted the minutes as they dragged by, praying for it to be tomorrow morning. Every now and then a customer would put his head outside and say, 'It's black as pitch. You'd need to be a cat to get about without a lantern on a night like this,' and she would tremble afresh.

Then a traveller who was stopping in the house came into the general room and said angrily:

'My horse hasn't been watered.'

'Indeed it has,' said Mme Thénardier.

'I tell you it hasn't, mistress,' the man said.

Cosette scrambled out from under the table.

'But he has, monsieur. I took him water myself, a whole bucketful, and I talked to him.'

This was not true. Cosette was lying.

'No higher than my knee and lies like a trooper!' the traveller cried. 'I tell you he hasn't, my girl. I know it for sure. When he's thirsty he snorts in a particular way.'

Cosette stuck to her guns, speaking in a voice so stifled with terror as to be scarcely audible.

'All the same, he has.'

'Look,' said the man angrily, 'there's not much in watering a horse, is there? Why not just do it?'

Cosette dived back under the table.

'Well, that's right,' said Mme Thénardier. 'If the horse hasn't been watered it ought to be. Where's the girl got to now?' She peered under the table and saw her crouched at the far end, almost under the drinkers' feet. 'Come out of there, you!'

Cosette crept out again.

'Now, Miss good-for-nothing, go and water that horse.'

'But, madame,' said Cosette faintly, 'there's no water left.'

Mme Thénardier's answer was to fling open the street door.

'Then go and get some,' she said.

Disconsolately Cosette fetched an empty bucket from a corner of the hearth. It was larger than herself, large enough for her to have sat in it. Mme Thénardier turned back to her stove and dipping in a wooden spoon tasted the contents of the pot.

'Plenty of water in the spring,' she muttered. 'No trouble at all. I think this could have done without the onions.'

She went over to a drawer in which she kept small change and other oddments.

'Here, Miss Toad,' she said. 'Here's a fifteen-sou piece. While you're about it you can get a large loaf at the baker's.'

Cosette took the coin without a word and put it carefully in the pocket of her apron. Then, with the bucket in her hand, she stood hesitating in the doorway, as though hoping someone would rescue her.

'Get a move on,' cried Mme Thénardier.

Cosette went out and the door closed behind her.

From *Les Misérables by* Victor Hugo

Although the article talks about child labour in general terms while the extract from the novel is about one child in particular, they both show how unfortunate the child worker can be.

In the article, child labour is defined 'first as an economic practice and second as a social evil'.

Referring to **both** passages, explain how child labour is:
a) an economic practice
b) a social evil.
You are advised to write about a page and a half **in total**.

Marking scheme

The following is typical of the mark schemes used by examiners to check how many of the main points from the facts have been included in your summary.

Points which can be mentioned:

'An economic practice'
1 huge number of child workers

2 statistic in national workforce

3 low pay

4 sometimes no pay

5 sometimes supplementing the family income

6 regarded as efficient – sharp eyes/nimble fingers

7 in industry which is a big foreign exchange earner

8 other political factors such as rapid urbanisation

9 Cosette is an example of exploitation

10 She receives no pay

11 huge profits/national economy

'A social evil'
12 contravenes the law in India

13 lured in by lies

14 contract various diseases – of the lungs, etc.

15 danger/lack of safety

16 girls exploited by families

17 has a lasting effect/criminalised the children/Cosette a liar

18 caused by dreadful poverty

19 Cosette is an example of a child sent into danger

20 work she is not capable of doing/heavy burdens

21 fear/at the slightest movement of Mme T

22 physically abused

23 stunted development/very small

24 subject to verbal abuse

25 not properly clothed

26 she felt trapped/in a prison

27 no way of speaking to anyone about her troubles

28 apparently lived under a table

29 education

30 appalling conditions/foul jobs

31 stunted emotional development/deprived of childhood

Number of points made	Marks
13–14	9–10
11–12	7–8
9–10	5–6
7–8	3–4
5–6	1–2

If only one passage is referred to in the answer deduct two marks.

Key
■ Errors of expression
▨ Spelling/punctuation
errors

Examples of candidates' work

Candidate's response: 1

The examiner's comments refer to the marking scheme on pages 116–117.

A former president of India explained the term 'child labour' in two phrases: first as an economic practise. This signifies employment of children in gainful occupation with a view to adding to the family income. Where poverty is high, children are often sent out to work, as a pair of extra hands to supplement the family income. Many of these children have had no education and are often illiterate. Many industries regard children as invaluable, because of their sharp eyes and nimble fingers. The carpet industry has been involved in a recent argument because it employs over 300,000 children. India has the largest number of child labourers in the world. Estimated figures range from 13.59 to 17.36 million. Child labourers comprise 6.22 per cent of the national work force. Because of the growing poverty problem in many third world countries and the rapid pace of urbanisation, child labour will continue to grow.

The second way child labour is defined is a social evil. This is a broader aspect and takes into account the dangers children are exposed to and the resultant denial of opportunities for development. Many children find employment as domestic helps and in factories, mills, small tea shops and construction sites. They are persuaded into these jobs by false promise of high pay. The result is most of these children work in terrible conditions, with low wages and poor food and shelter. The carpet industry which employs over 300,000 children, have poor working conditions. Often working in ill-ventilated rooms, where the wool fluff circulates resulting in many breathing problems. Other industries which employ children on a large scale are those manufacturing locks, glass and bangles. These children are exposed to many health hazards. Labourers working in brick kilns develop lung diseases. Other fatal accidents occur with little or no safty procedures. After 14–16 hour days the mental and physical pressure on child labourers, result in a stunted development, and many grow up to become criminals. These children are been denied a proper education especially girls who are kept away from education, and encouraged to work. Many of the children are subjected to physical abuse, been hit when not working hard enough and starved are common problems.

Marks awarded

This summary shows a very good understanding of the whole passage; it is clear that the writer has a secure grasp of what the two requirements actually mean and has selected relevant points to support this understanding.

In all, the summary makes fourteen out of a possible thirty-one points and, as you will see from the mark scheme, achieves full marks for this part of the question.

The style mark awarded was seven. Relevant points have been made and developed; understanding is clear and the explanation has been well expressed and is detailed. However, there are some inaccuracies of expression and some of the earlier ideas are not as logically developed as they might have been and so the answer does not quite qualify for the top band style mark. Overall, however, this is an impressive achievement, particularly under timed examination conditions, and is of a clear **grade** A standard.

Key

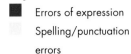

Errors of expression

Spelling/punctuation errors

This summary is limited in range and not very focused. The writer identifies only two points relevant to the section about 'economic practice' (numbers 3 and 9), one from each of the passages. However, he/she uses 118 words to make these two points. This is a clear indication of a failure to select appropriate material and to focus on it.

In the 'social evil' section, the few points which are made appear to have occurred almost by chance. Point 29 is found in the middle of a generalised statement at the start of paragraph five. It is not particularly clear which of the two original passages this statement refers to and some people might consider that an examiner would have been generous to allow it here. The only other relevant point is 14 which is found in the final paragraph.

Candidate's response: 2

a) Child labour is been increasing throught the years. It is most common in countries underdevelopt as India.

When it reffers to economic practise, it talks about the boys and girls that are employed by fabrics or industries. There they work between 14 and 16 hours a day for a miserable pay when sometimes there is just no one.

The children don't always work in fabrics only they can work in someones house and help in the most appropriate way possible. They do cleaning, washing, cooking, etc. If the owner of that house needs something and he can't go, here is the poor child, always there to help for only some coins at the end of a large exhausted day.

b) Social evil, as a famous president of India explained is: 'a broader aspect, takes into account the dangers children are exposed to and the resultant denial of opportunities for development.'

As this children are employed when they are too young, around 14 and 15 years old, they don't receive an education because they don't go to school. In the future, when the owners of the fabrics won't need them enymore, the children will have problems in finding jobs.

They already have some health troubles while they are young. The most common are breathing problems because of immalating wool fluff. Lung diseases are developed by children who work in brick Kilns. Some other problems that children have are anemia, myopia and night blindness cause by hard working hours.

The writer does not distinguish between examples and illustrations and the precise points relating to the question, so the reader is not sure that the writer's understanding of the task or the reading material is in any way complete.

Marks awarded

This total of only four points means that the answer would score zero for this section. Although the writer's expression is accurate enough to be understood, it is, nevertheless, somewhat dependent on using whole phrases taken from the original passages. The answer is not well structured — points appear to have been listed almost at random — and there are some serious spelling errors. Overall, the style mark awarded was three and this answer would fall into the **ungraded** category.

Practise summarising two texts

Exercise 1

Now that you have read these examples of candidates' responses, you could use the details of the mark scheme to write your own version of the summary question on pages 112–116. Of course, in the 'real' exam you won't be able to see the mark scheme, but this practice can train you to spot the crucial points that the examiner needs to see in order to give you marks.

Exercise 2

Read the two articles 'Apples and Pears' and 'Fat chance for kids . . .' carefully and then summarise what they have to say about:

■ why being overweight may not be a cause for concern
■ whether dieting is of any real value
■ the pressures put upon adults and children to be thin.

Write in paragraphs using your own words as far as possible. Write between 200 and 250 words **in total**.

The first of these two passages will be familiar to you as you looked at it as an example of persuasive writing (pages 44–45). However, you will need to apply different skills to the text for your summary work.

Text 1

Apples and Pears

Jay Rayner

Some recent scientific research has indicated that being overweight may not be as serious a health problem as it was once thought to be. The journalist Jay Rayner, himself a heavy person, investigated this issue. Some of his findings are printed below.

According to research conducted by, among others, Kay-Tee Khaw, Professor of Gerontology at Cambridge University, excess body fat is only really a problem when it's in your abdominal cavity, blanketing the vital organs. Laid there it's far more likely to cause health complications like heart disease or diabetes.

To assess it you need to find out if the waist measurement, taken at the level of your navel, is bigger than the measurement of your hips. If your hips are larger than your waist then you are classed as pear-shaped, and there's probably far less to worry about. Fat around your thighs and bottom is only likely to slow you down rather than kill you. It is worth noting that women, the real diet fanatics in Britain, are naturally pear-shaped; indeed it may come as something of a relief to know that, using the waist–hip measurement, the vast majority of women who are officially classed as overweight have nothing to worry about at all.

If, however, all the weight is on your stomach, you are apple-shaped. You'll see any number of apples in the saloon bars the length and breadth of the country, their beer bellies propped up on the tables. That's when there is cause for concern.

'Certainly if two patients are of similar weight,' Professor Khaw says, 'I would put more pressure on the person with the high waist/hip ratio to try and lose weight.'

But there are a growing number of academics who are prepared to be even more reassuring. Dr Tom Sanders is Professor of Nutrition at King's College London and co-author of the deliciously titled book **You Don't Have To Diet**, which has to make him a good bloke from the kick-off. His argument comes in two revelatory parts. Firstly, he says, 95 per cent of diets don't really work. Stick to boiled eggs and cabbage for three weeks, chew celery stalks and swallow milk shakes with the consistency of wet concrete and you may well lose weight, but it will probably be in the form of water and muscle rather than fat. What's more it will all go back on again very quickly. The only people to gain from diets are the people flogging them to you.

The second part of his argument is even more intoxicating. It is this: most overweight people do not even have a problem. 'The health risks of obesity have been greatly exaggerated,' he says. 'It does depend on age. The longer you are fat the greater the risk, because weight does go on as you get older. But it's a small risk compared to that of, say, smoking. I would argue that if giving up smoking made you put on a stone in weight it's still healthier to give up smoking.'

'Most experts do not regard obesity on its own as an independent risk factor for heart disease, in the absence of raised blood pressure, raised blood cholesterol or diabetes.' And just because you are overweight doesn't mean your cholesterol levels will be through the ceiling; skinny people have just as much likelihood of having arteries swimming with liquid fat. One statistic is very revealing: while the incidence of obesity has doubled, the rate of heart disease has dropped by over 30 per cent. If obesity really was such a major factor in causing heart disease, we should have expected to see more of it rather than less.

'Put simply,' Professor Sanders says, 'we've taken eating, a perfectly normal physiological activity, and turned it into a problem.' This is not a prescription for just letting yourself go. You should keep a steady weight – rather than letting your weight yo-yo – and take some exercise: becoming vastly obese is not something to get neurotic about.

Indeed, beyond a certain age it's a positive boon to be overweight. 'Skinny people of between 50 and 55 have a higher mortality rate. The older you get, being underweight becomes a greater risk to health than being overweight.' With more flesh on your bones, you have a greater chance of surviving the illnesses that strike in later years.

From *The Mail on Sunday*

Text 2

Fat chance for kids when it's in to be thin

SHYAMA PERERA

If parents swallow the skinny-is-beautiful myth, there is little hope that children will plump for common sense.

Shots of modelling sensation Jodie Kidd last week, her anorexic looking frame swathed in glorious creations, have revived fears that other 17-year-olds will think starvation is the route to fame. Hey girls, this is how you meet gorgeous blokes and make lots of money. Jodie is quoted saying that sometimes she forgets to eat for a day or two. Her cadaverous face is strained as she threatens, on breakfast television, to leave the country because of press harassment over her size. She thinks she looks great.

As she drags on her twentieth cigarette of the day, one wonders if Jodie is right. Not all her peers want to look like her, but then they diet to mirror the sun-bronzed bodies of the Aussies and Americans in imported teen soaps, in a world where a spare tyre is something you stash on the back of a jeep. As the pressure moves down the age barometer, we are raising a generation of serial dieters.

As someone whose bottom was once likened to two boiled eggs in a navvy's hankie, the whole vexed question of obesity and our obsession with weight is a subject close to my heart. Now it has become an area around which I tiptoe with shakes of near-paranoia:

my four-year-old has become the butt of bullying in the playground. Very tall and with musculature like her mountain-climbing father, she has been labelled 'fat' by her peers.

She does not understand why the word is used as a term of abuse, but she is insulted, chastened and, most importantly, humiliated in the eyes of others, by this baiting. It is a subject of concern and embarrassment to her. For me, it provides cause for anger and fear because I know and understand the pressures put on women to conform physically. I am not a fat person with a thin person inside – the thin person got out of the Isle of Sheppey 10 years ago and we shared a joyous farewell.

That is quite hard for some people to stomach. The sort of people, that is, who furnish four-year-olds with a tick-list of social acceptability. I was once in a playground with a mother who, on being informed by her son of a nearby fat woman, told him he shouldn't comment but 'should feel sorry for her'.

The stereotypical ideas of my daughter's classmates can only be a reflection of their parents' body-image. I tell her not to eat sweets because they will rot her teeth. Her peers, whose mothers will have complained in a previous breath that they never eat anything, are told sweets will 'make them fat'.

Trickle-down works here: tell mum and dad that fat is bad and little Billy will believe it too. The only problem is that small children cannot differentiate between 'fat' and 'big', 'stocky' or 'burly'. The incomprehension will continue into young adulthood for many. Girls such as Jodie Kidd take it too far, but as long as they stand to be rewarded for their self-neglect, there will be a strong incentive to follow suit.

Given that most teenagers are not overweight, why do they need to diet at all? And what is to be done when children as young as four are being given complexes about their size? It is meaningless to tell an infant that her weight and height match perfectly on the centile graphs. For the moment, having been told all her life that she is beautiful (as indeed she is, if you'll pardon the motherly pride), my

daughter is easily reassured. But with each day and each new insult, the reassurances will soon be played out.

Then I will have to question my own role in all this. Should I remain large, in order to reassure her that 'fat people are nice too' – or should I bow to the wisdom of the playground bullies and lose weight, so that she views obesity as a problem that can be 'remedied' if needs be? I do not blame Jodie Kidd for this obsession with weight, but rather her critics – the tabloids, the fashion writers, the style gurus, the diet experts – who have perpetuated the cult of thinness in order to get fat on the back of our insecurities.

In the meantime, in the real world, my daughter's teacher is on the watch and the major bully, caught in the act, has been dealt with. He is small and underweight, though his mother is not. Perhaps I should ask her to sit on him, but I fear he would be smothered.

From *The Observer*

Exercise 3

Look closely at the articles 'Putting the boot in' and 'Give Us a Game' on pages 124–26, then summarise what they have to say about each of the following:

A ■ why mixed football teams are not allowed after the age of eleven
B ■ the problems of playing in and organising all-girls' teams
C ■ the attitude of the public, the media and the Football Association towards girls' football.

Use your own words as far as possible. Write about 250 words in total.

The first of these two passages is one which you have already seen in Chapter 3 (page 59), but you will need to apply additional skills here as you work with this text and another for summary practice.

Text 1

Putting the boot in

by Marcella Moray Araujo

A We all know football can make grown men cry. But the world's most popular game is reducing even small girls to tears. Zara Robins, 12, was selected to join 10 boys on her school team. So successful was the team that one sour defeated school complained to the Football Association. The FA contacted the school and enforced Rule No. 37: no mixed football in schools after the age of 11.

Although staff and other pupils supported Robins, the headmaster had no option but to remove her from the team, or lose the school's league points. Robins herself said she would rather see her side go through and, like all true heroes, took the suspension like a man. When her mother contacted the FA, she was told that Rule No. 37 was introduced to promote women's football. Girls
C will never learn to play well, the FA declared, while they are intimidated and bullied by boys on the football pitch.

There is a general agreement in the UK that boys are naturally better at football. This should come as no surprise – we only ever see men playing it on TV. For skilled female players, girls-only football is not challenging enough: it's slower and the style is not the same. Perhaps more importantly, not all schools provide opportunities for all-girl teams to train. Three years ago 35 per cent of schools had girls' teams. While the FA talks up the importance of women's football it may still be some time before school teams get the chance to play and train regularly.

There are signs of progress, but although girls can now use local club facilities,
B the clubs are not yet signing girls. It is still very hard for the few girls who are good to find an outlet for their talent.

The idea behind Rule No. 37 is that, at or about 11 years of age, boys become physically stronger and faster than girls and, therefore, if paired with girls in competitive sports, the risk of injury for the girls is higher. On the other hand,
A both little boys and grown men are frequently injured as well and girls play hockey, which is both tough and fast. The only trouble with football is that girls simply don't play it enough.

Adapted from *The Guardian*, 14 September, 1994

Text 2

Eleven-year-old Amy has a kick like a donkey . . . she can't find a girls' football team to play a match with

GIVE US A GAME!

by Sean Moriarty

Amy Shipton lives for football. Every inch of her bedroom wall is covered with posters of her sporting heroes and she spends most of her spare time kicking a ball around.

But the 11-year-old is not happy. Since moving to Simon Langton Girls' School where football is not on the curriculum, the sport she loves has been given the red card.

Amy, who lives in Castle Street, Canterbury, has become so desperate to play a match, she wants to move to another school where she can play football.

Now mum Lesley has asked *Adscene* to help find a team in which Amy can compete.

'Amy takes after her father; she has always been football mad. Since she was old enough to walk, she has been kicking footballs,' she said.

'While other little girls were playing with dollies, she was playing football with the boys.

I believe that Simon Langton is the best place for Amy to get an education. We don't want to change schools, but it is such a shame she is being denied the sport she loves.

She played football in friendly matches when she was at the Hersden and St Stephen's Primary schools and her games teachers called her their secret weapon. Amy's got a kick like a donkey and is really very good at the game.'

Lesley says she would like to hear from anyone who runs a girls' football team, or is thinking of setting one up.

▶▶

'I thought about setting up a team myself, but I haven't got the time it would take to do it properly,' she said.

'I don't mind travelling to take Amy to play. It would be worth it for how happy it would make her.'

'Not allowing girls of my age to play competitive football is sexist,' said Amy.

'Girls are just as good at football as boys. Something should be done to change these out-of-date laws.'

The Football Association said it actively encouraged girls to take up the sport.

 'We don't allow mixed competitive football at secondary school age because we want to encourage the growth of girls-only football teams, and you don't do this by allowing the girls to play in boys' teams,' said FA spokesman David Bloomfield.

'It's nonsense to say we are sexist in our approach – we are here to increase the number of people who play and watch football, and to maintain its popularity at all levels among both sexes.'

Anthony Stanton, head teacher at Simon Langton Girls, said there was a limit to how many sports his school could offer.

'We do offer as much sport as we can to complement our busy academic curriculum,' he said.

'The problem of introducing new sports is that it can spread our resources too thin, and we might find that splitting up the girls makes it difficult to field a team in any sport.

'We realise many of our pupils pursue other sporting interests outside school hours, and I wish Amy every luck with finding a football club to play for.'

Adapted from articles in
***Adscene,* September 1994,**
Kent Regional Newspapers

6

Writing essays and coursework

Essays and coursework are different types of 'continuous writing'. Your general writing skills are essential for both, and for both you will need to be able to show that you can:

- order and present facts, ideas and opinions
- articulate (explain or convey to your reader) experience and express what is felt and what is imagined
- communicate effectively and appropriately.

For your IGCSE English course you will either be taking an essay paper (Paper 3) or be putting together a folder of three pieces of coursework (Paper 4). This chapter looks separately at the special skills you need for each of these.

Section 1 *Essays*

You will almost certainly practise writing essays during the preparation for your IGCSE examination. However, there are some important differences between this type of continuous writing and the essay writing that you will be asked to do in the examination. Although the tasks are similar, in the exam you have extra challenges to face, and this chapter will try to help you meet them.

- **Challenge 1: You don't know what the topics will be**
  You will not have had the opportunity to prepare the subject of your essay in advance because you won't know what you will be asked to write about until you open the question paper.
- **Challenge 2: You have to write within a time limit**
  In the exam you must complete your essay within a certain period of time: usually one hour, or one hour and thirty minutes.
- **Challenge 3: Writing to a particular length**
  The exam paper includes a guideline telling you how long your essay should be. Does it matter if it's too long or too short?
- **Challenge 4: There's only one chance to get it right**
  When you write essays as part of your schoolwork you have the opportunity to produce a first draft, which you can revise and improve until you are satisfied that the final product is as good as you can possibly make it. Under exam conditions the time limit makes it impossible to draft several versions, but you should try to allow time for certain important checks. We all make technical errors of spelling, punctuation and expression at times, and such errors are much more likely to occur when you are writing under exam conditions. Stress can lead to mistakes! It is important to check through your work so that you don't lose marks unnecessarily for this kind of error.

▧ Some practical guidelines

Meeting Challenge 1: Choosing from the topics on the paper

From your preparation for the exam you should have a good idea of the **type** of essay you are best at writing. This should help you to choose which topic to write about in the exam itself. This may not be the topic that immediately looks most attractive – remember that you only have to write about 400–500 words, and if you choose a 'favourite' topic you may find that you have too much to say and your answer is in danger of becoming too long and unstructured. The exam paper will contain different types of essay for you to choose from. There will always be an **argumentative** topic or two, a **narrative** and a **descriptive** topic. As well as these, there will sometimes be a few lines of **poetry** and there will usually be a **photograph**; you can use one of these as the basis for your writing.

Tips   Choose your topic on the basis of two points.

1 Your skills – are you best at description, narrative, imaginative writing, or arguing a case? Think about this before the exam so that you can make the best possible choice when you see the paper.
2 Your interest in the topic and any experience of your own that enables you to comment on it – **but** still make sure you focus really closely on the question. Your own experience can be an inspiration, but don't let it become a distraction!

Meeting Challenge 2: Writing within a time limit

The time limit means that planning is even more important than usual, not less! Make a skeleton plan of the main points that you intend to include in your essay before you start to write. Doing this will show you whether you have enough to say about the topic, as well as providing you with a paragraph structure. It is worth spending ten minutes on your plan.

Tips   1 Don't write full sentences in your plan, just brief notes. Jot down one key idea per paragraph, backed up by very brief notes on how you will explain or argue that idea. Overall, five to eight paragraphs should be adequate, plus . . .
2 Your **conclusion**. Don't forget to include this in your plan; it is a very good idea to know how you intend to finish the essay before you start to write it!
3 You could use a spider plan to sort out your ideas for your essay. There's an example of this on page 53.

Meeting Challenge 3: Writing to a particular length

The advice about the number of words you should write is there as a guideline for you, but it is not an absolute requirement. It is possible to write *slightly less* than the suggested length (say, 40–50 words less) and still gain a grade A mark if the expression, content and structure of your essay are of the required standard. Similarly, you will not be penalised if you *exceed* the suggested word limit, but by doing so you are increasing the chance of making careless slips and errors which may reduce your potential mark. (Example 1 on pages 132–134 is a very good example of a candidate successfully writing more than required.)

If you plan your essay carefully, staying clearly focused on the topic, you should not have much difficulty in keeping to the suggested length.

Meeting Challenge 4: Make time to check your work!

Try to keep at least ten minutes at the end of the exam to check your work. Check:

- punctuation
- spelling
- paragraphing
- tenses.

(Chapter 3 outlines some key points to remember on these aspects of your work.) A few mistakes are inevitable but a large number of mistakes will affect your marks. Finally, **make sure your writing is clearly legible** – if you write a brilliant piece that the examiner can't read, it won't score the marks you deserve.

Writing the essay

Quite simply, the main concern of the examiners will be to assess how effectively you can convey your thoughts about your chosen topic by using written Standard English. The examiners will want to be interested in what you have written. The more easily they can understand your ideas, the higher the mark you are likely to gain. Always try to see your work from the reader's – i.e. the examiner's – point of view!

Expressing your ideas

Remember that the examiners are looking carefully at **how you have expressed your ideas** as well as at **what you have written**. The exam tests your **ability to communicate** in written English; it does not test the level of your imagination and creativity. Look back at Chapter 3 for some basic reminders about how to structure your work and keep the level of accuracy in your writing as high as possible. Below are a few more guidelines which are particularly useful when writing essays.

Use paragraphs logically

Make sure that your writing is divided into paragraphs and that the paragraphs are logically developed.

The opening paragraph should provide a valuable introduction, both to the topic and to the person writing about it; it should set the tone for the essay and make clear the direction it is going to take.

The middle section of the essay should be clearly structured and logically sequenced.

Your conclusion should give evidence of being clearly planned for and the essay should finish with a definite statement.

The more simply, the more clearly and the more precisely you communicate your ideas to the reader, the higher your mark will be.

Write in complete sentences

While you are writing your essay, always try to **think in complete sentences**; never start to write a sentence until you know how it is going to finish.

Make sure you use full stops to separate sentences correctly. You must be able to convince the examiner that you understand how to separate sentences in order to achieve a C grade or above for your essay.

Take care with punctuation

A common error is to confuse the use of commas with the use of full stops. Other serious punctuation errors result from misunderstandings about how to use the apostrophe and how to use inverted commas to punctuate direct speech. Make sure you know how to use these punctuation marks correctly and check them when you have finished your essay.

Check your spelling

You will be penalised if you misspell, or confuse, basic vocabulary (*there/their*, *too/to/two*, *quite/quiet*, etc.), or if you spell simple words in more than one incorrect way. Nevertheless, you should not let your worries about spelling prevent you from using what you know is the best word for the job. The examiners will usually recognise the word you intend to use, even if it is incorrectly spelt. Although they may mark it as a spelling error, they may also give you credit for choosing and knowing how to use the word in the first place.

▦ What do examiners reward in an essay?

You will be relieved to know that you will not have a mark deducted for every technical error that you make. As mentioned earlier, examiners mark your essays by impression and are constantly balancing the positive and negative qualities of your writing in their minds. The main positive features that the examiners will reward are:

1 **The ability to structure and organise your ideas clearly**.
  A well-controlled, well-developed essay with a positive opening and a strong conclusion will usually be well thought of by examiners.
2 **A wide range of appropriately used and precise vocabulary**.
  This does not mean that you should fill your essay with the longest and most complicated words you can think of. On the contrary, it means that you should have a clear understanding of what you are going to say and a good vocabulary, so that you can choose the right word to convey the exact shade of meaning that you want.
3 **A good range and variety of sentence types and structures**.
  This helps to avoid monotony in your writing. Try not to let every sentence take the same form, or begin each paragraph with sentences of the same pattern. To achieve top grades you need to show evidence that you can handle complex sentences confidently. However, the ability to use short, simple, direct sentences when your essay requires it is also important. So, vary the length and type of your sentences (compound, complex, simple) to suit your meaning.

▦ But *what* do I write?

We have been concentrating on 'how' rather than 'what' to write. You may be wondering about content. Content is certainly important, but some candidates tend to worry too much about it and create unnecessary problems for themselves. The main points to remember are:

1 **Be realistic**. You do not have time to write a novel during an exam and examiners will not expect you to. So, don't make things more difficult for yourself by trying to think of obscure or totally original ideas: the originality of your writing will be found mainly in the way you express yourself.
2 **Keep it clear and simple**. What you write should be well planned, carefully structured and organised, and clearly focused on the topic you have chosen. Your main intention should be to think how best to use the language to put across your ideas as clearly and as vividly as you can. Keep what you write simple and manageable; base your content on and within your own experience and you won't go far wrong.

Tip If you choose a question that requires you to respond to some lines of poetry or a photograph, make sure you put some personal response into your answer. Just paraphrasing the poetry or describing factually what you can see in the picture will not be enough to achieve a good grade. The poetry or photo is there to help you produce an imaginative response, which usually requires you to respond to the mood of the poetry or the character pictured in the photograph. Use this as the starting point for your writing and then develop your ideas as you think best. Remember, it is on the quality of your written expression that you will be assessed.

■ Examples of candidates' work

Here are examples of three essays actually written by candidates for their IGCSE examination. Read them through carefully. You might like to decide what grades you think they were awarded and why before you read the examiner's comments.

The original spellings and punctuation have been retained and major errors of spelling, punctuation and expression have been indicated. **It is important to remember however that the examiner is just as concerned with rewarding positive merits of style, vocabulary and so on as with penalising errors**. For this reason, it is unlikely that any examiner would ever mark every error made by a candidate and the marking of these examples reflects this principle.

Example 1

Write a story in which severe weather conditions play a significant part.

Key

■ Errors of expression

Spelling/punctuation errors

The perpetual wailing of the Hawaiian winds was no novelty to the professor; a veteran scientist whose name was renound in the field of meteorological studies. Seated on a brown leather eighteenth-century chair, the hollow cries of wind outside were a constant reminder that weather was supreme. Though the powerful evening breeze could uproot the studiest of trees, however, it could not touch the thin delicate clouds of smoke rising from Professor Dean's pipe, a thought at which he could not suppress a smile. It was to him,

wrong word ('secret')

ironic that he was the creator of the 'Typhoon Eye', a secretive government project under his authority. Outside the complexe, atop a remote mountain on the island of Waikiki, in the Hawaiian Archipelago, the skies darkened as small droplets of cold rain began to fall on the island from the heavens above. At sea, some distance away, a rumble of thunder

Repetition

of thunder was heard, an omen of events to come.

Seated in his office, in serene relaxation, as thick smoke escaped from his lips, a loud series of knocks at his door revived the tired Prof. Dean from his quasi-slumber. 'Come in', he called with a bored tone of voice.

The hinges creaked with a dull sound as a tall, youthful figure entered in the office clad in thick clothes and a clean white labcoat.

'Oh, what is it, my boy?' inquired the professor without turning to face his guest.

'I just came to tell you, sir, that our guest from Washington is anxious to activate the device' replied the young assistant.

'Are all preparations complete?'

'They are, sir.'

'Well then', continued the arthritic, greying scientist, 'I'll be there shortly.'

With a nod, the youth left, carefully shutting the door as he egressed. Removing his cashmere jumper and preparing to don more formal attire, Prof. Dean glanced

►►

outside his window. He saw a tangled mass of tropical trees, swaying in the wind. Evidently a hurricane of some sort was indeed approaching.

'Welcome to Command Central. Please Indentify yourself.'

Walking through the dimly lit corridoors as he was observed by the highly disciplined guards which flanked the hallway, Prof. Dean reached into his pocket and inserted his access card into a brightly-lit panel.

'Thank you, Professor Gordon H H Dean . . .' replied the wall in a mechanistic tone of voice. The thick titanium doors shuddered open. Walking through them, he entered a new environment all together: at Command Central, several dozen scientists and researchers were hastily preparing for the prototype test. Moving back and forth between the project itself, a huge device named the 'Typhoon Eye' and the terminals of advanced computers which controlled it, the men moved with almost robotic efficiency. No voice could clearly be heard, sideline conversations and idle chattering darted chaotically across the room.

'Professor, you're here at last!' cried an enthusiastic diplomat seated some distance away.

Emerging from the trance the mayhem of the room had caused him, Dean recognised him as Murray Bunton, their liaison to Washington.

'We're ready to activate the device!' he said as the room fell silent.

After a brief pause, Dean moved towards the main control module and pressed the large button labelled 'BEGIN'.

Immediately the device shook and emitted many sounds.

Standing dumb in awed silence, the scientists let out a collective cheer.

'This is a great moment for mankind', whispered Bunton, 'Now, at last, men control the weather! With this device, mankind can manipulate the elements to our advantage!'

The atmosphere slowly ionised the surrounding area, releasing strange types of energy in all directions.

After toasting to their success with glasses of Martini, the group retired for the night, expecting a clear sky the next day.

Awoken from his sleep, Dean stumbled out of bed to replace his clothes. Looking at his clock with sluggish, blood-shot eyes, it read five o'clock in the morning.

'Hurry, Professor!' came the voice again.

Rushing through the security doors, his eyes were greeted by a room of haunting silence, the only sounds a series of murmurs from the main control panel operators. Outside a terrifying clap of thunder roared across the ocean.

'What's happened?' Inquired the professor, highly concerned despite his condition. There he was told that far from dissipating the storms, Typhoon Eye had had the reverse effect. Tropical cyclone 'Lethea' was now being drawn to Waikiki.

'How could this happen?' demanded Bunton, still half-dressed.

Silence was his only reply.

humorous

effective short sentence

▶▶

Key

■ Errors of expression

Spelling/punctuation errors

Some time later, while the weather outside continued to worsen, Dean sat down to drink a final cup of malt whisky. The room was deserted, a collection of empty chairs and dysfunctional machines with paper strewn al over the floor. And of course, there was me, the youthful scientist who had summoned the Professor to Command Central. I had stayed behind too, when offered a chance to evacuate. I could not deny my own responsibility for this disaster.

Outside, the cyclone had once again grown in strength, and had wiped out everything in the Hawaiian Islands.

The storm would remain here, its source of strength was this island, as it had now been polarised and filled with this energy. The storm would grow, slowly but surely gaining strength, eventually covering the entire planet.

Having gone to fetch some coffee, I heard a sudden gun shot, and a dull thud. I collapsed in a corner and wept. I could not bear to see the professor's corpse. Outside, the storm began to tear the building apart. I would soon be dead. As the outside breeze slowly infiltrated the room from holes in the roof, I pondered on man's underestimation of the wind. And now I realised that I had as well.

Examiner's analysis

This essay is a long (945 words) but well-sustained narrative. This is obviously written by a candidate who enjoys writing and has relished the opportunity of entertaining the reader. It opens forcefully, and immediately engages the reader's attention. The vocabulary is wide, varied, ambitious and fully appropriate. The writer uses a good range of sentence structures and types: there are well-controlled complex sentences, for example:

Outside the complex, atop a remote mountain on the island of Waikiki, in the Hawaiian Archipelago, the skies darkened as small droplets of cold rain began to fall on the island from the heavens above.

and some effectively used short, simple sentences, for example: 'Silence was his only reply.'

The writer has chosen to write a long and involved narrative and does so with confidence. There is no doubt that this candidate is consciously trying to impress the examiner with his/her mastery of the English language and he/she does so in particular through a plentiful use of adjectives ('The arthritic, greying scientist') and a deliberate use of literary language ('Preparing to don more formal attire'), although, in places, this approach is somewhat overdone. It is an extremely confident piece of writing; there is a clear narrative flow which is emphasised by the controlled use of long and short paragraphs for effect.

Direct speech is used convincingly and correctly punctuated, apart from a tendency to misplace commas (' "This is a great moment for mankind", whispered Bunton'), and the writer is not afraid to risk a humorous touch ('replied the wall.'). The essay is not without blemishes, both of spelling (renound, complexe, studiest) and expression ('Seated in his office . . . a loud series of knocks') but these weaknesses are very much the product of first-draft writing and the writer's ambition. They do not impede the reader's understanding and are more than compensated for by the essay's many merits, not least the way it remains clearly focused on the title throughout. The story is original and well developed.

Perhaps the most disappointing part of the essay is the end: the writer could obviously have written more had there been more time, but what is here is a most impressive achievement for the limited time available, and the examiner would have no hesitation in assessing this as a high **grade** A piece of writing.

Example 2

'The only worthwhile thing in life is going to parties.' What are your views?

I reckon this statement is rubbish. Many factors influence me in beleiving this way. As much as partying is fun it can equally be exhausting and unhealthy in some cases. By, keeping on partying, you are causing a huge deteriaration in your health which could (inturn) be quite life threatening. Certainly almost every party will have some alchoholic beverages in entertain it's customers, and definitely, if you are a drinker, you would'nt hesitate from staying away from the booze. It is just almost impossible to do so and therefore you would'nt refrain.

two words not one

At the age of fifteen, partying may seem the most worthwhile thing to do in life as an adoloscent, but looking ahead to the future, it does indeed seem quite bleak for someone partying all the time at this age.

A student that party's all day is certainly not going to get good marks or grades in their examination, and this (inturn) will reflect upon the student's causes. A bit of common sense and awareness of the present situation is all that is needed to realise exactly what the main objective is at this point of our lives. Studies should (unduly) be the priority right now. (Ofcourse) socialising is another aspect of life that is quite important as inter-personal communications and relationships could be demanded all our lives, but is it really the priority right now? Do our social commitments have to overshadow our whole future in front of us? I would say not. When the time comes to party, you can party but it is definitely not the only worthwhile thing in life at the adoloscent age of fifteen.

wrong word
two words not one

Other than the health factor and the education factor, I would believe that partying would be joyful. But only someone who is either peripherally blind or intellectually numb would say that it is the ONLY worthwhile thing to do in life. How many years will you party for? Is it going to get you anywhere in life? I would'nt think so. 'Going to parties' may seem as 'fun' at the time but in the long term, I really doubt as to how far in life it is really going to help you.

Also, most parties occur during nights and drag on till midnight or past. This will be a huge drain of energy from the party goer's part. It is definitely worth it at the time, but the after-effects are rather disturbing and uncomfortable.

Is it really worth wasting your whole life that way? Especially at this age, I would reckon, that it is much more of a use to prioritise as to what is worthwhile now, now instead of regretting it in the future.

Examiner's analysis

This essay begins with a forceful and unambiguous opening which is expressed directly but is not entirely appropriate in its tone of voice: 'I reckon this statement is rubbish.' As the essay develops, it becomes clear that the writing is poorly organised.

The writer possesses quite a wide vocabulary, but it is not always used with precision ('Studies should be unduly the priority now.') The word the candidate should have used is 'undoubtedly' or 'indubitably'.

Some statements, which sound linguistically quite impressive if read superficially ('inter-personal communications and relationships could be demanded all our lives') do not make clear sense on closer reading.

The development of the writer's argument is uncertain and lacking in cohesion; the ideas, although potentially interesting, are underdeveloped. The end of the penultimate paragraph is a good example of this; more details could have been included as to how the after-effects are disturbing and uncomfortable – the writer's meaning has not been made entirely clear to the reader.

There are several technical errors of spelling (Beleiving, alchoholic, adoloscent) and expression ('Going to parties may seem as fun').

The inappropriate tone of the opening sentence has already been referred to and this over-colloquial approach appears at other points throughout the essay, where it sits rather inconsistently with some over-formal expressions ('Many factors influence me'), with the result that the essay lacks a clear focus on the audience.

The reader is required to re-read passages to understand fully what the writer is trying to say, with the result that communication becomes blurred. The whole of the third paragraph is a good example of this.

This essay is an ambitious attempt but, in this case, the writer lacks the linguistic security to communicate the ideas clearly. The ending of the essay is also disappointing as the writer has run out of time and has not managed to produce a satisfactory conclusion. This candidate has made a fundamental mistake: he/she has chosen to write a difficult type of essay (an argumentative one) and has made the task harder than it need be. Had he/she chosen a descriptive or narrative topic the outcome would most probably have been more successful, as less time would have had to be spent on constructing arguments and more time would have been available to concentrate on making the most of the writer's positive merits of vocabulary. The essay which was written could be assessed only as *grade* E.

Example 3

Hidden Treasure.
Write in any way you like about this topic.

'Runners for the 800 metre race, please go to zone 3,' announced one of the judges at the scoring table.

I knew that was my call. Once I stood up, I hurrily turned to a slim, tall girl called Mary Anne. Eversince, she joined the training team, I had this bad feeling and imagined that I would be beaten by her.

two words not one

As I walked boldly, I looked up at the cloudy sky. It had such a dirty grey colour. But I told myself no matter what the weather was like it wouldn't influence me because I was going to win!

'Can you all stand separately? The race is about to start,' shouted a woman with a grim face. I found myself in an excited crowd. Out of them, my eyes found themselves on Mary Anne who was quietly doing warm ups.

THUMP! THUMP!

My heart was hammering at my ribs. Why was I nervous? I had success in numerous races before, and this would not be an exception.

CONCENTRATE, EVA, YOU MUST WIN THIS RACE!

'On your marks, get set . . .'

YOU ARE DEAD, EVA.

. . . go!'

All I saw was darkness. I opened my eyes and found myself running as fast as I possibly could.

DRIP! DROP! DRIP! DROP!

I felt waterdrops. It wet my dried throat when I opened my mouth to breathe. Amazingly, the rain drops gave me a rush of energy. I was on the road again. Not only did I keep a good pace, I ran faster and faster. The track in front of me seemed like a mile long. I ran all I could towards the finish line. Suddenly I felt a great pain in the ankle. I kneeled down desperately and found out that I twisted the ankle while running. Other runners ran pass me and I saw Mary Anne had this worried look on her face as she ran pass. It was hopeless, now, even though there was only 100 metres left to the finish line, I cannot possibly finish it?'!

'were' not 'was'
Inconsistent tenses – was (past), cannot (present)

Before, I felt like I was going to cry. I saw a shadow, a person, coming towards me in the rain. The person's hands helped me up and I saw the face just above mine was Mary Anne's! She kindly comforted me and said, 'Come on, Eva! You can do it!' With her help I was able to topple along and before long, I finally reach the finish line. It was like a door to paradise! If it wasn't Mary Anne's encouragement and help, I wouldn't have done it.

From this memorable event, Mary Anne and I became very close friends as I found after talking to her that we were a lot in common.

wrong word ('had')

I realized that I have gained a treasure, it was not the winning medal or any prize but a caring and trustworthy friend.

This was the hidden treasure that I have never known before and I am so glad that I found it!

Key

■ Errors of expression
  Spelling/punctuation
  errors

Examiner's analysis

This essay opens confidently and leads into a controlled, well-structured story which develops towards a definite conclusion. There are positive merits in its structure, particularly the skilful way in which the details of the race are woven into the action of the story ('YOU ARE DEAD, EVA' . . . 'go!'). The story is sufficiently clear to engage the reader's interest and to sustain it. There is quite a wide range of vocabulary which is appropriately used ('rush of energy', 'I was able to topple along'). The writer's expression is secure and confident enough for him/her to concentrate on selecting words and phrases which are designed to appeal to and interest the reader.

However, despite its many good qualities, this essay lacks a variety of style. Instead of a wide range of sentence structures, the writer tends to be over-reliant on short, simple sentences (there are many in the second paragraph, for example) and it would appear that the writer is using them as a result of linguistic limitations rather than deliberately to create a sense of tension and excitement.

Overall, this essay is the work of a writer who is aware of his/her limitations and strengths and, in general, does not try to go beyond them. Assessing this essay involves balancing the good and less good qualities. On the whole, the good qualities outweigh the others and the essay was assessed as a sound **grade C**.

▩ Writing in response to a photograph

Here are some key points on how to obtain a good score when writing in response to a picture or photograph.

1 **Don't** just describe what is shown in the photograph.
2 **Don't** try to adapt a story you may have written earlier, hoping that it will fit the picture – it won't, and your marks will suffer as a result.
3 **Don't** start off with the first idea that comes into your head.
4 **Do** write about **your own response** to what you see.
5 **Do** try to imagine what the 'story' behind the picture might be and look for details in the picture to help you.
6 **Do** jot down a plan, as you would for any other exam essay.

Ask yourself some questions before you start to write to help you focus your mind. For example, look at the picture on the right. You might ask yourself the following questions:

- Where is this picture taken?
- What does it show us?
- Who is the woman on the right of the picture?
- What is her job?
- How old are the children?
- What might be the relationship between the children?
- What might they be buying?

These questions will provide you with the basic material to start your writing. Next, you might want to start adding details, so you will begin to ask more specific questions such as: *The shopkeeper seems happy; why? Is she a friend of the children?* And so on. Once you have built up some background, you can develop your ideas and decide upon your approach. You could write a story. Perhaps the children are not buying anything at all; perhaps they are returning something to the shopkeeper which she has lost and they have found. Your story could deal with how they found whatever it was (it could be a box containing a valuable piece of jewellery) and how they traced the owner, who turned out to be the shopkeeper.

You do not have to invent a story, however. The picture might remind you of a favourite shop you go to or used to go to. You might, therefore, want to write about your memories or impressions of the shop, the people who work(ed) there, some of the regular customers and what they buy/bought.

Know where you are going

Either of these approaches would be perfectly acceptable, as both start from the characters in the picture. What is important to remember about this type of topic, however, is to organise your approach carefully before you start to write. This is why asking yourself questions is helpful. If you do not plan your approach, there is a danger that you will produce a rambling and unfocused piece of writing, which will lose you marks. As with any other piece of writing for an examination, it's important to know where you are going before you start.

■ Practise writing essays

Now that you have looked at some essays produced by other candidates, here are some more titles which you can use for practice. To help you, we have indicated next to each essay whether it is narrative, descriptive or argumentative (in some cases, you will notice, the same topic could lend itself to more than one approach). Two of the topics are **discursive**, which means you can approach the question in any way you choose.

Tip You can plan your essays in different ways. For example, you can produce a straightforward skeleton plan or use a spider diagram. Examples of both types of plan are shown opposite – they relate to the first two questions on the list. You could use them as the basis for writing your own practice essay, and then as models for writing your own plans for other essays. Remember, the points in each plan should provide you with the topic sentences for your paragraphs. It is up to you to add the details which make the paragraphs interesting!

1 'Television is a bad influence; it stops people thinking and ruins family life.' What are your views about the value of television? (Argumentative)
2 Which is your favourite day of the week and why? (Descriptive)
3 Write a story beginning with the words 'The noise was growing louder and louder,' and ending 'And then there was silence.' (Narrative)
4 What have you taught yourself that is not taught at your school? (Argumentative/Descriptive)
5 Do we spend too much time watching games instead of playing them? (Argumentative)
6 Describe a place you know well at two different times of the day. (Descriptive)
7 Castles in the Air.
Write in any way you like about this topic. (Discursive)
8 Write a story called 'The Empty House'. (Narrative)
9 Decisions.
Write in any way you like about this topic. (Discursive)
10 *Outside the window footsteps fall*
Into the ordinary day
And with the sun along the wall
Pursue their unreturning way

That was ordained in eternity.
Sound's perpetual roundabout
Rolls its numbered octaves out
And hoarsely grinds its battered tune
What thoughts or feelings do these lines inspire in you? (Descriptive/Narrative)
11 Make the scene shown in the picture an important part of your writing. (Descriptive/Narrative)

Examples of essay plans

Skeleton essay plan for Question 1: 'Television is a bad influence; it stops people thinking and ruins family life.'

Introduction: General comments on TV; its popularity, ubiquity; it is now a focal point in most households; it has become a major part of our lives.

Points against: It stops conversation and limits communication among people; it can cause family arguments over what to watch; it stops families doing more constructive things together; many of the most popular programmes are superficial; it is very easy to become addicted to certain programmes (soap operas, etc.) with the result that studies take a back seat. It tells you what to think.

Points for: It provides company for people who are on their own; it brings news and sporting events direct into the home and allows you to feel as though you are present at them even if they are on the other side of the world; it has some educational value – in fact, something can be learnt from most programmes; it can develop and refine one's analytical powers; it provides a ready topic of conversation with your friends.

Conclusion: sum up the main points made above, refer to own experience and that of friends and state conclusion re how much truth there is in the topic statement.

Spider diagram essay plan for Question 2: Which is your favourite day of the week and why?

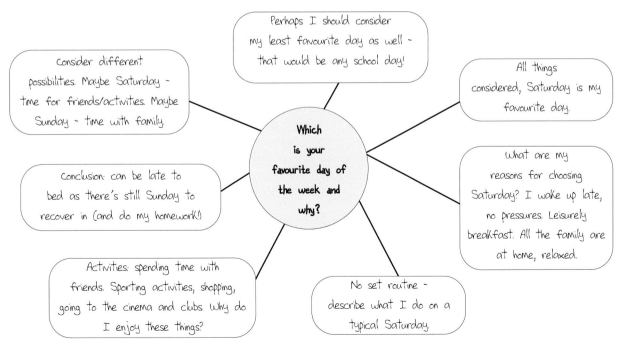

Section 2 *Coursework*

■ Why do coursework?

When following a course in IGCSE First Language English you are asked to show that you can produce a piece or pieces of continuous writing. Section 1 of this chapter dealt with continuous writing for the written examination (Paper 3). Alternatively, you may produce three pieces of continuous writing and submit them as coursework. (This is called 'Paper 4' in the syllabus.) But why do coursework? Isn't it easier just to sit down for an hour and a quarter and write? Not necessarily! If you do coursework you have the opportunity to plan and check your work, and you can draft and re-draft the piece of writing. You can be sure that, at the end of the process, your work is as good as you can possibly make it.

■ What do you have to do?

The syllabus requirements for coursework are as follows:

■ Candidates will be required to submit a folder of three pieces of writing, each of about 500 words.
■ One piece of writing should be factual: informative or argumentative.
■ One piece of writing should be expressive: descriptive, narrative or imaginative.
■ The third piece of writing is an entirely free choice, but should demonstrate some variety of style, skill or genre not already shown in the other two pieces.

Let's consider these requirements one by one.

Length

The syllabus states that each piece should be about 500 words. Will you be marked down if you write more or fewer words than this? The answer is 'no'! Your pieces of writing need to be as long as is necessary to complete the task and to demonstrate the range of your writing skills. Remember that you are not awarded marks just because you have written a lot; in fact, writing that has started well can sometimes lose its effectiveness and get worse the longer it goes on.

The three types of coursework

Doing coursework gives you the chance to demonstrate your skills in writing in different ways and styles. In everyday life we write for a variety of reasons. We might be required to write formal reports during our working life. We might be asked to write an article for a community newsletter, possibly an account of something particularly interesting we have done, perhaps a funny anecdote. We might have the job of writing the monthly newsletter for a club or group. In each of these situations we would have a different audience and a different purpose, so we would need to write each piece in a different style.

This is why you are asked to write three different pieces; it reflects the reality of how writing is used in everyday life. When you are choosing the different pieces to include in your coursework folder, remember this point and think:

■ Who am I writing for in each piece?
■ What is the purpose of each piece?
■ Am I choosing pieces that are different?

The factual piece

You must write an informative or argumentative factual piece. It could be in the form of an essay, but it might be more interesting to choose a different format, such as a letter, a report, or the words of a talk (there is advice on writing these in Chapter 4). Some other ideas include:

■ a publicity handout or leaflet
■ a set of instructions explaining how to perform a task
■ a programme for a cultural event
■ a travel guide to a place or area that you know
■ an account of a particular real-life experience.

What should I write?

There may be a topic in which you have a burning interest and you may feel that you can sit down and get going without any preparation. Don't! Doing coursework gives you the important opportunity to do your research and make sure that all the facts you use are 100 per cent accurate. So get your facts together and sort through them before you start.

If a topic doesn't spring to mind immediately, then there is a whole range of sources to give you ideas. You might get your inspiration from:

■ a programme on the television
■ a discussion of a topic suggested by your teacher in class
■ something you have read
■ something you have heard on the radio.

The following text is a short story in the form of a dialogue which could start you thinking about relationships and social issues and be a springboard for a piece of writing on a related topic, such as:

■ Discuss how the conventional family unit is becoming a thing of the past.
■ Teenagers are often more responsible than their parents!
■ Abortion is murder and should never be allowed.

Well, Well, Well
by Kate Hall

'Well you obviously can't keep it.'

'What do you mean, CAN'T keep it? Who says I can't?'

'It's obvious – you'll have to have an abortion.'

'I don't want an abortion. I want to . . .'

'You can't, just think about it for a minute.'

'I have thought about it, I've thought about it a lot.'

'But you've just started college.'

'I know I've started college but there's a crèche there.'

'Oh, I see, you're going to go in pregnant and have the baby in between lectures.'

'It's due in the holidays and anyway I can get time off, other people have done it before, you know.'

'That doesn't mean you have to, though, does it? And what about money?'

'I'll manage.'

'What, on a grant, with a baby and no father?'

'Yes on a grant, with a baby and no father – that's what's really worrying you, isn't it? Bloody hell, in this day and age!'

'Well, it would help if you would say who the father is, or don't you know?'

'Of course I know, but I don't want him to.'

'Why not for Christ's sake, he ought to pay for it – you could get maintenance you know or he could pay for an abortion.'

'I don't want him to pay for anything and I am NOT having an abortion.'

'He's not married is he?'

'No, he's not married.'

'Then I don't see . . .'

'I just don't want anyone interfering, that's all.'

'Well you needn't worry on my account – I'm not having anything to do with it and don't expect me to baby-sit either.'

'No one asked you to.'

'Not yet, but just you wait. Honestly, I thought you were old enough to know better. It's embarrassing.'

'You'll be saying "What will the neighbours say?" next.'

'I don't give a damn about the neighbours but they will think things if there's no father.'

'There is a father.'

'Oh yes, an anonymous one.'

'I KNOW who he is.'

'Well at least tell me.'

'No. Look, I made a decision; I got pregnant on purpose. I want to have this baby, okay?'

'BUT MUM – at your age!'

From *The Stench of Kerosene – Short Stories* by Steve Bowles, Cambridge University Press, 1991

If you are inspired to try writing a dialogue by pieces like the one opposite, then go ahead. **However**, it is more likely that a dialogue will be suitable for submission as your 'free choice' piece rather than as your 'factual' piece, because it is difficult to convey detailed information successfully in a dialogue. If you really want to write a dialogue as your factual piece, then try writing the script of a radio interview, where you can include real information in a natural way.

Tips
1 Make sure that you use your research and make it belong to you. Don't just copy out the information. In your planning make sure that you get the points in the order you want. If you fail to do this, it will look as if you are just copying out your sources rather than the work being your own.
2 You should always list the sources you have used if, for example, you have researched information in books or on the Internet, or used particular sources as your inspiration. For each source, you should give the title and the author's name. For a website, give the title and www.address.

How should I write?

You should write in a style that allows a reader clearly to follow the information you are giving or the opinion you are putting forward.

Tips
1 Each sentence should make one important point.
2 You won't need many descriptive words, adjectives and adverbs in this piece of writing because you need to concentrate on facts and keep your purpose clear.

▨ The expressive piece

You must write an expressive piece: descriptive, narrative or imaginative.

What should I write?

The great thing about the expressive piece is that, provided you remember the key words **descriptive**, **narrative**, **imaginative**, and make sure your piece matches at least one of these descriptions really well, you can choose any theme you like! Still, it's not always easy to come up with an idea that works, or to choose between different ideas that occur to you. Here are a few examples of ideas which have been used successfully by IGCSE English students for their coursework:

■ a story involving a place you remember from when you were younger
■ a story about a particular episode in your life which has had an impact on you (e.g. an accident or illness)
■ a piece about family relationships and their importance
■ a piece about friendships, perhaps when a person has proved themselves to be a friend – or has not!
■ a science-fiction story.

How should I write?

This second piece should be written in a very different style from the first. Here there are no constraints. You can let your imagination take off. Use all the descriptive words and images, similes and metaphors, that you like. You don't have to write a series of points but can make your writing really vivid. You can experiment with using sentences of very different lengths, for instance. A journal or diary version of one of the ideas on page 145 might be one way to structure your writing.

The Toy Girl
by Paula Clark

The grass was wet against her face and smeared her as she looked up. Irregular shifting shapes surrounded her in the darkness and laughter grew from one side and shimmered over her head. One of the shapes reached out and touched her shoulder – 'Paula?'

The voice, incredibly loud, ricocheted inside her head. She winced and squinted to focus on the blank face, dissolving into helpless, wheezy giggles when the shape became Helen, her eyes wide and amazed. Arms lifted her (or pulled her down) and half carried her,

mumbling and weak, across the damp park. She could hear voices swirling through the vapour in her mind, some familiar, some not, some from outside, some from within. 'Drunk? She's blasted! What was she doing?'

Her kitchen appeared from somewhere and she was sat down, blinking in the hard electric light. She looked absently at her hands. They were bruised with the cold but she felt nothing and the uncomprehending giggling bubbled uncontrollably out of her.

The house seemed full of people. Their voices and movements blurred around her and vaguely she heard the cupboard doors open and hungry hands reach inside and take. The words asking them not to formed in her mind but diffused into confused sobbing and mumbling before they reached her mouth. She could hear pop music from somewhere and a muffled fear turned in her stomach, but then the light began to dim around the edges and the sound to spin away and darkness flowed over the room.

The wrenching in her own head woke her up. Aware of a throbbing silence and, strangely, the heavy smell of paint in the room, she ached her eyes open and blinked painfully around her. The image which faced her made her recoil in horror, taking a sudden, frightened breath. The walls . . . oh my God the walls . . . paint . . . Random sprayed lines dribbled across them, coating the ripped wallpaper as it hung like jagged leaves around her. The pounding in her head grew and her stomach tumbled as she saw the room completely now, smashed and littered, a red wine stain seeping like blood in the corner of the carpet. She sat up, spinning, trembling, her mouth horribly dry as fear burned in her throat. She walked almost dreamlike through the house as though it were some weird, undiscovered cave. It was totally unfamiliar, a sickening mixture of garish, hateful colour and destruction.

What had they done? She stared disbelievingly around her, a cold numbness spreading inside her and beginning to squeeze hot tears down her face. The sweet, gluish smell of vomit grew in the hallway and as she heard the crunch of her parents' car in the drive she stood, uncertain, caught between the two. As the key scraped in the lock, the discarded Toy Girl wiped her eyes and, reaching down, gently picked up a torn piece of paper from the floor. She curled herself up in the corner by the stairs and pressed her face into her knees, her trembling hands tightly clutching the tiny fragment of a birthday card.

From *The Stench of Kerosene – Short Stories* by Steve Bowles, Cambridge University Press, 1991

This passage has some useful ideas. It is short but it very cleverly deals with all the things that a short story needs to do. It has a number of the features of a short story which you might want to imitate.

- It has a good opening which leads you to want to read on as questions are left hanging: what is she doing; who or what are the shapes around her?
- It develops the situation with some very effective expressions. 'She could hear voices swirling through the vapour in her mind', 'her stomach tumbled'.
- It leaves us wondering who the others are right up to the last two words of the story, which are an effective and poignant end. We are, however, left with the very big question, what will the reaction of the parents be?

When writing your own stories, pay special attention to the beginning and the end and think about every word and phrase. Ask yourself if it is the best word or phrase you can use. Don't always be content with your first ideas.

Tips   You can approach the process of drafting and redrafting in a variety of ways; remember that redrafting does not mean just writing something out again and correcting any technical errors that were in the first effort.

1 You might ask your teacher to read the first version and suggest whether any parts could be improved. You could ask a friend or classmate to do the same. They might notice, for instance, that in a story, you have created one character rather more strongly than another, and you might consider trying to give the second character more life. In an argumentative essay, you might have presented one side of the argument very much more strongly than the other, and you should try to balance them a bit more. Don't expect your teacher or friend to tell you **exactly** how to change your piece – it is, after all, your work and the final decision is up to you.

2 Try reading through the piece, asking yourself over and over again, 'Is this sentence necessary and is it as good as I can make it?'

▦ The free-choice piece – something different!

What you choose to do as your third piece of coursework is entirely up to you, but it should demonstrate some variety of style, skill or genre not already shown in the other two pieces.

What should I write?

What you need to produce is something 'different'. In pieces one and two you have already shown your ability to write factually and expressively, so . . . how about trying some **poetry**?

You might enjoy writing your own poetry – many people do. If so, why not submit some of your poems? Two or three will be enough. It is up to you whether to submit poems with a shared theme or stand-alone poems. It would probably not be sensible to submit a series of haikus or limericks. There is nothing wrong with these forms of poetry but they are likely to be very personal, very short and very difficult to assess.

The main problem with poetry for exam purposes is that, because it is a very personal form of writing, you have to take particular care to make sure your reader understands what you wanted to convey. To help overcome this, if you submit your own poetry it would be very sensible to write a brief commentary to go alongside it. In your commentary you should explain:

- what the poem(s) is (are) about

- why you wrote the poem(s) in the way you did

- what you were hoping to achieve

- any particular features you are proud of – vocabulary, imagery, verse form, etc.

- why you think the poems are successful.

Another possibility for your third piece is to submit **a literature essay**. It is probable that, as part of your English course, you are studying some literature: a novel, a play or poetry. You may even be preparing for IGCSE English Literature, as well as IGCSE English. If you are studying literature, you will almost certainly be writing essays developing your thoughts about it. This is a different sort of writing, analytical writing. If you are studying for IGCSE English Literature, and are doing coursework for literature, a real bonus is that you can use the same essay for both subjects. Simply photocopy the essay and put the photocopy in your English folder. However, a word of warning: if you do this, make sure that this piece is different in style from your other coursework pieces. For example, you should not include two factual essays in your folder.

How do I write?

The free-choice piece gives you the chance to show your personal strengths. You might want to be very experimental with your choice of words and the way you put your thoughts together. Be prepared to experiment. Ask your teacher what you do really well in writing which you could exploit here.

Tips

1 **Checking word-processed work.** You are allowed to use a word processor to produce your coursework and many people do. There are, however, a few things to remember. A word processor is not the answer to all your linguistic problems. To use the spell check effectively, for example, you have to have a clear idea of the word that you want. It is amazing how many students scan the list of possibilities and pick the wrong word, so that what they end up with is nonsense. The same applies to a grammar check. Computer checks are not a substitute for your own knowledge.

2 **Don't copy!** We all read things that influence us and, if the model that influences us is good, it can have a positive effect. However, copying out sections of other people's writing is called plagiarism and it is a form of cheating. Your teacher knows what your own writing is like and will immediately question work that is very different. In the same way, although you are encouraged to write in different styles, a moderator will be able to see quite easily if something does not belong to you. Cheats are nearly always caught out. If you have used ideas from books or the Internet, remember to list your sources.

In this section we have provided a poem and a leaflet, which you might like to use as models to get you into your third piece of writing.

Writing a poem

Use the following as a source of some ideas for your own poetry. The poem overleaf was written when the poet was being taken to prison. Consider:

■ its shape

■ its use of short phrases

■ its use of adjectives

■ its contrasts.

Cold

by Dennis Brutus

the clammy cement
sucks our naked feet
a rheumy yellow bulb
fights a damp grey wall
the stubbled grass
wet with three o'clock dew
is black with glittery edges;
we sit on the concrete,
stuff with our fingers
the sugarless pap
into our mouths
then labour erect;
form lines;
steel ourselves into fortitude
or accept an image of ourselves
numb with resigned acceptance;
the grizzled senior warder comments:
'Things like these
I have no time for;
they are worse than rats;
you can only shoot them.'
Overhead
the large frosty glitter of the stars the Southern Cross flowering low;
the chains on our ankles
and wrists
that pair us together
jangle
glitter
We begin to move awkwardly.

From 'Letters to Martha 18' in *Simple Lust, Collected Poems of South African Jail and Exile*, Heinemann, 1973

What do you think of the word 'sucks'?

How would you describe the grass on a cold early morning, or the scrubland down the road?

Would you want to put speech into your poetry?

How would you get the details of sights and sounds into your poetry?

Being taken to prison was a very intense experience which clearly affected the writer very much indeed. Very often this sort of experience, a vital moment in our lives, can trigger the most effective writing.

Practise writing a poem

Think of a very important, perhaps traumatic, experience in your life and try to express your emotions about what happened in a poem.

Writing a leaflet

The leaflet opposite was produced by the pharmacy chain UniChem and was sent out to pharmacies, doctors' surgeries and other health clinics. It has been carefully written and designed to make the information accessible.

SPORTS INJURIES

Grazes and Skin Burns

These occur as a result of friction.

A graze (abrasion) is a superficial skin wound commonly caused by a sliding fall. The top skin layers are scraped off, leaving a raw, painful area. The palm of the hands or knees are common sites for grazes. Foreign particles sometimes become embedded in the grazed area and pose an infection risk.

Friction burns of the skin may be due to rope burns or sliding falls on synthetic sports surfaces.

First aid treatment for grazes and friction burns of the skin involves careful cleaning of the wound, preferably by rinsing dirty grazes under gently running water. Glass or grit may be gently picked off the surface of the graze, but do not attempt to remove embedded debris – seek medical treatment. After rinsing, cover the wound with sterile gauze, clean the surrounding area and apply a plaster or light dressing.

Cramp

Cramp is a painful muscle spasm that may arise following any exercise, but particularly swimming and running. Muscle spasm occurs when muscles contract for too long, or when profuse sweating causes water and salt loss. Lactic acid accumulates in muscles following strenuous exercise and this also causes cramp. Massage of the affected muscle often helps to relieve the spasm and pain.

First Aid

First Aid: following an injury to the soft tissues, including sprains, deep bruising and muscular injuries, first aiders should follow the R.I.C.E procedure as follows: **R**est the affected part: **I**ce, apply a cold pad to the injured part. Alternative 'ice packs' could include a bag of frozen peas or vegetables, wrapped in a tea-towel. **C**ompress the injured part by means of a supportive bandage. **E**levate the part that is injured.

Prevention: many sports-related injuries may be prevented by:
- Wearing correct footwear for your particular sport
- Replacing worn sports shoes
- Practising your technique and obtaining professional guidance if possible
- Wearing protective clothing or equipment (where applicable)
- Warming up before strenuous exercise and cooling down afterwards
- Devising your own loosening up routine to increase blood flow to the muscles, allowing sufficient time for old injuries to heal.

Always read the label.

You can obtain professional advice and a variety of treatments at your Unichem Community pharmacy.   From UniChem Pharmacies

The information is broken up into short sections, each with a large heading. There is plenty of space around the headings, to make them stand out.

The language is simple and clear, and short sentences are used. This helps to make the information easy to understand.

Bullet points are used to help readers pick out relevant details.

Practise writing a leaflet

Use this leaflet as a model. Think about: how information is made to stand out; the order the information is given in, and why; the vocabulary used, and so on. Then prepare your own leaflet, advising students about how to plan and pack for a two-week trip – you decide on the nature of the trip and the destination.

■ Examples of candidates' coursework

The rest of this chapter provides a wide range of examples of coursework for you to read through. The teacher's annotations and comments are printed in red. The examiner's comments and the grade awarded to the work are printed in blue after each piece, so that you can see how different strengths and weaknesses in the writing have an effect on the marks.

In the coursework samples that follow, there are examples of:

■ informative/persuasive essays (capital punishment, vivisection)
■ autobiographical writing
■ short stories
■ writing in response to literature
■ diary writing
■ a package of items related to the process of getting a job
■ a poem.

As you get down to your own coursework, consider these along with all the other ideas that have been mentioned and decide on your way forward.

Coursework folder: Example 1

The three pieces submitted in this coursework folder are as follows:

■ Factual piece: 'Capital punishment'
■ Expressive piece: 'Surviving victim'
■ Free-choice piece: 'Pygmalion'

CAPITAL PUNISHMENT
Discuss the arguments FOR and AGAINST capital punishment

Capital punishment, as defined in Encyclopaedia Britannica, is the execution of a criminal convicted of a crime. It is the lawful infliction of the death penalty, and, since ancient times, it has been used to punish a wide variety of offences. The methods used to inflict this death penalty, with those of the past now regarded as barbaric and forbidden by law almost everywhere, range from stoning in biblical times, to crucifixion under the Romans, and beheading in France, to those used in the United States today: hanging, electrocution, the gas chamber, firing squad and lethal injection. That aside, the use of capital punishment in modern times has declined markedly, and the death penalty is now inflicted only for the most serious crimes such as murder or treason. Indeed in much of Western Europe capital punishment has been abolished altogether, and it is seldom used even where it is legal. In the West, where complete abolition could not be achieved, laws which distinguished first-degree and second-degree

▶▶

murder and limited the death penalty to murders committed with premeditation or in the case of carrying out another felony were adopted. In contrast, there are about 125 nations which retain the death penalty including countries in Asia, Africa and the Middle East (except Israel) and most of these nations adhere strictly to the traditional practices of Islam with beheading or stoning still occasionally employed as punishment. Despite all this, the subject of capital punishment is still hotly debated and is frequently on the minds of both politicians and the public. It is a subject

Good.

of immense complexity as there is no clear relationship between crime and punishment. The alternative, however, to capital punishment is long-term or life imprisonment and it is here that fundamental questions raised by the death penalty start.

Those in favour of the retention or reintroduction of the death penalty claim that is has a uniquely powerful deterrent effect on potentially violent offenders for whom the threat of imprisonment is not a sufficient restraint. As defined by Encyclopaedia Britannica, a general deterrent is 'a punishment, the object of which is to deter other persons from following the example of the offender, by fear of the same consequences that have been inflicted on him'. Proponents defend capital punishment mainly on this ground – that because taking an offender's life is more severe than any prison term, it must be a better deterrent – the potential murderer would think twice before committing the act if he knew that he might also die when caught. With the death penalty, an armed bank robber might become as simple bank robber leaving his shotgun at home, argue those in favour of capital punishment. Public opinion, which in the U.S. currently supports the death penalty for murder by a more than two-to-one margin, rests on this conviction. Supporters also argue that there is no adequate deterrent in life imprisonment for those already serving a life term who can potentially commit murder while incarcerated and not receive further punishment; those who have not been caught but who would be liable to a life term if arrested; and terrorists, traitors, revolutionaries, and spies.

Equally important, argue those in favour of capital punishment, is the idea of protection or incapacitation. The idea is simply that the offender should be dealt with in a manner that will make it impossible for him to repeat his offence – by execution or banishment in earlier times, in modern times by execution or lengthy periods of incarceration. Attacking the weak point of life imprisonment, those in favour of capital punishment argue that executing the criminal is the only sure means of preventing a murderer

▶▶

from being released or escaping and committing further murders. Life imprisonment, supporters of capital punishment say, would not be equally as effective as a deterrent and would expose prison staff and fellow prisoners to dangerous murderers. This risk later extends to the community, as such people may escape or be pardoned or paroled. Under capital punishment, however, the convicted murder who is executed will never be set free after 20 years of his life sentence and go on to murder again. It is the only objective of punishment for which there is any certainty. Thus the public would be safer, protecting both civilians and police. They also claim that society has the right to kill in defence of its members, just as the individual may kill in self-defence.

The following two arguments used by the pro-capital punishment lobby are a lot murkier in their motives. Retribution, as interpreted by Encyclopaedia Britannica, 'is that there should be relation between the gravity of the crime and the severity of the punishment'. 'Whoever sheds man's blood, by man shall his blood be shed' (Genesis 9 : 6) has usually been used by those who defend the death penalty as a divine warrant for putting the murderer to death. 'Let the punishment fit the crime' is its secular coequal statement; both sources imply that the murderer deserves to die. Proponents of the death penalty argue that those who have committed a crime which goes against *The Declaration of Human Rights* cannot then expect to defend themselves by that Declaration. The state/country, they say, must show it disapproval of serious lawbreakers by executing them. The whole of the retribution theory is closely linked with revenge and has the Old Testament concept of an 'eye for an eye and a tooth for a tooth and a life for a life'. The idea also states that the state must punish offenders in order to satisfy the demand for punishment that is natural among members of the public, particularly among those who are the victims of the crime and who, in the absence of official punishment given by the state, are likely to take the law into their own hands and seek revenge by direct violence. It is not fair for the victim's family that a murderer of its members should go on living.

The fourth main argument included by those in favour of the death penalty is the most cold-blooded. It makes economic sense, they say, to execute convicted prisoners, rather than have them in prison wasting taxpayers' money. While it can take between £400–£1000 to keep a criminal in high security prison for a week, it takes less than a fraction of this amount to execute him. Those, however, who are violently against capital punishment reply that the public has the right to pay tax money in return for their protection.

▶▶

With the arguments for capital punishment put aside, it can be seen that the arguments against the restoration of the death penalty are largely based on humanitarian grounds. But there are also statistical reasons to oppose it, for the deterrence figures presented by those in favour of the death penalty do not add up. For example, in Britain, 1903 was a record year for executions yet in 1904 the number of unjustifiable homicides actually rose. 1946 saw an unusually high number of executions followed in 1947 by another rise in the murder rate.

Those against the death penalty point out that there is no evidence of its being a more potent deterrent than the threat of a sentence of life imprisonment. The U.S. is a perfect example of this. The first point in the argument cites that two adjacent states, in which one has a death penalty and the other does not, show no significant fluctuation in the long-term incidence rate of murder – the presence of the death penalty in one state should, theoretically, mean a lower murder rate, however this does not prove to be case. Moreover, the second point declares states that use the death penalty to seem to have a higher number of homicides than the number found in states that do not use it. The third point shows that states which abolish and then reintroduce the death penalty do not seem to show any significant change in the murder rate – on abolishing the death penalty, a rise in the murder rate is expected and on its reintroduction, a decrease is expected. In addition, no change in the rate of homicides in a given city or state seems to occur following an execution. Moreover, all statistics indicate that very same fact – in the early 1970s, some published reports purported to show that each execution in the U.S. deterred eight or more homicides, but subsequent researched has proved the finding wrong. The whole of this argument, however, should not and does not rest on statistics. Those violently against capital punishment state that most of the criminals who commit serious crimes are terrorists, desperate and insane. The desperate, they say, will risk being caught in order to end their despair. This class won't be deterred by the fear called for by the death penalty. As for those who are insane, they do not have rational thought processes (i.e. psychopaths) to be deterred in the first place. Furthermore, terrorists will not be deterred as they are deeply committed to a political or religious cause and capital punishment only further emphasises this cause. The deterrence theory the pro-capital punishment lobby talks about will thus not influence these people which represent a majority of the murderers. What remains to be accepted by criminologists is that there is no conclusive evidence showing that the death penalty is a more effective

▶▶

deterrent to violent crime than long-term prison. Instead, opponents of the death penalty say that prolonged detention over decades is a harsher penalty than death.

Equally important, and not to be underestimated, opponents of the death penalty argue, is the fact that the death penalty is naturally subject to caprice and mistake in practice and that it is impossible to administer fairly. Capital punishment has always been used unfairly, in the U.S. at least, in three major ways. First, women are rarely sentenced to death even though they are responsible for 20 percent of all homicides – Karla Faye Tucker was the first woman to be sentenced to death this century in Texas's history. Second, a disproportionate number of nonwhites are sentenced to death and executed. Before the 1970s, when the death penalty for rape was still used in many states in the U.S., no white men were executed for raping non-white women, whereas most black offenders found guilty of raping a white woman were executed. Third, that the death penalty tends to be imposed in a discriminatory manner on the poor and friendless defendants and on members of minority groups, and those with inexperienced or court-appointed counsel.

Not to be forgotten, critics of the death penalty have always pointed out that the death penalty creates the risk that an innocent person is executed and while we can let someone out of prison we cannot bring them back from the dead if we have executed them. Although definitely established cases of this sort are rare, they include (1) Timothy Evans – hanged 1950 for murder and later proved innocent by Scott Henderson's inquiry into the case and (2) Mahmood Hussien Mattan – hanged September 1952. Timothy Evans received a posthumous pardon and Mahmood Hussien Mattan also had his conviction quashed on February 24th 1998 (both were of course dead by then).

The next argument against the retention or reintroduction of the death penalty is that the death penalty prevents any possible rehabilitation of the offender. In Encyclopaedia Britannica, this is the idea that 'through treatment and training the offender should be rendered capable of returning to society and functioning as a law-abiding member of the community'. Those violently against the death penalty argue that it does not allow enough time for the offender to truly repent the crime(s) he has committed, and with that, society loses one of its members that might have been liable to rehabilitation. The idea began to establish itself in legal practice in the 19th century. Although seen by many as a humane

►►

improvement, it did not always mean that the offender received a more lenient penalty than a retributive or deterrent theory would have given him. For many offenders, rehabilitation meant release on probation under some form of condition instead of a period in prison or a case in which the length of detention was governed by the degree of reform exhibited.

In conclusion to all these arguments for and against capital punishment, there remains the fact that many of the theories explained come into conflict. A lenient sentence (such as probation), designed to rehabilitate the offender, may fail to express society's rejection of his behaviour or to provide an effective deterrent to others. A sentence of unusual severity, designed to make an example of the offender as a warning to others, is in conflict with the principle of rehabilitation. A sentence whose object is incapacitation may fail to satisfy those who believe in rehabilitation. Criminologists have never succeeded in producing convincing evidence to resolve these issues and it may well be that criminology will never provide the information on which to base a scientific choice between the different objectives of punishment as no single theory provides a system suitable for all cases – there is no clear relationship between crime and punishment.

Teacher's comment

A* An outstanding essay. You discuss these complex arguments with maturity and express your ideas clearly and elegantly. You manage many very complex sentence constructions which show that you are in complete control of the language.

Examiner's analysis

The essay on capital punishment is clearly well planned and extremely well written. It is longer than the minimum length of 500 words which is suggested in the syllabus, but remember that this is only given as a guide. There is no problem with writing being longer than the guideline – the quality of your writing is more important than its length. Technically it is correct; words are correctly spelt and sentences are well constructed. The student has been asked to present a balanced argument and she does this very well in quite a simple structure. We have an introductory paragraph which explores the situation which exists in various parts of the world; there is then an exploration of reasons for keeping the death penalty, followed by an equally detailed exploration of reasons for getting rid of it; there is then a very measured conclusion which neatly ties back to the introduction. The tone throughout is formal, careful and entirely appropriate.

SURVIVING VICTIM

The Galactic Empire was falling.

It was a colossal Empire, stretching across millions of worlds, millions of light years apart. Its fall was colossal too – and a long one, as Hari Seldon had predicted . . .

The memories were fragmentary at first, as they always were . . . He had been walking the dirty, scorched streets in silence since twilight first began to gather. His steps were steady and monotonous. Pain streamed like liquid fire through every cell of his body – but he locked it away in a corner of his mind, ignored it and walked. It was all a shock to him. All was new. All was horrific.

Dim soft sunlight barely reached the soft black soil beneath his silent steps. Its rays were blocked by fine glittering dust like mist on a humid day, only it wasn't. There was little, In fact nothing to please the eye in his surroundings. In fact, it was the exact opposite. He looked to the falling dust in hatred and screamed, '*Who* and *why*?' only it was as silent as his dead surroundings. Questions upon questions, mysteries upon mysteries heaped themselves up in his mind, with this question plaguing him as fiercely as the pain.

He continued, threading his way through the clatter and glitter of the streets, thronged with shrivelled corpses clustered around the tawdry attractions offered to space-weary visitors – everything from ordinary holoscreens to shadowy, semi-illicit drug dives. Vegetation was grudgingly available, or what was left of it. Trees were left bare and naked in the dim light as if to say 'come what may come,' only it already came.

Broken, fleeting visions of landscape passed his mind as he had seen them from his spaceship – a bleak inhospitable world, dominated by chill expanses of desert, by towering ranges of rock-fanged mountains. His name was Elijah Bailey. It was his world – the planet Aurora. It had had breathable air, with water, and vegetation sprawled all over its surface. it also had had a variety of its own life forms – the venomous reptiles of many weird shapes, the deadly jungle cats, the huge, horned mammoths of the mountains, the tangled vine growths that fed on flesh – all alien beasts, all threatening, all dangerously elegant. Now, this was non-existent. It was now a dead and deadly world.

His memories were gathering pace now, and Elijah writhed in his chair, powerless to stop his unconscious mind from forming images that he had ▶▶

re-lived so often before, in horror and despair. Elijah Bailey's memories shifted back, as they always did, and the broken, fleeting visions gathered, held steady . . . ✓

As he studied the face of the planet Aurora looming and filling his view-screen, all seemed puzzlingly calm and normal. There was a faint, hazy aura round the image of the planet and the spaceship's sensors reported unknown radiation, but Elijah discounted that as a possible minor malfunction of the screen and the sensors, to do with the lack of repairs that resulted from the lack of funds the falling Empire suffered from. The planet had been attacked and unknown radiation released over the entire surface. The planet was bathed in a glowing haze of lethal radiation, in which everything and everyone that Elijah had loved had met their deaths.

Now, Elijah's face twisted, his body hunched, aching, torn with a fury that was beyond bearing, a grief that was inconsolable, and a physical sensation – pain. It seemed to emanate from his very bones – faint, but tangible and definite. A deep-lying sensation of burning pain. Horror and savage rage tore at his sanity. But in the end as the hours passed, something else – not intuition but a physical sensation itself, from within his body – told him that even though he had survived, it was not likely to matter to him for very long. He was to meet with his fellow victims of the falling Empire soon. He was to meet them in nowhere but heaven – he was dying a slow and painful death...

The medic had made exhaustive tests. And the gloom that appeared on his face was enough to tell Elijah the results. The radiation – from some altered isotope unrecognised by either Elijah or the medic – had reached Elijah despite his wearing a radiation-proof suit and settled in Elijah's bones. There it was creating cellular changes and breakdowns that were surely, inevitably, killing him now.

"A month more." Elijah remembered the space medic saying, "Two at the most."

Time was now his most precious possession. Every minute gone was ✓ another step towards the day – soon now as the medic had said – when the pain would grow strong enough to batter down his control, when the radiation within him would overwhelm and quench his life.

Elijah began looking forward to the end – not only as a release from the pain. It would also release him from the memories that came to torment his

▶▶

nights, in which he relived the terrible day when he thought he was rushing to visit his planet and found he had come to join it only in death.

And it would release him from the despair which came with the growing realisation that the Galactic Empire was certainly falling. Hari Seldon's prediction was no joke. But afterall, who would think that such a powerful empire would disintegrate to rubble.

The flavour of that anticipation reached into the memory, filled it, changed it. For the first time in weeks, the surviving victim of the Empire's fall sank deeper into peaceful, undisturbed sleep, moving closer and closer towards his fate.

The fact was inescapable. It was that many more wars were happening, everywhere, than should have been happening. Entire solar systems were erupting with violence. A large industrialised planet would move suddenly and inexplicably attack a smaller, under-developed neighbour. Alternatively, two small planets came to invade – without clear cause – a third, and then after their victory fall out and fight between themselves. Elijah had witnessed it right before his very eyes. Hari Seldon had foreseen it. The Galactic Empire was falling. Its people had to *accept* it, as a religion is accepted. No sane human could deny it.

Teacher's comment

A* An effective short story – well written and making effective use of description. You capture and sustain the genre. Well done!

Examiner's analysis

There are some delightful phrases in the piece of imaginative writing which is a sophisticated piece of science-fiction writing. We could pick out so many but here is just one: 'the venomous reptiles of many weird shapes'. What is perhaps surprising is that the note at the beginning says that it is a first draft. Normally a second draft might have improved the vocabulary and one or two of the ideas might be reworked but there is no necessity for that here. This student understands science-fiction writing and can employ exactly the right tone.

PYGMALION
BERNARD SHAW

DISCUSS THE CHARACTERS OF ELIZA AND HIGGINS FROM BERNARD SHAW'S PLAY 'PYGMALION'. TRACE THE DEVELOPMENT OF THEIR RELATIONSHIP AND EXPLAIN HOW ELIZA AND HIGGINS FEEL ABOUT EACH OTHER AT THE END OF THE PLAY.

Professor Henry Higgins is the central male figure in Bernard Shaw's play 'Pygmalion'. He has an important role in the play and his character may be described as a complex one. Equally, Eliza Doolittle must be considered as the female central character and acts as a counterpart to Henry Higgins who is at the heart of this comedic drama. The mainspring of the comedy lies in the fact that this self-opinionated professor, who has the ability to correctly identify any accent from Selsey to Hoxton via Lisson Grove, has not the faintest idea about human thoughts and feelings – what goes on in peoples heads and heart. This is despite the fact that he has received the highest quality of education being a wealthy member of the landed classes and treated on the same footing as the aristocracy. In contrast to him, Eliza is an outcast from good society, a destitute flower girl. In the play, Professor Higgins is Pygmalion. Eliza Doolittle is the woman he creates and gives life to. As in the myth, Higgins creates a beautiful object out of crude raw materials, but the last great gift of a living soul is more than he has power to give by himself. These two conflicting characters (at first) are brought together by Shaw during 'torrents of heavy summer rain'. From this small scene the play grows. It is the seed from which the three-way relationship involving Higgins, Pickering, and Eliza Doolittle develops.

When Higgins boasts about how he could pass off a dirty, ignorant flower girl as a duchess at an ambassador's garden party, he has not the slightest idea of putting such a plan into execution. He is only using this particularly dramatic example to demonstrate what can be accomplished by applying the science of phonetics in a practical way. Henry Higgins, the hero of 'Pygmalion', is a professor of phonetics. That is, he is an expert on human speech sounds, the way they are produced, and the means by which they are perceived. He is so deeply involved in his work, his goal is to be 'the greatest teacher alive'. His work, which seems to be the only activity that brings him joy and satisfaction, is:

> 'Simply phonetics. The science of speech. That's my profession; also my hobby. Happy is a man who can make a living by his hobby.'

►►

Higgins has said that he could make her into a duchess – or, he adds ironically, even into a saleslady or a lady's maid, which requires better English. Eliza is not interested in becoming a duchess, but she would like to be a saleslady in a florist's shop, employment now impossible for her because of the way she speaks. As a result of Higgins' casual remark, Eliza presents herself at Higgins' house the next day to start lessons. She means to pay for them in a businesslike way.

Higgins' character is expertly outlined by Shaw in the brief scene with Eliza and Pickering. He is entirely unconcerned about Eliza's feelings. He shouts fiercely at her when her complaints start to annoy him. He refers to her as a 'squashed cabbage leaf'. His eloquence and his finer feelings are all reserved for the English language. When he speaks of it he becomes a passionate idealist saying to Eliza that:

> 'A woman who utters such depressing and disgusting sounds has no tight to be anywhere – no right to live. Remember that you are a human being with a soul and the divine gift of articulate speech: that your native language is the language of Shakespeare and Milton and The Bible; and don't sit there crooning like a bilious pigeon.'

To Higgins, English is not only the language of a noble literature, of Milton, Shakespeare and the King James Bible, but also the vehicle of man's humanity. Man has a soul, and his soul appears in his gift of speech. Thus, the English language is to Higgins a supreme spiritual treasure; he has no patience with those who do not treat it with the reverence it deserves.

Higgins is characterized so far as a man who has little understanding of human feelings, but whose comprehension in the field of his work is exceptional. Even Shaw himself comments explicitly on the fact that:

> 'He is, infact, but for his years and size, rather like a very impetuous baby'

Higgins certainly is like a small child and I strongly agree with this description of such a character – like an infant with a new toy as the idea of transforming Eliza takes hold of him. Again and again he unconsciously reveals that he does not think of Eliza as a human being with feelings. He orders her to be scrubbed and then wrapped in brown paper until her new clothes come, as though she were a doll or some other inanimate object.

▶▶

When Mrs. Pearce protests that she has no place to put Eliza, he tells her to put the girl in the dustbin. He does not mean this, of course, but it does show his flippant attitude. He also discusses her in a completely tactless way while she is in the room with him.

Yes! Henry Higgins, as Shaw portrays him, has many characteristics that we would find unattractive if we were to meet them in real people. He is rude and inconsiderate, even to harmless strangers like the Eynsford-Hills, when he meets them in his mother's drawing room. He acts as if other people have no feelings. We remember the way he talks about Eliza in Act II;

> 'She'll only drink if you give her money.'

He pays no attention to her vigorous protests, not to those of Pickering such as:

> 'Does it occur to you, Higgins, that the girl has some feelings?'

Thus Mrs. Pearce feels a heart-to-heart talk with Higgins is necessary if an impressionable young girl is to live in the house. This description reveals the vices of Higgins' character for first of all, his language is terrible. He swears constantly. It is interesting to note that Mrs. Pearce is not worried by his use of the word 'damn.' What she objects to is the adjective 'bloody.' In England it was (and is) considered offensively vulgar. Mrs. Pearce will not even permit the word to pass her lips. She refers to it indirectly, indicating that it begins with the letter 'b.' Of course, it is well known to Eliza; she has heard plenty of rough language in her lifetime. But she later learns new and better behavior; this will be almost impossible if Higgins uses bad language in front of her.

He is ruthless about getting his way, whether he has to do it by giving an exhibition of bad temper or by wheedling and coaxing and he answers Pickering's above protest by saying:

> 'Oh no, I don't think so. Not any feelings that we need
> bother about. [Cheerily] Have you, Eliza?'

an answer similar to all his responses to complaints. When he wants Eliza for his experiment, no obstacle stops him. Yet, in his description of Higgins, Despite his petulant nature, Shaw says that he:

> 'remains likeable even in his least reasonable moments.'

Furthermore, this is actually so. Higgins is appealing throughout the play, even when his ignorance of human feelings causes us to pity Eliza and feel angry towards him. This shows that Shaw has excellent control over his dramatic materials.

▶▶

Professor Higgins is also socially inept, not because he is unable to be otherwise, but because he does not know his own self sufficiently to be able to detect any error. When he meets resistance, Higgins resorts to coaxing and bribery. He promises Eliza chocolates, beautiful clothes and unlimited taxi rides. He invents fantasies in which men kill themselves for her and she marries the handsome heir of a noble family. (The young nobleman does not interest Eliza very much; the taxi rides are a real temptation.) He also coaxes Mrs. Pearce to let him have his way. He suggests casually that she can adopt Eliza as a daughter!

The main reason that Higgins remains appealing is that he means no harm. He is neither vicious nor cruel. His intentions are never evil, even when his behaviour is most unreasonable. Also, he himself does not realise how unreasonable he sometimes is. He sees himself as

> '. . . a shy, diffident sort of man. I've never been able to feel really grown up and tremendous, like other chaps. And there she is firmly persuaded [Mrs. Pearce] that I'm an arbitrary overbearing bossing kind of person. I can't account for it.'

Besides this, Shaw makes his bad temper and bad manners so extravagant that they are comical. His rudeness at his mother's 'at home' is an example of this. An excellent comic touch is the way Shaw turns upside down this meeting between mother and grown-up son. Whereas we would expect to see the mother passionately happy to see her child, and even perhaps reproachful that he has not come more often, Mrs. Higgins is horrified to see Henry show up on the day that she expects visitors. She reminds him that he promised not to come and urges him to go back home immediately. She says that:

> 'You offend all my friends: they stop coming whenever they meet you.'

Higgins paces up and down, fidgets, and bangs into the furniture. He is a disturbing element in his mother's gracious home. He abruptly breaks it to her that he has invited a flower seller to her 'at-home'. Higgins, however, is irritated at the Eynsford-Hills' arrival. He tries to get away, but his mother is too quick for him. She introduces him to Mrs. Eynsford-Hills and Clara. His irritation turns to despair when Freddy enters the room, for anyone can see that Freddy, though amiable, is not too bright. Higgins mumbles to himself:

> 'God of Heaven! another of them!'

►►

Higgins is annoyed simply because he hates aimless chatter with strangers. He treats them with spectacular rudeness, making no secret of their hopeless stupidity and his boredom. He is still appealing even now, for he does not realize what he is doing. His reactions are not unkind. To me, they display the innocence of a child on a visit who says: 'I don't like that lady! I want to go home!'

Yes, within this formal society.

To summarize, Shaw shows Higgins to be well meaning and entirely free from malice. His misbehavior is so unconventional as to be funny. And also, he feels pain, as well as inflicts it, when his own emotions become involved. For all these reasons, we find Higgins likeable throughout the play.

I believe that Higgins' faults are a result of him being too involved in his hobby, which results in him spending too much time dwelling on his experiments keeping him isolated from the outside world. With his time being occupied by teaching, the pronunciation of the English language, he is always in the position of the superior and I consider this to be the cause for his character's limitations – he is uninterested with the manners that are the key for starting and maintaining successful social relations. I am convinced that in this process, and only through it, has he developed an egotistic sense of his own importance since – he is often in interaction with people that beg for his knowledge of linguistics and pay large amounts for this or become the victims of his experiments. In both cases, it is this sense of superiority that I understand to have deprived him of the opportunity to develop virtuous manners. Finding no incentive in being kind and courteous, he has developed into a flamboyant, egocentric specialist in phonetics. However, excuses and exceptions can be made to him because he is seen by society as a personality who enjoys full and proper understanding of his field of study. He is referred to, by Miss Eynsford at Mrs. Higgin's house, as:

'Your celebrated son!' √

As is easily seen, 'Pygmalion' has a strong resemblance to the old fairy tale of Cinderella as well as to the Greek myth mentioned previously. Eliza Doolittle is a perfect embodiment of Cinderella. She begins as a lowly, dirty creature. Then her transformation takes place. She is clean. Fine clothes are bought for her. She exhibits the behavior of a duchess. Most important of all, her speech is changed. To Shaw, this is the most important part of the fairytale transformation from flower-seller to duchess, though the original fairy tale has nothing to say about it. At last, she becomes the sensation of a great ball, magnificent in fine clothes and jewels.

Teacher's comment

A* A long and very competent analysis of the key characters and their relationship. Your personal response which you revealed in class is evident. Your knowledge and enjoyment of this text shine through in every paragraph.

Examiner's analysis

The third piece, which is a response to literature, is a response to a massive question; you might say that it is a number of questions which have been put together. It is obvious that it is a very good piece of writing and it might give you something to aim at. If there is a fault, the original here was excessively long and we have not printed it all. The important thing is that the student is in control of the essay throughout, analysing the characters and their relationship with careful reference to the play, using quotations where they are appropriate.

Examiner's grading decision

The grade awarded for each piece, **A***, is indisputable. This coursework folder is exceptionally good and must be marked at 40 out of 40.

Coursework folder: Example 2

The three pieces submitted in this coursework folder are as follows:

- Factual piece: 'My Autobiography'
- Expressive piece: 'The Englishman'
- Free-choice piece: 'Animal Vivisection: A Cruel Science'

My Autobiography

First Draft

The Early Years (1983–85)

I was born on a sunny day in Keighley General Hospital, (Yorkshire, England) at 10:02pm on Friday, the First of July, 1983, weighing in at five pounds and eleven ounces and measuring nineteen and a quarter inches. According to my parents I had curly, jet black hair and deep azure-blue eyes, which is funny as I now have straight, straw-blonde hair and greyish-green eyes. I had long, thin arms and legs, so much so that my Mum used to call me her 'little spider; and I did not have a high-pitched cry like most babies, but a lamb-like 'bleat'.

My parents are both teachers at this school. My Mother, Jennifer Lees is from Manchester and was born on February the twenty-ninth, 1952 and is an artist currently teaching here at the Continental School as acting-head of Art and Design, and is the deputy Head of the upper School, so as you can imagine she's a pretty busy woman! Of my two parents, I am probably more similar to my Mother than my Father, and have been described as the 'male version' of her. My Dad's name is David Rogers and he is two days older than my Mum. He is a fully qualified Physical Education instructor who played county rugby, and

▶▶

represented Great Britain in athletics at the European Catholic Schools Championship before I was born, at which he met, and was presented with a medal by, Eamon De Valera, the first president of the Republic of Ireland, and is currently head of the Swimming department here at Conti.

Of the three months I lived in Yorkshire after I was born I remember very little, only the rolling hills of lush green grass, and that it was nearly always raining. Where I moved after Yorkshire was a stark contrast to the cool air and green grass of Yorkshire; it was Dhahran, Saudi Arabia, where my parents had been working for the past eight years. I spent about a year and a half in Dhahran, where my Dad was head Volleyball coach and Recreation Manager and my Mum was the Art Specialist, both at the UPM University. Something that always sticks in my mind about the time there was the humidity and the heat of the place, and how much like a big Desert the whole place was, and that it was so different to Yorkshire, replacing the green hills of grass with dusty-brown sand-dunes, and the cool air with the stick, almost nauseating humidity.

Another thing that I remember vividly was learning to swim, the hard way! It was during a weekend and we were out by the pool, my Mum was asleep and my Dad was messing around in the water with me. I had my arm-bands on and was perfectly happy just playing in the water, when my Dad asked my if I wanted to jump off the diving board. I said I did and so he took me over to the diving board, walked me to the top of the big one, and dropped me off! Now, bearing in mind that I was only one and bit, you can imagine my feeling of confusion as the entire world rushed up at me and I felt my armbands fly off! My Mother who had been watching me and thinking my Dad was taking my to the smaller diving board was surprised to see me floating there without my arm-bands, instantly panicked; yelling, 'what are you doing to him?' at my Dad. She then dived in and pulled me out of the water as soon as possible, and although it was a funny way to learn to swim, I never wore arm-bands again.

During the time spent in Dhahran my Mum and I developed a routine; everyday at about five o'clock, when it was cooler, we went down to the campus supermarket and did the shopping together. Mum would push me in my push-chair, facing away from her so I could see where I was going, while she was talking to me and shopping. Everyday she would buy me a little 'dinky' car from the checkout, some of which I still have in storage. Anyway, one day we were doing the usual, mum had paid and we had just left the shop, when she looked at me and saw that my pram was full of various cans and packages, which I must have picked up as we strolled down the shopping aisles! Well, after that incident she made sure that I hadn't picked up anything by the time we reached the checkout.

Over all I spent about two years in Dhahran and then we moved to a house in Spain.

A– Excellent!

Examiner's analysis

The factual piece of writing is straightforward; this is what makes it factual rather than expressive writing. Some of the sentences are rather tortuous in their construction, especially in the second paragraph. They are, however, under control and the corrections which the teacher makes are generally to put capital letters to titles, such as 'Upper School', which are not serious errors. The piece of writing fits the requirements of the syllabus but it is the weakest piece of writing. The student might well have done some more work on it, redrafting it before submitting it for marking. In a redraft he would have been able to change some of the sentences to make them more straightforward and would have been able to develop some of the ideas a little more.

The Englishman

Having spent the last six weeks of my life in these desolate trenches I feel that telling this story is my last stab at sanity after the suicidal attack on the German trench that has been the major focus of the last six weeks of my life.

I am Edward Molden, a soldier in the 3rd regiment of King George V's army, stationed on the French frontline. It is 1917 and we have been at war with the Hun for three years now. I was drafted last year and was transferred here six weeks ago, and the strange thing is that I still have no idea where I am, only that it is the north of France; I have heard mention that we are near Ypres, but no one is sure anymore. In the regiment to which I am assigned I have one friend with whom I am close, name Robert Paulson, or Bob for short. He and I have been together since basic training and I feel that he is the only one in this regiment who I believe I could trust my life to in this slow-moving, pointless war.

I will begin my story when Bob and I were transferred to this area of, I think, Ypres in which we are now stationed. My first view of the area was one of grim desolation; trees stripped bare by the impacts of shelling; land trodden underfoot, brown and muddy with quagmires littering the area of no-mans land that lay between us and the German trench; and the vast stretches of barbed wire, coiled around rotting corpses and bones, which were picked clean by rats, stretched as far as I could see. The damp, cold wind whipped my face and I could already smell death in the air. I saw what was left of the regiment we were replacing, the 5th I think, ambling, some limping, away from the trenches, coughing, cursing the Kaiser, the King and even God for bringing them to this terrible place. As we stepped off the train, behind me Bob mumbled something or other and I turned and faced him. He was almost as tall as me, with azure-blue eyes and short, black hair. He was a very handsome man, and thin before the war he had married a woman and had a child.

'God Eddy, look at this damn place! It's like a little slice of hell, right here on earth,' he said, frowning, 'and have you seen the troops we're replacing?' He shook his head; 'They're broken men.'

►►

I gazed out across the shell-shocked, the crippled, the maimed and felt for the first time, a deep sense of foreboding about this place.

We were quickly marched into the trenches, re-briefed on the 'Don'ts' of trench warfare: don't stick your head above the parapet; when on nightwatch don't light a cigarette; don't ever retreat until the order is given; and all the other orders we had heard a thousand times before. Soon we were off and setting up our sleeping quarters.

About four days after our arrival at the trenches, we experienced a gas attack and, although I remained unhurt, we lost four men, so replacements from other regiments were transferred to ours. On of the men transferred to our regiment was and Irishman named Patrick O'Flannery, a charismatic man; not the brightest I've known, but a good man, and some one who I got along with very well. He was of medium height with short, curly hair, and was well built. The most memorable thing about him was his strong Cork accent, which was mocked furiously by the rest of the regiment, but I found very endearing. Bob found his optimism towards life refreshing and was always laughing about the fact that he never stopped talking about 'after the war'.

It was about ten days after the arrival of the Irish troops and the rain had set in. The rain has always made me miserable and this was no exception. I thought of home, my friends who I has left behind, my house in Dorset and then remembered where I was; in some muddy trench, probably getting trench-foot in these cheap leather boots I was wearing, all around me people dying for a cause no-one cared about anymore.

We had been given the order to attack the German trench by the start of next week and were all busy preparing for the attack. In the days leading up to our charge on the Germans, there wasn't one of us who wasn't quaking in his boots at the thought of running out into the German machine-gunners' firing line. Over this time Patrick and I had become better friends and had constant conversations about everything. On the second day before the attack we were having one such conversation after Patrick had returned from the gun post:

'I tell ya Ed, I was looking t'rew that periscope over there, and I haven't seen that much dirt in all me life! It's like a nightmare, all them dead men, just rotting there, it ain't right!'

'I wonder how many,' Interrupted Bob.

'How many what?' I asked.

'How many have died so far?'

'It most be at least t'ree million,' guessed Patrick, 'But as long as I ain't one of them, it don't matter to me.'

'I tell you something though,' started Bob, 'I'm bloody worried about Monday; the attack'll be pure suicide; they've got machine guns you know.'

►►

'Yeah but as long as God's on our side, we'll get t'rough!'

Proclaimed Patrick, as optimistic as ever, and walked off to get some food from the mess.

Poor lad, I thought, doesn't know what he's in for . . .

This was it. Monday. The day we had all been dreading. As I stood waiting for the Sergeant to blow his whistle, thoughts of home raced through my mind: Would I make it out alive? What would happen to my friends? Would we be victorious? Before I could consider the outcome of these worries I heard the deafening whistle for attack and before I realised what was happening I was over the parapet, screaming at the top of my lungs and charging towards the Hun. I saw a spray of bullets come out of the German trench and watched five of my allies drop to the ground in agony, clutching their chests as they fell. To my right were Bob and Patrick, both making good ground, dodging machine gun fire and various explosions. Patrick was making particularly good ground and was almost on top of a machine gun post, with a grenade in his hand as he approached the panicking German. He raised his arm, threw the grenade, blowing up the post and gunner. Just as he began to slow his pace and dodge another blast of machine gun fire, he disappeared in a flash of smoke and an almighty bang. He had stepped on a landmine and been blown apart right before my eyes. I slowed to a stop and, frozen with horror, stood motionless trying to make sense of what had just happened.

I suddenly felt a powerful jarring of my shoulder and the world became a blur as I slammed into the wet, muddy ground with a thud. When I regained vision I saw Bob's familiar face, looking panicked with a stream of bullets whizzing above his head. He had seen me get shot and rushed to my aid, dragging me into the shell hole in which we were now hiding.

'We've gotta get out of here Ed!' he said in a frantic tone, 'The Hun's killed most of the regiment and they're still shooting at us! I think we'll have to wait until it's dark and then crawled back, ok?'

I mumbled some attempt at recognition and threw up, the pain in my shoulder making me sick. I felt my eyes becoming heavy and then lost consciousness.

All I can remember of the four or so hours in which we took getting back to the trench, dodging sniper fire and hiding in shell holes, was a deep sense of gratitude that I felt for Bob, who was carrying me back to the trench on his back. When I came to I was lying on my back in a stretcher in this trench with Bob by my side.

'The train I'll be here in a couple of hours,' started Bob, 'then you should be ok. I heard talk that the Hun was badly hit during the attack and they're launching a counter offensive, with the 9th regiment' he continued, his face suddenly looking very worried again, 'and me; along with what's left of this one . . .'

A- Lovely! well done!

Examiner's analysis

The imaginative writing, possibly a response to having read some First World War poetry, is good. There is an understanding of the atmosphere in the trenches and a feel for the characters involved. They seem real and might well have behaved in the ways suggested. When you are creating a character, it is so important that the reader can believe that this is a real person. The speech, including the lines written in dialect, works well. There is some nice phrasing including, 'the world became a blur as I slammed into the wet, muddy ground with a thud.' One thing which is shown once or twice here is the importance of proofreading if you choose to word-process your work; there are several careless typing errors.

Animal Vivisection: A Cruel Science.

Animal Vivisection is an under-publicised, yet widespread problem about which something must be done. I will begin with the UCLA's 'spinal research centre' in California. I ask you to imagine yourself as a fifteen-month-old cat; you are in an underground lab along with hundreds of other cats. Your back has been crushed violently by lead weights, your entire body has been shaven, and electrodes have been implanted in your head and tail. You have just been subjected to twin blasts of hot air to your face and electric shocks to your paws and tail. You are in for 119 more before you are finally put out of your misery, if you don't die from the electric torture first.

This is called the 'fear test'; the electrodes monitor a current passed trough the cats' spines and monitor the response from the brain and change in heart rate throughout the experiment. These experiments have been going on for many years now and yet there is still no evidence that they have any connection with treating human back pains.

Other examples of this torture are in uncounted labs across the world where cruel and heartless experiments are being carried out by doctors on rats, dogs, cat, rabbits and even our closest relatives in the animal kingdom; monkeys. For the rats there is 'the maze'; an experiment where a rat is placed in a maze at the end of which are two doors, behind one, a piece of cheese, behind the other, a wire giving an electric shock. You can imagine the results when the rat finds the wire. This is bad enough, but what happens then the doors are switched? Or when there is a shock behind both doors? The poor rats are eventually driven mad, or die from shock. Dogs and cats have medical drugs tested on them, sometimes resulting in great sickness or even death. This experiment is pointless anyway as dogs and cats have differing reactions to that of humans regarding medicines. An example of this is the drug Paracetamol which has healing properties to humans but is lethal to dogs! Monkeys are being subjected to tests in relation to smoking, usually developing lung cancer, or tar lined lungs, eventually killing them. The saddest thing about these experiments is that most of

▶▶

them go unpublished, so even if the results were relevant, they are never released to the public, so the same experiments are repeated over and over again.

In the cosmetic world, make-up is tested on animals such as pigs and rabbits. Make-up found to be corrosive usually dissolves an animal's face before they are removed. Hairspray is sprayed up Rabbits' noses to find out if it is harmful to the sinuses; those that are usually result in sneezing, causing convulsions so great that they break the animal's back.

My request to those reading this article is this: Please think on these examples of cruelty to animals, and the pointlessness of most of them, the very fact that we are a different species to those we are testing OUR products on, and take action to ban Vivisection world-wide. A positive example of people taking action to halt the pain caused on animals is the recent banning of the sale of fur taken from slaughtered animals, and if we just follow this example, and remember that it was on the request of everyday people that brought about this banning, we can bring the cruelty of Animal Vivisection to an end.

Teacher's comment

A- Well argued! A powerful catalogue of examples to shock the reader! Your 'introduction' reads rather like the opening paragraph of the body of the essay – this is the only weakness in the piece.

Examiner's analysis

The first question you might ask about the piece on animal vivisection is whether it is suitable to be included in the coursework submission. It is a piece of factual writing and would have been perfectly OK as the first piece. It can, however, be accepted as piece three because it is a real contrast to the piece of autobiography. It is clearly a subject about which the student feels strongly and he writes well. There are again occasional typing errors which ought to have been corrected.

Examiner's grading decision

This is not a very easy folder to grade as the quality is not even. The second piece is the strongest and it has to be balanced against the piece of autobiography which is the weakest. The strengths mean that we are looking at a high grade and it is very much on the borderline of A/B. It goes into the top of the **B grade** with a mark of 35.

Coursework folder: Example 3

The three pieces submitted in this coursework folder are as follows:

- Factual piece: 'Water Safety'
- Expressive piece: 'Zoo Story'
- Free-choice piece: 'What would you say Eliza and Higgins feel about one another at the end of the play . . .'

Water Safety

Ladies and Gentlemen, have you ever wondered about the dangers of swimming? As we all know, a swimming pool is a classic source of rest and relaxation during a hot day. A pool can also be a prime source of danger. Many children drown while swimming every year. A child's risk of drowning is much greater than most people like to think. Some amazing statistics show that children under the age of five are fourteen times as likely to die while in a pool than in a motor vehicle. To me that figure is absolutely astonishing and these deaths must be prevented. Children are not the only ones that fall victim to the pool, anyone can have accidents in and around the pool.

If you are in a swimming pool, do not let children run around the pool edge or they could slip over and fall causing severe injuries to themselves or others. It is dangerous to jump into the pool. Check first that there are no swimmers in the area. It is a dangerous act to duck and dunk people in the pool because it can destroy their confidence as a swimmer. Think about the other swimmers and try not to collide with them. If you do not look where you are going, especially if you are using equipment, you can hurt someone.

Style

If your children are in or around the pool, someone needs to be watching them at all times. You can <u>never</u> ensure that <u>no one</u> will need assistance or help while in the pool but you can take the responsibility and the proper precautions to assure that if someone does need assistance, they are able to receive help rapidly and efficiently. Some of these precautions are as follows: place a fence around the pool, or cover the top of the pool when it is not in use. This has reduced the risk of drowning by 70 percent in some areas around the world. You as the responsible adult must remain vigilant by constantly watching your children while they are in the pool. Most deaths are due to the fact that the children panic and as they try to yell for help, water is swallowed and as they try to cough up the water, they swallow more. As a result they are not able to be heard and will sadly drown. According to past personal experience, children can not be

▶▶

left alone even for you, as the adult, to go and answer the door. Anyone taking care of children that are in the water should know Cardiopulmonary Resuscitation or CPR and should be prepared to use it in an emergency.

We must learn to become our own lifesavers and should always prepare for emergencies. For example, mark the pool's deep end; place a circular buoy on a rope, a long handled hook and a rescue ladder at the poolside. You should also have a poolside telephone with emergency phone numbers posted next to it because it is both a convenience and a critical safety feature.

Some essentials that you need to know are getting into the water when the depth is unknown and while wearing clothing, how to undress and remove heavy articles of clothing while keeping the light ones on, and know how to swim or float in clothing. A few more precautions that should be taken are to teach your children not to panic when they are in and around the pool. They should know when to yell for help, and to be patient and cooperate to the person trying to help them. Teach them how to stay erect with their head clearly above the water.

Say you see a person yelling for help, do you think it is safe for you to jump into the water to save them? In these situations, you cannot follow your instincts and instead, you must use your head. If you jump in after someone, it could result with both of you in extreme trouble. This is because of the panic factor. Every human being, when in trouble, start panicking. When people panic, they can not control their actions and two out of three end up hurting the person that is trying to save them. If it is possible to reach the person from the side of the pool, do it. Find anything, like a plank or a beach ball, which could be used as a floatation device. Give help by voice and tell the person who needs help to keep his or her arms under the water and not to struggle. Stay aware of the situation all the time because statistics show that many people drown within ten metres of safety. Helping someone calm down may save a life.

It is impeccable that the safety precautions that were explained are not only taken notice of but they must be put into action as well. This information has not been given to you to scare you, but on the contrary, it has been given to you to ensure that your time in the pool is made more fun because now you know that you and your children are safe.

Examiner's analysis

The factual piece of writing states clearly situations which can exist around and in a swimming pool. The tone is good in that it remains serious and clear. However the material is not as well ordered as it might be and is a little repetitive. There are also errors of expression and the occasional clumsiness. There is some misspelling.

Zoo Story

Synopsis

Mr. Moni, the head keeper of a small zoo in Zimbabwe, is drinking again. Mr. Moni is a tall, old, and always grumpy man. He has been the keeper of the zoo for about 25 years, as long as any of the animals can remember. He also has a tradition in which he gets drunk each and every evening on his night shift at the zoo. He mistreats all of the animals, especially when he is drunk and because of this all of the animals hate him. He loves to terrorize the animals when he is drunk and he likes to pick on one in particular every night. Her name was Jennifer and she is a ten-year-old chimpanzee with extreme intelligence. Jennifer is liked by all that see her because she the famous monkey who has been taught to eat with a fork and knife.

After two weeks of observing the actions of Mr. Moni, Jennifer formulated a plan to rid the entire animals of human oppression forever. She called a meeting of all of the animals and explained he plan to them. They were all excited to rid themselves of the humans they hated so much and were anxious to get the plan underway. The plan was every night a different animal would take turns distracting Mr. Moni while Jennifer used the one tool that had access to, her knife, to cut the bars of her cage. Their plan worked well because of Mr. Moni's reliability.

After two weeks of this every night, Jennifer finished her work. She, Alex and Suhail escaped from their cage and freed the bear, the lion and the tiger so that they would be able to attack Mr. Moni. That night, it was Bijan, the parrot's turn to distract Mr. Moni. Mr. Moni however had a different idea and was desperately trying to hit Bijan with a tick he had acquired from a nearby tree. Jennifer and the others came up behind Mr. Moni without making a sound and attacked him before he knew what was going on. Finally, Claire, the bear, carried him behind some bushes and that is where Mr. Moni screamed his last scream.

Chapter 1

After the death of Mr. Moni, all the animals were freed and they all celebrated until Alex said, "Friends, we still have one more minor problem. What about the other keeper, Mr. Salman? He starts work at seven."

Then Jennifer said, "Don't worry, we will be ready for him. I've got another plan."

For the remainder of the night the animals assembled everything that they would need to destroy Mr. Salman. At seven o'clock the

▶▶

following morning, Mr. Salman entered the zoo. He started his usual rounds of the zoo when he realized that there was no animal in any of the cages. To his shock, he was the only one in sight. In a panic he began to run back to the office to call Mr. Moni. Just as he turned the last corner before the office he skidded to a halt. He was frozen stiff. All of the animals were in front of him in a barricade. They all just stood there and stared at him. He saw the red in their eyes and could not move a muscle. Suhail swung to the gate and made absolutely certain that it was licked securely. Mr. Moni and Mr. Salman were hung on the outside of the gate as an example and a sign of the animals' new found independence.

Jennifer, after much effort, quieted the group of animals and said, "We have just taken a great step to the independence of this zoo and I am extemely proud of each and everyone of you, but, we still have one complication, Mr. Amin will be very upset."

Mr. Amin is the rich owner of the zoo. Jennifer continued, "Soon he will be receiving a lot of questions and complaints about the status of the zoo. He will most definitely come to see what is going on in here. The problem is that it is impossible to tell when he will come or whom he will bring with him, so we must be prepared at all times. You might be asking yourself how we are going to eat and live but do not worry, Bijan has been sent to search for the storage room. There will be a truckload of food coming every month but Mr. Amin can not know about this. If he does, he will put a stop to it and we will starve."

Chapter 2

Two weeks passed and the storage room was found. The animals did nothing but playing around and having fun. The animals were able to come and go to eat whenever they were wanted. Jennifer was extremely reserved as she stayed in her cage most of the time and she kept to herself. No one except Suhail understood Jennifer very well and this is how she liked to keep it. Suhail and Alex were spending a tremendous amount of time together.

One day, the two animals that were lookouts spotted Mr. Amin on his way to the zoo. They went and warned the rest of the animals. As Mr. Amin approached the gate, he spotted the two dead bodies, screamed and ran to his car.

Three days later, the animals spotted him again but this time six vans, two police cars and a fire engine followed him into the parking lot. The vans had painting on the side that read 'ANIMAL CONTROL'. People were getting out of the vehicles with all kinds of weapons.

▶▶

The animals saw them coming so they all decided to hide in the storage room. That way, they would have all of the food and water they would need for a long time. Most of the animals had never seen a gun before therefore they did not there was any reason to be scared. Jennifer's plan was to wait until Mr. Amin and others opened the storage door and the animals would attack them with all of their brute strength. The men arrived and they flung open the door, more the one hundred animals came running out of the door trampling half of the men. Some of the men turned and ran away while others stayed and began shooting.

During this tragic battle only 35 animals survived and half of the food was destroyed, along with most of the zoo. If there was a second attack on the zoo, the animals would not stand a chance against the attackers. The animal did not celebrate after their first great battle because of the deaths of their fellow animals, including Alex and Claire.

Bijan was sent to other zoos around the country to inform them of their continued success. A few months past and Jennifer and Suhail spent more time together and fell in love. Everyone else were enjoying themselves immensely, just eating and sleeping. All of the animals new Mr. Amin would come back and that he would bring others with him so they were making the most of the time they had left.

This is the beginning of my story. The rest of the main events in the story are listed below.

1. Two years past and Jennifer was the leader of the zoo.
2. There was a shortage of food so she decided to put rations.
3. The zoo got very dirty so the animals had to work and clean the place up.
4. Two months past and there was no electricity and there was not a lot of food left.
5. The other larger animals did not treat Bijan very well so he became very angry and decided to leave.
6. Bijan told the other zoos of their situation and that the animals will not last long.
7. Some other zoos started to help them and sent them some gifts like little scraps of food.
8. Now the animals in the zoo do not have food, electricity or any connection to other zoos.
9. Suhail and many other animals were getting old and were very sick. They knew they would not be able to survive another attack from Amin.

▶▶

10. Suhail died and Jennifer lost all her hope and thought it was not worth living anymore.
11. Two weeks later Amin came in with an army of men. The animals, including Jennifer, ignored them and did not even try to fight. All the animals were caught. Some of them were slaughtered or sold. Jennifer was about to be sold to an English family but one day she was found dead.
12. Amin decided to reopen the zoo.
13. Two new monkeys were placed in Jennifer's cage and they saw a crossed out note carved in the wall. It was from Jennifer saying 'If anyone sees this, always remember not to give up and always have faith in yourself, even if there is not a big chance in achieving your goal. My goal was to become free from this zoo and I did not have a big chance but at the end, I achieved it.'

Examiner's analysis

'Zoo story' works quite successfully, although it rather lacks substance in its middle section; we don't get much idea about how the animals live and the idea of a regular delivery of food continuing with Mr Amin not realising he is paying for it is not very successful. There are errors, although some of them may be the result of failing to proofread.

What Would You Say Eliza And Higgins Feel About One Another At The End Of The Play, And As A Result Of Shaw's Writing, Where Do Your Sympathies Lie?

The relationship between Eliza and Higgins changes drastically throughout the play and goes from bad to worse in the last scene. Higgins feels that Eliza has finally grown up, she is 'a tower of strength' by the end of their conversation and refuses to be put down by Higgins bullying. She finally gains some respect from Higgins. As she absorbs that little bit of respect she gains even more strength and has an obvious advantage over Higgins. Higgins becomes infuriated and strikes Eliza, she caused him to lose his temper and not many people have been able to accomplish that. Eliza has made a decision to leave Wimpole Street and this maddens Higgins beyond words. Higgins has learned to rely on Eliza as she does everything and anything for him, he also says that he enjoys her presence because of her appearance. When Eliza announces her engagement to Freddy, Higgins calls him a fool. Eliza now has the ability to change her mood whenever she feels like it and she does, Higgins tells her not to play the game he taught her with him. Eliza says goodbye and leaves.

▶▶

By the end of the play, Eliza has lost her independence and could never return to her old way of life. Higgins and especially Pickering have spoiled her and after their success at the ball, she realizes this. She says,

> 'You know I can't go back to the gutter, as you call it, and that I have no real friends in the world except you and the colonel.'

In other words, she is saying that she has no where else to go and that she does not want to remain on Wimpole Street. She wants Higgins to give her a solution to her problem and when he does not she becomes frantic. Higgins offered to adopt her or for her to marry Colonel Pickering but she refused both offers. She can not marry Pickering because of the fact that he is to old for her. Higgins feels that he has the right to tell her what to do and to make decisions for her. This is because he paid her father, Mr. Doolittle, five pounds. He feels that she is his and she can not leave whenever she wants and so when she does he is furious.

If Eliza married Higgins, she would most probably end up alone or being ignored by him. Eliza is still young and attractive so she does not feel any pressure to get married and she feels that she will not have any trouble finding a husband. Eliza follows her instinct and decides not to marry Higgins. This is because he invests all of his love in his mother and phonetics and he has no love left for a woman in his life.

Eliza decides that she is going to marry Freddy. She bases this decision on the fact that he likes her and will treat her as an equal instead of like a servant, and this is all Eliza wants out of life. To Higgins, Eliza will always be a flower girl from the gutter; he will never look at her on the same level he is. Higgins' mother, in his eyes, is perfect and his problem is that he always compares the women that he meets to his mother. This is why he will always remain a bachelor. Eliza needs someone that will respect her as a person but also she needs to have more control in the relationship. Another reason why she decides to marry Freddy is because he is a weaker person than Eliza and he needs her to be there for him as well. Eliza is a very strong person and so she would search for all the other qualities in a partner but strength and she finds this in Freddy. She would

> "look forward to a lifetime of fetching Higgins' slippers or to a lifetime of Freddy fetching hers."

All Eliza ever wanted from Higgins was a little bit of respect and for him to treat her as a normal lady. She wanted Higgins to change her to a lady but all he could do is teach her how to speak like a lady. He can not teach how to act like a lady because he was not able to treat her like one.

▶▶

Since she was never treated in that way she could never feel like a lady and so she could not act like one. She went to Higgins in the first place because she was trying to improve her lifestyle by obtaining an education. She actually got a large lesson about life. She learned that it takes more then being able to speak in an amiable manner to move up in the world, money also plays a major role in life.

Higgins shows Eliza two choices that she has to choose from and he has set opinions about both. The two options that he sees are one, to come back and live with Higgins and Pickering and if she stays with Higgins, he thinks they can grow old together and she will live comfortably without a care in the world, except for his. The other option is to go live with Freddy and if she that, then she will probably end up supporting him for the rest of his life and will not have the same luxuries as she would on Wimpole Street. Eliza's reaction is that of complete shock, she explains to Higgins that if she continues to live with him she will never be truly happy because she will always be treated as if she is a flower girl, he will never see her as anything more than that. If she marries Freddy she will live with someone who truly loves and respects her as a lady and not just some girl off of the street. Even to this point in the conversation Higgins still has not learned to respect Eliza for all that she has become.

Higgins has taught her all of his secrets about the English language and when Eliza threatens to marry Freddy and teach Phonetics she hurts and angers him. Higgins believes that Freddy is a fool to begin with but when Eliza begins to see him as a potential husband Higgins does not believe that Freddy would be able to support her, let alone make her happy. He does not want lose his experiment. Instead, he wants to show off his work to the rest of the world.

Eliza's transformation from a flower girl on the streets to a refined lady has allowed her to be able to change her moods effortlessly. She can go from being hysterical to being elegant and refined in a matter of seconds. When Eliza realizes that she has found Higgins' weak spot she uses it against him to make him even madder. As soon as this happens she becomes "a tower of strength" against Higgins and refuses to be put down by any thing that he might say. All of a sudden, she becomes the more dominant of the two and so there is no turning back for her now. She will never look back on her time spent at Wimpole Street. She is determined to move on with no restrictions to hold her down from obtaining her goals.

Higgins reacts violently to Eliza's defiance of him and so decides that if she wants she can marry Colonel Pickering. This new suggestion shows that he has no understanding of her and has learned nothing

▶▶

about her character in the last six months. He does not care what is best for her he just wants Eliza to come back so she can watch over him. Eliza can not make Higgins understand why she must leave so she only tells him that she must.

As soon as Mrs. Higgins re-enters the scene Eliza becomes a dignified lady again, she has obtained the ability to switch her anger on and off from Higgins. She not only has learned how to speak but also when and what to speak about. Higgins finds the instantaneous change of behaviour and he tries to investigate another argument by giving her some orders. She turns around and gives him the answers to most of his orders with grace and then says.

"What you are to do without me I cannot imagine."

Higgins' final reaction is just to laugh at her because she has just shown her first bit of being an upper class women by being a bit of a snob. Eliza chooses Freddy because he will love her the way she wants, with respect and he will treat her with dignity. Higgins just laughs at the whole situation, he finds it extremely amusing.

In conclusion my sympathies lie with Eliza because of the position that she has been forced into by Higgins' teachings when, Higgins knew the consequences of his actions. Higgins did not think twice about what was going to happen to Eliza after he was finished with her. Eliza is now caught between the two classes and there is nothing she can do about it. She does not want to go back to selling flowers on the street but the upper class will not accept her because she does not have any social status or any money. This means that Eliza is not accepted into any one part of the city and so will end up being an outcast. She will probably never be an accepted part of the upper class and she understands this but she does not know where to go or how to behave.

Examiner's analysis

The third piece is a response to literature, and knowledge of the play *Pygmalion* and the characters is shown. The essay is not as well ordered as it might be and there is a substantial amount of repetition. Some people would disagree with some of the points made but this does not matter as the essay is being assessed here for the quality of the writing, not the ability to analyse literature.

Examiner's grading decision

This coursework clearly meets the requirements of the syllabus well. The writing is competent but there are weaknesses. Overall this folder is assessed in the *C Grade* range with a mark of 26.

■ Further examples of coursework pieces

Example of a factual piece: looking at the process of getting a job as office secretary

This piece consisted of four items related to a successful job application: the advert (below), the letter of application and CV (pages 183–184), a reference letter (page 185) and a letter from the candidate to a friend (page 186).

SECRETARY REQUIRED FOR RELIANCE AGENCIES

Responsibilities: Answering phone calls, typing using electric typewriter, faxing, telexing, computing and other basic secretarial skills.

Necessary Qualifications: A typing speed of 90 words per minute, and a shorthand speed of 110 words per minute. Familiarity with an IBM computer system would be an advantage.

Terms of Appointment: A salary of K2000 per month (excluding bonus), working days Mon–Fri, 8.30am to 6.30pm. One month paid holiday. A company car will be provided. Benefits include a sickness scheme and insurance. You will be trained on an upgrading scheme while you are at the job. You will be working in a modern spacious office.

Closing date for receipt of completed applications is 18th May 2002.

For further details and application form, please write to Mr Peter Green, Appointments Officer, Chayamba Building, PO Box 123, Lilongwe. Tel: 654 321 123 456.

PO Box 277
Lilongwe
Malawi
Telephone: 987654

19th April, 2002

Appointment's Officer
Chayamba building
PO Box 123
Lilongwe Malawi

Dear Mr Green,

I would like to apply for the post of secretary, which I saw advertised in the 'Daily Times' on 18th April 2002.

I am a single, but intend to get married in two years. I am 22 years old. I have a typing speed of 50 words per minute, and a shorthand speed of 110 words per minute. I have passed 8 GCSE's and 3 'A' levals. I have my own IBM computer, and fully know how to operate it.

I am applying for this job as I wanted a higher salary, than my previous job. Also your office is idealy situated for me as I live 3 minutes away from Chayamba building.

I have worked at ICI for 3 years and enclose a referance from the Manager and from my headmaster.

Yours sincerly,

S------- T--------

CV

Name: S------- T--------

Address: PO Box 277, Lilongwe, Malawi

Telephone number: 987654

Date of Birth: 14th February 1980

Nationality: British Citizen

School's Attended: Central Secondary School, Speed typing school Lilongwe, Shorthand School Lilongwe.

Exam Results: (GCSE) 4 A's, 3 B's, 1 C ('A' level) 3 B's, typing school certificate: 50 word's per minute, shorthand certificate: 110 words per minute.

Experience: Further on the job training for 3 years with IBM, Blantyre. Office Secretary at ICE for 3 years

References: Headmaster of school, Manager of ICI

The Headmaster
Central School
P.B. 999
Lilongwe

20th April, 2002

Appointments Officer
Chayamba Building
PO Box 123
Lilongwe

Dear Mr Peter Green

This is a letter of Reference to S------- T--------, who has applied
for the job of a secretary.

S------- has achieved high grades in his exams, and has done well
in his academic school career. Although at times his standards did
drop; he just needed a push to come back up again. When he first
came to the school, he did not display a mature and sensible
approach towards his studies. However after his seven year stay at
Central, he has developed a serious attitude, and shows promising
performance in the future.

When it came to sports, S------- was not too keen, but later on he
did participate in team sports such as tennis and cricket. Although
he did not exeed on the field, S------- won several awards on
weight lifting.

S------- is a polite and well manerred boy.

I have enclosed his last Report and period work order book.

Yours sincerly

A.B. Davies

PO Box 277
Lilongwe
Malawi
Telephone: 987654
Office: 456789
3rd June, 2002

Dear Mark,

Yo! Mark, you know that job you told me to apply for? Well thats what I did, and guess what? I got it! The company first changed my place, so I'm going to be moving into the new house soon. They are still trying to organise a car for me. I should be coming over to South Africa soon for a month's paid holiday.

Anyway when I first went to work, I met this really friendly man. He showed me my office, and how to operate the fax, telex and the typewriter. I have one of those phones where I just transfer the call to whoever the caller wants, it's like a switchboard. When I received my first caller for the Manager, by mistake I sent it to the general manager but still they weren't too angry about it, because they know I'm new. Every half an hour this man comes from all the offices to give me letters to type, or put on the computor, or the fax machine, so I try to do all that in half an hour before the next lot come's in. It's difficult so I asked him to come every 45 minitus. If I still can't finish it. I take it home. At the Lunch Break, everyone was asking me how I was getting on. After lunch 2.00pm to 3.00pm I get a special training course. After this I carry on with the usual routine. I finish the work and go home.

They really work hard here!
your mate,

S-------

Examiner's analysis

The work is well structured and there is enough content to fit it for its purpose. There is variety of style. Spelling is not good: 'levals', 'referance', 'sincerly', 'computor'. Maybe this task would not easily show evidence to justify a grade A, but it is confident enough for mid **C Grade**, despite the errors.

Example of an 'expressive' piece: Diary entry on *Gregory's Girl*

This is an interesting example of a coursework item because it was submitted as the 'expressive piece' but in fact was not suitable for inclusion under that category: it is more appropriate for the 'free choice' category – as pointed out in the examiner's comment.

2nd November

Dear diary,

Life . . . is a disaster! Maybe I should go drown myself in my bathtub; or even since there are three steps leading to our garden I should jump off the very top to commit suicide. I think I'll use up some of my cornflakes to make my mum a pair of earrings! I am so fed up?! I used to enjoy football so much but now it's all becoming a drag. It's just the same old thing over and over again. Me mates feel the same way too. So now we are just not enthusiastic about playing, so we end up loosing matches and the coach goes bonkers when this happens!

Maybe I should just hold out on playing since I think I'm the best player on the team, he'll come pleading for me to play on the team! I'll set him some conditions and those are I want new recruitments! Yeah! That's what I'll do.

7th November

Dear diary,

I think the idea of not playing football went a bit too far. I've been doing it for about a week now and today coach came and told me in more complicated parables than in the Bible . . . that History repeats itself and King Louis has been threatened to be abdicated if he refuses to meet up to terms set. It was not until now that I realise he was implying that he would remove me from the team if I went on the way I was behaving.

He didn't even seem sorry about the idea of loosing me! We are having trials tomorrow to see who stays on the team. I don't think I care.

9th November, 8 am

Dear diary,

Oh what the heck . . . cut the formalities . . . I am stressed, and I want to stay on the team. I have my pride I will not cry! If anything he should be the one begging for me to stay and not the other way around. Who needs who more?

On second thoughts I am scared . . . heck . . . I can't find my boxers! Will I have to go play with a loose third leg? OK, I'm going now with my boxers!

10 pm

Dear diary,

Check this out, the coach didn't let me try out because he said I wasn't in proper gear for try outs! I can't believe it. To make it even worse, this other girl (she's beautiful) anyway she walked onto the field like she owned the world and when asked what she was doing . . . she said that she was there for try outs! The nerve of her . . . Can't she see she's a girl? Me and the boy's will show her whose job it is to play football and whose it is to stay at home! Just wait n' see.

▶▶

13th November

Dear diary,

Oh dear, for a moment I thought I was dining at the horses stables. Today I saw a fly playing in my football in my saucer, I went to ask her why this was so and she said it was practising for world cup?! OK jokes aside . . . That girl is in my geometry class. She acts like a miss 'know it all.' Oh the nerve! She just has to have an answer for everything. Why if she were a boy, I'd knock her head in! Can't stand her!

15th November

Dear diary,

Today was the day pigs flew because I passed her in the corridor today, I thought she would snob me. But she actually said hello! She's not as bad as I thought. She's quite nice. I found out her name is Dorothy.

17th November

Dear diary,

Her name is like a magical note tinkering in spring time air. We had a practise as a football team and she plays absolutely beautifully. I think I'm in love with her but I won't let her know it. Can't have it this way with me having a girl in the football team. I'm the man around here.

20th November

Dear diary,

I've decided I can't stand the thought of my mates laughing at me because of Dorothy, even though I heard she likes me too! But I like her sooooo much!!!!

22nd November

Dear diary,

Dorothy came and asked me if we could go out on a date. I nearly died! I wanted so much to say yes but I just acted like a total jerk and I actually told her to make like a bee and buzz off! Why? I was with my friends and there they were sniggering their heads off. I wanted to look macho for my friends so I ignored her. She looked at me then walked off! I messed up?! So have I lost her forever? What a schmuck I am what will I do? Maybe I'll send her this poem:

> I know a girl and Dorothy was her name,
>
> Since I met her I've never been the same,
>
> Because I love my Dorothy, please understand me

23rd November

Dear diary,

I gave her the poem today and she asked me if we could go out for lunch and talk. We went to a cafe down the street and there they gave us these rolls of towels to wipe our hands (I found out later) so I took mine and bit, thinking it was a spring roll. Dorothy just laughed. I was so embarrassed, but we ended up laughing about it and we got along well that day.

►►

27th November

Dear diary,

Andy came over. Andy the randy dandy. He just went on about this woman he had spied on in the shower . . . Is that love for him? I guess in his on way. But what I feel for Dorothy is remarkable! Billy who is a close mate of mine told me to go easy on things. I like Billy, he's old and seems to know what he's doing in life. I trust him.

30th November

Dear diary,

Some wretched young boy came today feeling so sure of himself, to ask Madelaine for a walk. My sweet sister is still too young to be dating. So I put the guy off and told him to get lost and go play with toy's or something. Now I feel guilty, I mean if two of them are in love who am I to stop them? No one's stopping me and I'm in love with Dorothy.

1st November

Dear diary,

Billy gave me a tip off for my date last night. In the beginning it was a disaster. Billy had told me that I should be aggressive as Dorothy seemed pretty independent and if she could join the football team she could pay for her own supper.

So I acted everything of the aggressive male date. We got our table and she stood there, like she waiting for me to pull out the chair, but I didn't instead I sat down and began to order. She gave me a puzzled look then followed suit. We received our orders and proceeded to eat in silence. Our first date had already gotten off to a bad start.

I decided to heck with Billy's advice. Halfway through the meal I apologised to her, then we began to talk like nothing had happened. Our date turned out very well . . . we're so comfortable with each other.

I'm happy we got together and my mates don't even make noise about the two of us!

Examiner's analysis

This is really a piece of re-creative writing and should come under 'Free choice'. Very difficult to mark because of inconsistencies of style and content. It starts very well, dwelling over the initial matters of concern and fitting them together interestingly. The language is varied but does give examples of interesting usage ('that history repeats itself' . . . 'Oh, what the heck . . . cut the formalities'). Then the entries become shorter and the candidate begins to follow the narrative events of *Gregory's Girl* more slavishly. The reader is less engaged at this point. There are stylistic oddities ('threatened to be abdicated . . .', 'meet up to terms set'). Again, there is little error. *Grade C*

Example of a free-choice piece: The process of writing a poem

As a contrast, this sample is a 'free-choice' piece which is completely different. It shows an approach to the use of the candidate's own poetry which is interesting and very successful.

Planning Poem One

Most of my good poetry requires a bit of sitting back and relaxing, thinking long and hard about what I really want to say. As with most writing, one idea sparked another in my mental process. Originally, I had heard the quote, 'I have no proof that God does not exist, but I rather He not,' by an atheist. The very fact that this man said that he has no proof is saying that God does indeed exist! Here he is unwisely contradicting himself and in my opinion, making himself seem very ignorant. Thinking that there is no God does *not* mean He doesn't exist. A human can not control that. God is God and that's final no matter what humans have to say.

From this quote, I had the idea to use other quotes said by famous people in a poem *about* God. This was done through research on the Internet. A man had set up a website about Albert Einstein. There were about fifty quotes that he had compiled that Einstein had made in his life. I copied the ones that I thought could be incorporated into a poem (see below).

Quotes Made By Albert Einstein

'God is subtle but he is not malicious.'

'The most beautiful thing we can experience is the mysterious. It is the source of all true art and science.'

'Nature to him was an open book, whose letters he could read without effort.'

'Nature hides her secrets because of her essential loftiness but not by means of ruse.'

'Science without religion is lame, religion without science is blind.'

'When I am judging a theory, I ask myself whether, if I were God, I would have arranged the world in such a way.'

Quotes which I ended up using.

Other Quotes that I Have Also Heard Before

'Faith is the evidence of things unseen.'

'I have no proof that God does not exist, but I rather He not.'

'Everything around us points to a higher wisdom.'

Getting Started on Poem One

It was unclear at the beginning of this poem which quotes I wanted to and would be able to use in the poem. First I tried out the quote of, 'I have no proof that God does not exist, but I rather He not.' Following are some ways I experimented with to incorporate it into the first verse.

This is what I wanted to say, but somehow intermix the quote within the verse.

> She says there is no God
> and yet she screams
> and curses Him; demanding
> to be heard.
> The non-existent I thought
> was said.
> *I have no proof that God*
> *does not exist – but I rather*
> *He not.*

An attempt at inserting the quote, which didn't come out as clearly as first intended. Some words were also changed.

> She says there is no God,
> with no proof that He
> does not exist; and yet she screams
> and curses Him, demanding
> to be heard. Rather He not
> be, and so He isn't. The
> non-existent I thought
> was said.

This is the beginning of a slightly different version. I decided not to develope it further as I realized it wasn't going anywhere.

> She says there is nothing,
> having no proof that God
> does not exist; screaming
> and cursing Him; determined
> to shut Him out

All of these variations didn't seem to quite 'connect' and smoothly flow into other verses. The second variation was the most likable, but in many ways seemed too wordy and confusing for the reader. When trying to use this as the starting of a poem, I wasn't able to get anywhere with it. None of my ideas for the other quotes followed the way I put the first verse. Therefore, I decided to make a fresh start and banish all of my first intents.

My God in Einstein's Words

Lost people
of this world; holding vague images
of an obscure being, watching
with an etched scowl, white hair
robe billowing as a cloudy dust bowl
up, up in the sky; a silent observer who
strikes with lighting bolts every
so often.
True, my **God is subtle** – understated and
misunderstood by man – **but He's not mallcious**.

Small minds of humans, engrossed
in their favorite preoccupation: denying my God.
Rippling muscles, beating
bloody hearts, brains with complex turns
and twists all came from nothing
with nothing – **science without my God is lame**.
Locked away, not turning the key
of probing and exploring
to discover the wide
open doors – **religion without science is blind**.

Musty books, laced
with crinkly old smells, bug-eyed
florescent screens, lined with information,
and yet we have only made
a dent in this metallic ocean of unknown.
Nature hides her secrets
because of her essential loftiness, the reminder
of who the Creator is; not deceptively, but plainly
supreme.
Sound waves bouncing
back and forth; leaking out
of the atmosphere into space,
vigorously leaping further
and further to nameless places. Dying
stars, ticking human thoughts, sizzling
energy; brimming with the
mysteries of my God –
the most beautiful thing
we can experience.

* Words in **bold** are quotes that Albert Einstein made in the course of his life.

The parts that I used from some of Einstein's quotes are in bold. Some are changed or cut off a bit, but the original meaning is not lost.

Examiner's analysis

This piece is very original. It is a clear account of how the candidate planned and wrote her own poem and a very competent explanation of some of the images within it. The piece of explanation at the end is not trying to write a formal poetry commentary but a personal analysis of how the poem was put together. The poem itself is beautifully constructed, using strong images and provoking lots of questions. It really is a very striking piece of work and would gain a **grade** A.

Commentary on 'My God in Einstein's Words'

The length of this poem is deceiving as it is only one page long, but could easily have ten pages of explanation. 'My God in Einstein's Words' is all about God. On the surface, the poem has two characteristics. One is the spacing. I tried to imitate Margaret Atwood's style of spacing and use of punctuation, especially the semicolon. None of my previous poetry has included the semicolon. In some cases, I think that it is good to use it. It gives the right type of pause and flowing connection to certain parts of poetry. The second characteristic of this poem is that I included quotes from Albert Einstein. I incorporated parts of the quotes in certain areas. These quotes are what ultimately sparked and shaped my ideas.

Everything said in 'My God in Einstein's Words' is about *my* God. Whenever 'God' is mentioned in it, 'my' follows before. This is important as it means that I am not talking about somebody else's god, but mine. I do not have the universalistic view that all gods are the same one God.

To explain this poem, we must concentrate on what the quotes mean. In the first stanzas, the quote is, 'God is subtle, but He's not malicious.' This quote is used as a correction to what was said before it about God. People think very vaguely about God and see Him as a being up in the sky who looks down and punishes them. I used the image of 'robe billowing as a cloudy dust bowl' to describe part of it. It compares a dust bowl in a desert to the white robes of God that so often flash into people's minds. I used the semicolon twice in the stanza. I wanted a longer pause than a comma, but not a complete full stop. The semicolon connects the two parts together in the desired way.

The next quote was, 'Science without religion is lame, religion without science is blind.' I changed it a little bit as the poem is supposed to be *about* God, *not* religion. The two can be very different things. There is a comparison made in this stanza. While humans are always trying to deny that there is a God in science, they are forgetting that the very thoughts and brains that they are thinking with are from God, 'rippling muscles, beating bloody hearts, brains with complex turns and twists.' The 'b' sound is repeated here to make it sound as if the heart is actually pumping. 'All came from nothing with nothing,' is referring to the 'Big Bang Theory'. What is my view on this? 'Science without my God is lame.' The last part of the stanza goes on the reverse side. On the other hand, it is also wrong to turn a cold shoulder to science and the knowledge about our world it has to offer us. The next stanza explains this more fully. Books with 'crinkly old smells' and computers with 'bug-eyed fluorescent screens' have a huge amount of information that Science has explained. Every day, new things are being discovered. Science makes us realize that there is so much that we do not know. It is as if we have only made a small imprint in a sheet of metal, 'a dent in this metallic ocean of unknown.' As Einstein says, 'Nature hides her secrets because of essential loftiness.' In other words, nature is so complex because of the Creator (God). The complexity proves that there must be a higher wisdom behind all of it.

The last stanza is full of unusual, peculiar images. I used the image of sound waves seeping out of the earth's atmosphere to show the vastness of the universe, 'vigorously leaping further and further to nameless places.' Sound waves along with 'dying stars, ticking human thoughts, sizzling energy' are strange things that are happening all of the time without anybody paying attention to or thinking about them. If we were to sit back and think about these things, we would see God in all of them. This, as Einstein's quote says, is 'the most beautiful thing we can experience.'

▧ Coursework checklist

When the examiner assesses your coursework, the following points will all be taken into consideration. If you take them into consideration, too, when you check and revise your work before handing in your folder, you could gain yourself a better grade!

1 Is the content:

- interesting?
- entertaining?
- enjoyable?

2 Does it achieve the assessment objectives for continuous writing, proving that you can:

- order and present facts, ideas and opinions?
- articulate experience and express what is felt and imagined?
- communicate effectively and appropriately?

3 Is it well structured? Is it easy to follow and does it move sensibly along from beginning to end?
4 Is the style appropriate for the purpose of the piece?
5 How accurate is the writing? How good is the:

- spelling?
- grammar?
- punctuation?

Speaking and listening skills

What is tested and how?

Assessment in oral work (i.e. speaking skills) is not compulsory and your teachers might have decided to enter your class only for the written examination. However, whether they are assessed or not, speaking and listening are bound to be an integral part of your English lessons, and being able to speak in English and understand what is said to you in reply are hugely important skills. It's also worth remembering that if you write a script for your written papers, you will produce a better piece if you have thought about how to speak interestingly and communicate clearly.

In Chapters 3 and 4 we looked at the skills involved in writing for different purposes and for different audiences. Similar skills are needed for speaking. If you are a high court judge about to sentence someone to ten years in jail, you are going to speak rather differently from someone who is talking to a group of friends about whether to go to the cinema or to go shopping. Even in school, you adapt your speaking style to different situations – perhaps without really thinking about it: you are bound to find yourself in a mix of formal and informal situations, talking with adults and with your peers, talking about school work and your leisure time, and so on.

In IGCSE there are two methods of assessment of speaking:

- examination
- coursework.

You probably already know that for the written part of the examination you will receive a letter grade, A, B, C and so on. For the speaking part of the examination you will receive a number grade from 1 to 5, with grade 1 being the highest.

The exam is conducted by an examiner who is usually your teacher, although some schools do bring in specialists to do it. The exam lasts about fifteen minutes, broken down into:

- five minutes to **prepare for the role play** (explained below)
- five minutes of **role play**
- five minutes to **discuss a topic** which you will have chosen in advance.

How is the exam marked?

The role play and discussion are taped and the tape is sent to a moderator who is appointed by the examinations board. The moderator receives a number of tapes and compares them with the standards that have been set. He or she will decide whether you have been assessed at the right standard. If he or she agrees with your teacher's marks the results will simply be sent to the examining board; if the moderator doesn't quite agree with your teacher then he or she might adjust your marks slightly.

■ Role play

You are given five minutes to look at a card explaining the role-play situation and think about what you are going to say. Then you go into the exam room and the role play itself lasts about another five minutes. You play one part and the assessor (probably your teacher) plays the other. The situations you are put in are imaginary but perfectly normal and natural situations – you won't be expected to deal with unrealistic problems! Although it's a role play, you won't necessarily have to pretend to be someone else, although your assessor probably will! For instance, the assessor might play the role of your parent and your task could be to try to persuade him or her to give you a large amount of money so that you can go on a holiday with your friends.

Tip During the role play, **listen** really carefully to what the assessor is saying. You will be answering questions put by him or her and it is important that you have heard and understood the question properly. Sometimes candidates are concentrating so hard on what they are going to say that they forget to listen – and end up saying something that has very little to do with the question that has been asked!

How to use the preparation time

Here is one of the cards which was used in an examination.

> **Candidate:** Yourself
> **Teacher:** Your new next-door neighbour
>
> A new person has just moved into the house next door to you. He/she does not know the area and is keen to find out as much as possible about it from somebody who does.
>
> **The following suggestions may help you, but you are free to develop the conversation in any way you wish. The teacher will speak first.**
>
> 1 Describe the local facilities (e.g. shops, sporting/swimming facilities, school, library, park) and explain why this is a nice area in which to live.
> 2 Explain why you do/do not go to the local school.
> 3 Talk about two people who live nearby and what they are like as neighbours.
> 4 Describe one or two interesting places in the area that should be visited.
> 5 Say that the only thing lacking is somewhere for youngsters to go in the evening and explain why this is a problem.

How could you prepare for this role play?

1 **Concentrate on the essentials.** Think about the area you live in and make sure that you can describe it to a stranger. Remember, it is your job to make it sound as interesting as you can. You don't want to put your new neighbour off the area immediately.

2 **Anticipate what the assessor might say.** Put yourself in the place of the new neighbour and imagine what sort of introduction you might want. Your list might not match the assessor's questions exactly but there is a good chance that you will have anticipated some topics correctly.

3 **What are your ideas?** You have looked at and thought about the ideas that are on the card but it says 'You are free to develop the conversation in any way you wish'. This is where you can use your initiative and take the lead; for instance, there might be a very good local drama club which you are very keen on and you might want to recruit a new member.

4 **Think of the tone you will use in your talk.** In the example above you would want to be friendly and helpful. In another situation you might want to be crisp and business-like.

So use your preparation time well:

■ Read the card carefully.
■ Make sure that you can deal with all the points on the card.
■ Think of points of your own.
■ Think of the tone you will need to use.

Example 1

The assessor's role: Your fussy friend.
Your role: Yourself.
Your task: You have invited your friend to a meal you have prepared yourself, not realising that he/she is very particular about food.

Preparation

Part of your preparation will be to decide quickly what you have prepared for the meal. It would help to choose something a bit unusual or special, so that (a) your 'fussy friend' will have plenty to quibble about, and (b) you have something worth arguing about. However, don't spend too long on this as you have only five minutes to think about the whole conversation. In these five minutes you also need to think about:

■ what you are likely to say/ask
■ what your 'friend' is likely to say/ask

so that you are as well prepared as possible.

The role play

Your friend might comment that there is a strange smell coming from the kitchen and you might explain that it is the main course and a particular sauce which you have spent hours preparing. Your friend might react in a very unenthusiastic way, saying that he/she does not like rich food, at

It is very important to make sure that both you and your partner take the lead at different times. Don't get into a rut of just answering questions and always coming in second.

which point you will backtrack, saying that it is not *really* rich. You might then quickly describe the soup, which you will be having first, emphasising the simplicity of it.

You might try to change the direction of the conversation a little and ask your friend what he/she normally eats. It might be that he/she eats burgers and chips and other junk food all the time, and this might give you a chance to talk about healthy eating, fresh fruit, and so on.

Example 2

The assessor's role: Your friend.
Your role: Yourself.
Your task: You have very strong views about how we should treat animals, which are different from your friend's. You would very much like to change your friend's views. You are in a café. Your friend has walked in wearing a brand-new leather coat and has ordered a double beefburger; you are wearing a cotton jacket and are waiting for your order, a vegeburger.

The role play

Remember that it's up to both of you to change the direction of the discussion when necessary.

Your friend may accuse you of being obsessive about animals and this might annoy you. You might come back and try to explain why we should behave properly towards them. Explain why you don't eat meat and why you would never wear clothes made out of animal skin. You might get on to talking about the cruelty of hunting animals because so often it is not for a purpose, and your friend might come back at you because he/she is going off shooting rabbits when you leave the café.

You might get on to talking about the much wider problems of conservation and the dangers of some animals becoming extinct.

Example 3

Some of the situations which are set up are more formal than others and you should think about the right language to use in each situation.

The assessor's role: The chairperson of the committee (see below).
Your role: Yourself.
Your task: You are helping to arrange a visit to your town by some students from another country and are discussing the programme with the chairperson of the organising committee.

The role play

The students are going to be visiting sites of interest in the town. You might start by suggesting places they ought to visit; the chairperson might not agree with all of your choices. You should discuss reasons for your choice.

You can tell a friend not to be so silly, but here you must remember that you are talking to the chairperson of a committee who is probably your headteacher or another important adult!

When you get to the exam, always look carefully at the ideas on the card and use them. They are there to help you.

The programme might include a welcoming party and you should discuss who might be invited, whether there should be any entertainment and, if so, what type, and so on.

The students might be going to play some sports matches against the local school or might be coming to put on a concert in the town. You could discuss all these things and many more besides.

Example 4

The assessor's role: Your friend, who is a keep-fit fanatic.
Your role: Yourself.
Your task: Your friend is very keen to encourage you to take more exercise and has a whole series of suggestions, including cycling or jogging to school rather than being driven in the car, eating salads for lunch rather than your favourite burgers, going to an aerobics class in the evening and so on.

The role play

You know that what is being suggested is quite sensible, but you are very reluctant to agree to any of the suggestions. You like staying in bed as late as possible and, so long as your mother is willing to drive you, you would prefer to go on travelling in the car. You enjoy your food and want to go on eating what you like, and so on.

Your friend will bring in health issues and perhaps even try to frighten you with stories about what might happen if you don't improve your fitness. You might become more and more annoyed.

Example 5

The assessor's role: A new neighbour who has two very noisy and naughty children.
Your role: The owner of a house in a quiet street.
Your task: You are having very real problems with your neighbour. You cannot concentrate during the day on things you want to do and your neighbour's children don't even seem to sleep at night but keep you awake. You were working in the garden and a football came over the fence and hit you on the head; the children started yelling and screaming for you to throw it back. Instead you go round to see their parent to discuss the whole matter.

The role play

The parent is very sympathetic and explains that the children are virtually out of control; your view is that something must be done. You try to keep the discussion on an even keel but might be driven to suggest things like the authorities being called in, which might upset your neighbour. You might discuss your sort of lifestyle, which is quiet – perhaps you like listening to classical music – and how important it is for you to be able to relax at home because you have a great deal of responsibility at work.

Your neighbour is clearly in need of help and you become very sympathetic, but you don't really want to become involved.

Tip To build your confidence in speaking, record some practice pieces on cassette. You could start by reading something out loud, just to get used to the sound of your own voice on the machine. Once you have done this, make your practice as close to the situation you will face in the exam as possible – in other words, find a willing partner, do some preparation and then have a go! If you manage to do this a few times then you will feel much more confident when it comes to the exam itself.

■ Choosing a discussion topic

It is up to you to choose a topic that you want to introduce and discuss with the assessor. The only restriction on the choice is that your assessor must be happy to discuss the topic with you. Make sure you choose a topic that you know something about and are able to discuss. This may sound obvious but students have been known to choose topics which sounded impressive, but about which they knew very little, if anything! You might consider these possibilities.

1 Do you have a hobby?

You might collect stamps; you might go ballroom dancing every week; you might breed fish; you might have a pet boa constrictor which has to be fed on small live rodents; you might knit socks. The point about a hobby is that presumably it is something you enjoy and find interesting. You should be able to interest other people in it. By way of preparation, ask yourself the following questions.

- Why did I start this hobby?
- When did I start?
- How much time do I spend on my hobby?
- Why do I enjoy it?
- Is there anything I can take with me to help me introduce the topic?
- How else might I make my hobby interesting for the assessor?

Then you can plan your introduction. You might do it in such a way that there are some obvious questions for the assessor to ask.

2 Do you travel much?

Many of you might be lucky enough to have travelled widely; you may well have been to places that you have loved; you may well have been to places that you have hated. Either way, you should be able to talk about them in an interesting way. Again, you need to prepare, and the following points might help.

- Make a list of all the places that you have visited.
- Group similar places together.
- Pick out the places that you most liked.
- Pick out those places that you didn't like at all.
- Consider what was most important to you when thinking about a place – people, buildings, the scenery?
- If you were to pick your favourite place, which would it be?

3 What do you want to do as a career?

You may have a very clear idea about what you want to do as a future career, or you may have a part-time job that will provide you with material for your discussion. Do you baby-sit, work in the local shop, run your own computer website service? Some of you might be hoping that your part-time job will expand into a future career; for others it may be just a means of earning enough money to be able to go out with friends at the weekend.

Some of you might have been sent on work experience by your school. Again, through work experience you might have discovered your future career path. Alternatively, you might have been very bored or you might have hated every moment of your experience. Even so, you will have learnt something for the future.

However you have gained your experience, whatever your ideas, this might be a topic which would work for you. Ask yourself the following questions.

- Do I know what I want to do as a career?
- How did I get this idea?
- Was I influenced by others rather than making up my own mind? (For instance, do you want to do the same job as one of your parents?)
- Why am I sure I will enjoy this job?
- How important is the money to me?
- Do I think it will be a job for life?

4 Are you passionate about a particular issue?

'I am a vegetarian! No one should eat meat. It is unnecessary and barbaric.'

'Animals should not be used to test produce for us humans. The plight of animals that are used to test cosmetics is disgraceful. Even testing medicines on animals should not happen; use human volunteers.'

'All rubbish should be recycled. We are destroying our own planet with our pollution. People who abuse our planet should be fined huge amounts. We have to think of our children and grandchildren.'

'They are my favourite pop group. I would go to the ends of the earth to see them. Their last record was the most exciting thing I have ever heard. I know some people disagree with me but they simply don't have any soul.'

'School uniform should go!'

If you choose to talk about an issue that you feel passionate about, you must be able to talk without going off the rails and you must have clear reasons to use to convince your listener. If you start off by advocating that all school uniforms should be burnt and the assessor argues against you, you will not do very well if all you can do is keep repeating 'I hate it!' So decide:

- What is my subject?
- Why do I feel strongly about it?
- What do I need to say to make sure the listener understands the subject?
- What are likely to be the arguments on the other side and how will I answer them?

5 Is your family interesting?

It is perfectly possible that your aunt is an astronaut. Your father might have been an Olympic athlete. Your grandmother was possibly the first woman to sail around the world single-handed. Your brother might be the world pie-eating champion. In other words, there might be members of your family who have achieved outstanding success. If so, there is little doubt that you could talk about them in a fascinating way. You might even be able to bring in a lump of moon rock or an Olympic gold medal to help in your introduction.

However, you might believe your family to be interesting for far more simple reasons. Perhaps you have lived in a whole variety of countries and have had to adapt to frequent moves. Perhaps you come from a very large family who are involved in a wide range of activities, which means that your family life is a non-stop whirl.

If this is the topic for you, then you must decide on your way into it.

- Who or what am I going to talk about?
- Would others find the person I am going to talk about interesting?
- Are there things which I should keep private?
- If the assessor asks me a question I don't want to answer, how am I going to get out of it? (There is no problem with politely declining to answer a question and moving on.)
- Are there any small items I could take to the discussion that will be useful to illustrate my points?

6 Have you been fascinated by a book you have read, or a play or film you have seen?

If you were to choose this topic, you would find it quite straightforward because the first thing you would have to do is make sure that your partner or the assessor understood what you were talking about. You would have to reiterate the plot of a novel, however briefly; you would have to tell the story of a film or a play and say who was in it, and perhaps why their performances were so good.

You may well find that you have to take the lead more than with some of the other topics. One point remains central, though; you must not only be able to tell your partner what the book, film or play was about, but you must also be able to explain, perhaps in some detail, why it was so special for you.

7 Does a particular person interest you?

A wide-open topic if ever there was one, and many of the points and ideas above lead you in. Your person might be a member of your family, it might be a singer or an actor. It might be someone from history who fascinates you.

- Choose your person.
- Make sure you know about them in detail and can interest a listener.

Tip Remember that your talk is going to turn into a discussion. The assessor will have been listening very carefully to what you have said and will have some questions to ask. He or she may also have some ideas of his or her own and will want to see what you think of them. In order to respond well, you need to:
■ listen really carefully
■ take your time in answering thoughtfully.

■ Coursework

If your school has decided to assess your oral work by coursework, you will be assessed by your teacher three times during the course. Your teacher may choose to use the role play and/or the discussion activities that are used in the examination, but may also choose more natural situations.

■ You might be assessed while you are discussing a topic in class with your partner; for example, you could be talking about one of your literature texts and planning an approach to an essay together.
■ Your teacher could choose to have a formal class debate and assess the main speakers and/or the contribution of speakers from the floor.
■ You might not be in an English class at all, or even in school. For example, you could be interviewing your representative on the town council as preparation for an article you are going to write for the school newspaper. Your teacher might have arranged to be present so that he/she can assess you.

What is certain is that your teacher will want to give you the opportunity to speak and listen in a variety of contexts. It is worth thinking about the different purposes for which we need to talk. We might need to:

■ explain
■ describe
■ narrate, read or recite
■ analyse in detail
■ imagine something and interest the listener in it
■ put some ideas together and then explore them, either with a partner or in a group
■ discuss
■ argue (not in the sense of having a row but of putting forward your view)
■ persuade.

Remember that it is always your job to decide why you are talking and therefore how you should speak.

Remember also that with coursework there is no need to be nervous, because if things go wrong you and your teacher can always decide that you can have another go later. But then, things won't go wrong!